A YEAR FULL OF RECIPES

This edition published by Parragon Books Ltd in 2015

Parragon Books Ltd
Chartist House
15–17 Trim Street
Bath BA1 1HA, UK
www.parragon.com

ISBN 978-1-4748-0494-3

Printed in China

Cover design by Beth Kalynka
Cover photography by Max and Liz Haarala Hamilton
Cover food styling by Sara Lewis
Project managed by Natalie Coates
Internal design by Lexi L'Esteve
New photography by Mike Cooper
New home economy by Lincoln Jefferson
Additional design by Siân Williams
Introduction and additional recipes by Christine France

Notes for the Reader

This book uses both metric and imperial measurements. Follow the same units of measurement throughout; do not mix metric and imperial. All spoon measurements are level: teaspoons are assumed to be 5 ml, and tablespoons are assumed to be 15 ml. Unless otherwise stated, milk is assumed to be full fat, eggs and individual vegetables are medium, pepper is freshly ground black pepper and salt is table salt. Unless otherwise stated, all root vegetables should be peeled prior to using.

The times given are an approximate guide only. Preparation times differ according to the techniques used by different people and the cooking times may also vary from those given.

For best results, use a food thermometer when cooking meat. Check the latest government guidelines for current advice.

CONTENTS

INTRODUCTION

For any of us who regularly cook meals for family and friends, the one thing that can turn this everyday task into a chore is the repetitive nature of it. However good a cook you are, providing meals for a family all year round can soon drain your bank of ideas. Special occasions often provide an extra challenge, especially if you're not used to cooking more demanding, skilful recipes.

So if, like most of us, you suffer from a lack of culinary inspiration, this is the book for you. Every page is packed full of creative recipe ideas for every single day of the year, whether it's for those quick weekday meals or for dinner party dishes. There are tempting cakes and desserts, plus some classics for special occasions and festive celebrations.

Chilly Autumn and Winter days call for warming, hearty dishes that are slow-cooked and economical, too, making the best of comforting, seasonal ingredients. In the Spring and Summer months we tend to focus on lighter, refreshing dishes that use the best fresh young produce, either to cook outdoors or to take outdoors to eat when the weather allows. It's always good fun to cook on the barbecue or have an impromptu picnic, so inside you will find lots of easy dishes for al fresco eating of all kinds, including healthy, colourful salads, flavourful grills and even campfire treats.

EVERYDAY INSPIRATION

Feeding a family every day can be demanding, especially if you're catering for different ages and tastes whilst trying to ensure everyone maintains a healthy balanced diet. This book will prove to be an invaluable store of recipes to fall back on, any day of the week.

Whether you are looking for ideas for healthy lunchbox snacks when the children go back to school, or you are in need of nutritious, sustaining food to help you through the working day, there are plenty of ideas to choose from to keep your diet varied and interesting.

Cakes and bakes have their place in everyday cooking too, as well as on special celebrations. You'll find some irresistible sweet treats to cover every season, not forgetting those special occasions when you need an extra sophisticated, indulgent sweet dish to impress your guests.

STORECUPBOARD SENSE

A well-stocked storecupboard is invaluable at any time of year. Then, all you should need to buy are the fresh foods in season to complete the dish. Start with this list of basic standbys, then add your own useful favourites:

Canned foods:
- plum tomatoes
- sweetcorn
- beans and pulses, e.g. red kidney, cannellini, lentils

Jars/bottles:
- honey, golden and maple syrup
- olive oil
- extra virgin olive oil
- cooking oil, e.g. sunflower or groundnut
- Worcestershire sauce
- malt and wine vinegars
- soy sauce

Dry goods:
- flour, e.g. plain, self-raising and cornflour
- sugar, e.g. caster, muscovado, Demerara and icing
- dried pasta and noodles
- rice and grains, e.g. bulgur wheat
- porridge oats
- dried beans and pulses
- dried fruits, e.g. apricots, sultanas

Frozen:
- vegetables, e.g. peas, broccoli
- pastry, e.g. filo, shortcrust, puff

Herbs and spices:
- sweet spices, e.g. vanilla pods, mixed spice, cinnamon, nutmeg, ginger
- dried herbs, e.g. bay leaves, thyme, parsley, oregano, sage, rosemary

HOW TO USE THIS BOOK

Whether you're cooking everyday family meals or cooking to impress your friends for special dinner parties, this book will be an invaluable resource, ensuring that you always have a suitable choice of dishes to hand. It's designed so that you can easily dip in and out of the pages for ideas and inspiration.

You'll find this book is simple to use as there are two useful separate indexes. The first index lists all the recipes alphabetically by name in the usual way, for easy reference. A second index lists by the main ingredient or food type, so you can quickly check out all the recipes that use your main ingredient; for instance, all the beef recipes are listed together, all the chicken ones and so on. So, if you're trying to decide how to cook some chicken for dinner, it's easy to see at a glance what's in the book and find not just one, but several ideas for chicken dishes. All that's left to do is to start cooking and enjoy eating your way through the whole year!

JANUARY

BAKED HAM WITH HOISIN & HONEY GLAZE

SERVES: 6–8   PREP TIME: 20 MINS PLUS 20 MINS STANDING TIME   COOK TIME: 1 HR 45 MINS

INGREDIENTS

2 kg/4 lb 8 oz smoked gammon in 1 piece

2 bay leaves

2 garlic cloves, crushed

1 tbsp Dijon mustard

2 tbsp hoisin sauce

2 tbsp clear honey

1. Preheat the oven to 180°C/350°F/Gas Mark 4. Put the ham into a large saucepan with the bay leaves and cover with cold water. Bring to the boil, cover, reduce the heat and simmer gently for 10 minutes. Drain well.

2. Put the ham into a roasting tin and cover loosely with foil. Bake in the preheated oven for 1 hour.

3. Remove the ham from the oven (do not turn off the oven). Take off the foil and place the ham on a board. Carefully remove the skin with a sharp knife, leaving an even layer of fat on the meat. Score lines through the fat layer, criss-crossing to make a diamond pattern. Return the meat to the tin.

4. Put the garlic, mustard, hoisin sauce and honey into a bowl and stir to combine. Spread half the mixture over the fat layer of the meat, pressing it into the cuts.

5. Return the ham to the oven and bake for 15 minutes. Remove from the oven, spread with the remaining glaze, then bake for a further 15 minutes until golden brown.

6. Cover loosely with foil and leave to stand for 20 minutes before carving into slices. Skim the fat from the juices and serve them with the meat, as a sauce.

HEARTY BEEF STEW

SERVES: 4   PREP TIME: 30 MINS PLUS 15 MINS STANDING TIME   COOK TIME: 2 HRS 15 MINS

INGREDIENTS

1.3 kg/3 lb boneless braising steak, cut into 5-cm/2-inch pieces

2 tbsp vegetable oil

2 onions, cut into 2.5-cm/1-inch pieces

3 tbsp plain flour

3 garlic cloves, finely chopped

1 litre/1¾ pints beef stock

3 carrots, cut into 2.5-cm/1-inch lengths

2 celery sticks, cut into 2.5-cm/1-inch lengths

1 tbsp tomato ketchup

1 bay leaf

¼ tsp dried thyme

¼ tsp dried rosemary

900 g/2 lb Maris Piper potatoes, cut into large chunks

salt and pepper

1. Season the steak very generously with salt and pepper. Heat the oil in a large flameproof casserole over a high heat. When the oil begins to smoke slightly, add the steak, in batches, if necessary, and cook, stirring frequently, for 5–8 minutes, until well browned. Using a slotted spoon, transfer to a bowl.

2. Reduce the heat to medium, add the onions to the casserole and cook, stirring occasionally, for 5 minutes, until translucent. Stir in the flour and cook, stirring constantly, for 2 minutes. Add the garlic and cook for 1 minute. Whisk in 225 ml/8 fl oz of the stock and cook, scraping up all the sediment from the base of the casserole, then stir in the remaining stock and add the carrots, celery, tomato ketchup, bay leaf, thyme, rosemary and 1 teaspoon of salt. Return the steak to the casserole.

3. Bring back to a gentle simmer, cover and cook over a low heat for 1 hour. Add the potatoes, re-cover the casserole and simmer for a further 30 minutes. Remove the lid, increase the heat to medium and cook, stirring occasionally, for a further 30 minutes, or until the meat and vegetables are tender. Remove the bay leaf.

4. If the stew becomes too thick, add a little more stock or water and adjust the seasoning, if necessary. Leave to stand for 15 minutes before serving.

TURKEY & LENTIL SOUP

SERVES: 4   PREP TIME: 30 MINS   COOK TIME: 50 MINS

INGREDIENTS

1 tbsp olive oil

1 garlic clove, chopped

1 large onion, chopped

200 g/7 oz mushrooms, sliced

1 red pepper, deseeded and chopped

6 tomatoes, peeled, deseeded and chopped

1.2 litres/2 pints chicken stock

150 ml/5 fl oz red wine

85 g/3 oz cauliflower florets

1 carrot, chopped

200 g/7 oz red lentils

350 g/12 oz cooked turkey, chopped

1 courgette, chopped

1 tbsp shredded fresh basil

salt and pepper

sprigs of fresh basil, to garnish

1. Heat the oil in a large saucepan. Add the garlic and onion and cook over a medium heat, stirring, for 3 minutes, until slightly softened. Add the mushrooms, red pepper and tomatoes and cook for a further 5 minutes, stirring. Pour in the stock and red wine, then add the cauliflower, carrot and red lentils. Season to taste with salt and pepper. Bring to the boil, then lower the heat and simmer the soup gently for 25 minutes, until the vegetables are tender and cooked through.

2. Add the turkey and courgette to the pan and cook for 10 minutes. Stir in the shredded basil and cook for a further 5 minutes, then remove from the heat and ladle into serving bowls. Garnish with basil and serve.

HEARTY
BEEF STEW

BARLEY, LENTIL & ONION SOUP

SERVES: 6 PREP TIME: 20 MINS PLUS 30 MINS DRYING TIME COOK TIME: 2 HRS 40 MINS

INGREDIENTS

25 g/1 oz pearl barley

150 ml/5 fl oz water

1.7 litres/3 pints vegetable stock

500 g/1 lb 2 oz onions, thinly sliced into rings

140 g/5 oz Puy lentils

½ tsp ground ginger

1 tsp ground cumin

3 tbsp lemon juice

2 tbsp chopped fresh coriander

salt and pepper

TO GARNISH

2 onions, halved and thinly sliced

5 tbsp vegetable oil

2 garlic cloves, finely chopped

1. Put the barley into a large saucepan, pour in the water and bring to the boil. Reduce the heat, cover and simmer gently, stirring frequently, for about 30 minutes, until all the liquid has been absorbed.

2. Add the stock, onions, lentils, ginger and cumin and bring to the boil over a medium heat. Reduce the heat, cover and simmer, stirring occasionally, for 1½ hours, adding a little more stock if necessary.

3. Meanwhile, make the garnish. Spread out the onions on a thick layer of kitchen paper and cover with another thick layer. Leave to dry out for 30 minutes. Heat the oil in a frying pan. Add the onions and cook over a low heat, stirring constantly, for about 20 minutes, until well browned. Add the garlic and cook, stirring constantly, for a further 5 minutes. Remove the onions with a slotted spoon and drain well on kitchen paper.

4. Season the soup to taste with salt and pepper, stir in the lemon juice and coriander and simmer for a further 5 minutes. Serve garnished with the browned onions.

HOT SESAME BEEF

SERVES: 4–6   **PREP TIME: 20 MINS**   **COOK TIME: 10 MINS**

INGREDIENTS

500 g/1 lb 2 oz fillet steak, cut into thin strips

1½ tbsp sesame seeds

125 ml/4 fl oz beef stock

2 tbsp soy sauce

2 tbsp grated fresh ginger

2 garlic cloves, finely chopped

1 tsp cornflour

½ tsp chilli flakes

3 tbsp sesame oil

1 large head of broccoli, cut into florets

1 yellow pepper, deseeded and thinly sliced

1 fresh red chilli, finely sliced

1 tbsp chilli oil, or to taste

chopped fresh coriander, to garnish

cooked wild rice, to serve

1. Mix the beef strips with 1 tablespoon of the sesame seeds in a small bowl.

2. In a separate bowl, stir together the stock, soy sauce, ginger, garlic, cornflour and chilli flakes.

3. Heat 1 tablespoon of the sesame oil in a large wok. Stir-fry the beef strips for 2–3 minutes. Remove and set aside, then wipe the wok with kitchen paper.

4. Heat the remaining sesame oil in the wok, add the broccoli, yellow pepper, red chilli and chilli oil and stir-fry for 2–3 minutes.

5. Stir in the stock mixture, cover and simmer for 2 minutes.

6. Return the beef to the wok and simmer until the juices thicken, stirring occasionally. Cook for a further 1–2 minutes. Sprinkle with the remaining sesame seeds.

7. Garnish with fresh coriander and serve over wild rice.

06 JANUARY

BAKED TUNA & RICOTTA RIGATONI

SERVES: 4 | PREP TIME: 5 MINS | COOK TIME: 30 MINS

INGREDIENTS

butter, for greasing

450 g/1 lb dried rigatoni

200 g/7 oz canned flaked tuna, drained

225 g/8 oz ricotta cheese

125 ml/4 fl oz double cream

225 g/8 oz freshly grated Parmesan cheese

115 g/4 oz sun-dried tomatoes, drained and sliced

salt and pepper

1. Preheat the oven to 200°C/400°F/Gas Mark 6. Lightly grease a large ovenproof dish with butter. Bring a large, heavy-based saucepan of lightly salted water to the boil. Add the rigatoni, bring back to the boil and cook for 8–10 minutes, or until just tender but still firm to the bite. Drain the pasta and leave until cool enough to handle.

2. Meanwhile, mix together the tuna and ricotta cheese in a bowl to form a soft paste. Spoon the mixture into a piping bag and use to fill the rigatoni. Arrange the filled pasta tubes side by side in the prepared dish.

3. To make the sauce, mix together the cream and Parmesan cheese in a bowl and season to taste with salt and pepper. Spoon the sauce over the rigatoni and top with the sun-dried tomatoes, arranged in a criss-cross pattern. Bake in the preheated oven for 20 minutes. Serve hot straight from the dish.

07 JANUARY

SPAGHETTI ALLA CARBONARA

SERVES: 4 | PREP TIME: 10 MINS | COOK TIME: 20 MINS

INGREDIENTS

450 g/1 lb dried spaghetti

1 tbsp olive oil

225 g/8 oz rindless pancetta or streaky bacon, chopped

4 eggs

5 tbsp single cream

2 tbsp freshly grated Parmesan cheese

salt and pepper

1. Bring a large, heavy-based saucepan of lightly salted water to the boil. Add the spaghetti, bring back to the boil and cook for 8–10 minutes, or until just tender but still firm to the bite.

2. Meanwhile, heat the oil in a heavy-based frying pan. Add the pancetta and cook over a medium heat, stirring frequently, for 8–10 minutes.

3. Beat the eggs with the cream in a small bowl and season to taste with salt and pepper. Drain the pasta and return it to the saucepan. Tip in the contents of the frying pan, then add the egg mixture and half the cheese. Stir well, then transfer the spaghetti to a serving dish. Serve sprinkled with the remaining cheese.

PENNE IN TOMATO SAUCE WITH TWO CHEESES

SERVES: 4   PREP TIME: 20 MINS   COOK TIME: 35 MINS

INGREDIENTS

450 g/1 lb dried penne

115 g/4 oz Bel Paese cheese, diced

55 g/2 oz freshly grated Parmesan cheese

TOMATO SAUCE

25 g/1 oz butter

2 tbsp olive oil

2 shallots, finely chopped

2 garlic cloves, finely chopped

1 celery stick, finely chopped

400 g/14 oz canned chopped tomatoes

2 tbsp tomato purée

brown sugar, to taste

1 tsp dried oregano

100 ml/3½ fl oz water

salt and pepper

1. For the tomato sauce, melt the butter with the oil in a saucepan. Add the shallots, garlic and celery and cook over a low heat, stirring occasionally, for 5 minutes, until softened. Stir in the tomatoes, tomato purée, sugar to taste, oregano and water and season to taste with salt and pepper. Increase the heat to medium and bring to the boil, then reduce the heat and simmer, stirring occasionally, for 15–20 minutes, until thickened.

2. Meanwhile, bring a large, heavy-based saucepan of lightly salted water to the boil. Add the penne, bring back to the boil and cook for 8–10 minutes, or until just tender but still firm to the bite. Drain and return to the pan.

3. Add the tomato sauce and the cheeses to the pasta and toss well over a very low heat until the cheeses have melted. Transfer to a serving dish and serve.

WINTER SALAD SLAW

SERVES: 4–6   PREP TIME: 15 MINS   COOK TIME: NO COOKING

INGREDIENTS

140 g/5 oz white cabbage, finely shredded

140 g/5 oz carrots, coarsely grated

1 celery stick, thinly sliced

3 spring onions, thinly sliced

1 crisp red eating apple

2 tbsp lime juice

2 tbsp toasted pumpkin seeds

DRESSING

100 ml/3½ fl oz natural yogurt

2 tbsp mayonnaise

2 tbsp finely chopped parsley

salt and pepper

1. Put the cabbage, carrots, celery and spring onions into a large bowl and mix together. Coarsely grate the apple and discard the core, then sprinkle with the lime juice and add to the vegetables.

2. To make the dressing, mix together the yogurt, mayonnaise and parsley, then season to taste with salt and pepper.

3. Pour the dressing over the prepared vegetables and toss well to coat evenly. Sprinkle with the pumpkin seeds and serve cold.

HOT BANANA BUTTERSCOTCH

SERVES: 4   PREP TIME: 5 MINS   COOK TIME: 2–3 MINS

INGREDIENTS

55 g/2 oz unsalted butter

40 g/1½ oz demerara sugar

4 large bananas, thickly sliced

3 tbsp lemon juice

2 tbsp golden syrup

freshly grated nutmeg, for sprinkling

vanilla ice cream or Greek-style yogurt, to serve

1. Melt the butter in a wide saucepan and stir in the sugar. Heat, stirring, until bubbling, then add the banana chunks. Cook over a fairly high heat, stirring constantly, for 1–2 minutes until bubbling and golden.

2. Stir in the lemon juice and golden syrup, then cook for a further minute until bubbling and golden.

3. Sprinkle with nutmeg and serve with ice cream.

WHOLE ROAST RIB OF BEEF

SERVES: 8   **PREP TIME: 25 MINS PLUS 30 MINS RESTING TIME**   **COOK TIME: 2½ HRS**

INGREDIENTS

olive oil, for rubbing

3-kg/6 lb 8-oz joint of well-hung rib of beef on the bone

½ tbsp plain flour

200 ml/7 fl oz beef stock

200 ml/7 fl oz red wine

seasonal vegetables, to serve

YORKSHIRE PUDDING

250 g/9 oz plain flour, sifted

6 eggs

½ tsp salt

600 ml/1 pint milk

2 tbsp vegetable oil or lard

ROAST POTATOES

2 kg/4 lb 8 oz roasting potatoes, peeled

6 tbsp sunflower oil, goose fat or duck fat

salt and pepper

1. For the Yorkshire pudding, mix together the flour, eggs and salt in a bowl, then gradually add the milk as you stir with a whisk. When smooth set aside but do not chill.

2. Preheat the oven to 220°C/425°F/Gas Mark 7. For the roast potatoes, bring a large saucepan of lightly salted water to the boil, add the potatoes, bring back to the boil and cook for 10 minutes. Drain the potatoes and toss them in oil and salt and pepper. Put them in a roasting tin in a single layer.

3. Rub a generous amount of olive oil and salt and pepper into the beef, then place in a roasting tin. Transfer to the preheated oven and roast for 30 minutes.

4. Reduce the temperature to 160°C/325°F/Gas Mark 3. Transfer the potatoes to the oven and roast with the beef for 60 minutes. Remove the beef from the oven and increase the oven temperature to 220°C/425°F/Gas Mark 7. Cover the beef with foil and leave to rest for at least 30 minutes. Meanwhile, place a roasting tin in the bottom of the oven.

5. Remove the roasting tin from the bottom of the oven and add the vegetable oil. Put it back in the oven for 5 minutes, then remove it and add the Yorkshire pudding batter. Put it back in the hot oven for about 20 minutes.

6. Meanwhile, make the gravy. Remove the beef from the tin and stir the flour into the leftover juices, add the stock and wine, then simmer over a medium heat until reduced by about half.

7. Remove the Yorkshire pudding and the potatoes from the oven. Cut the Yorkshire pudding into eight pieces. Cut the rib bones off the meat and carve the beef. Serve with the roast potatoes, gravy and seasonal vegetables.

12 JANUARY

CHICKEN SOUP WITH LEEKS & RICE

SERVES: 6 — **PREP TIME: 15 MINS** — **COOK TIME: 40 MINS**

INGREDIENTS

2 tbsp olive oil

3 leeks, chopped

6 skinless, boneless chicken thighs, diced

55 g/2 oz long-grain rice

1.3 litres/2¼ pints vegetable stock

dash of Worcestershire sauce

6 fresh chives, chopped

6 thin bacon rashers

2 tbsp chopped fresh parsley

salt and pepper

1. Heat the oil in a saucepan. Add the leeks and cook over a low heat, stirring occasionally, for 5 minutes, until softened. Add the chicken, increase the heat to medium and cook, stirring frequently, for 2 minutes. Add the rice and cook, stirring constantly, for 2 minutes more.

2. Pour in the stock, add the Worcestershire sauce and chives and bring to the boil. Reduce the heat, cover and simmer for 20–25 minutes. Check the chicken is tender and cooked through. Meanwhile, preheat the grill.

3. Grill the bacon for 2–4 minutes on each side, until crisp. Remove and leave to cool, then crumble.

4. Season the soup to taste with salt and pepper and stir in the parsley. Ladle into serving bowls, sprinkle with the crumbled bacon and serve.

13 JANUARY

SAUSAGE & BEAN CASSEROLE

SERVES: 4 — **PREP TIME: 15 MINS** — **COOK TIME: 35 MINS**

INGREDIENTS

8 Italian sausages

3 tbsp olive oil

1 large onion, chopped

2 garlic cloves, chopped

1 green pepper, deseeded and sliced

400 g/14 oz canned chopped tomatoes

2 tbsp sun-dried tomato paste

400 g/14 oz canned cannellini beans

mashed potatoes or rice, to serve

1. Prick the sausages all over with a fork. Heat 2 tablespoons of the oil in a large, heavy-based frying pan. Add the sausages and cook over a low heat, turning frequently, for 10–15 minutes, until evenly browned and cooked through. Remove them from the frying pan and keep warm. Drain off the oil and wipe out the pan with kitchen paper.

2. Heat the remaining oil in the frying pan. Add the onion, garlic and green pepper to the frying pan and cook for 5 minutes, stirring occasionally, or until softened.

3. Add the tomatoes to the frying pan and leave the mixture to simmer for about 5 minutes, stirring occasionally, or until slightly reduced and thickened.

4. Stir the sun-dried tomato paste, cannellini beans and Italian sausages into the mixture in the frying pan. Cook for 4–5 minutes or until the mixture is piping hot. Add 4–5 tablespoons of water if the mixture becomes too dry during cooking.

5. Transfer to serving plates and serve with mashed potatoes.

CHICKEN SOUP
WITH LEEKS & RICE

CLAM CHOWDER

SERVES: 4   PREP TIME: 15 MINS   COOK TIME: 25 MINS

INGREDIENTS

900 g/2 lb live clams

4 bacon rashers, chopped

2 tbsp butter, plus extra for frying

1 onion, chopped

1 tbsp chopped fresh thyme

1 large potato, diced

300 ml/10 fl oz milk

1 bay leaf

375 ml/13 fl oz double cream

1 tbsp chopped fresh parsley

salt and pepper

1. Scrub the clams and put them into a large saucepan with a splash of water. Cook over a high heat for 3–4 minutes until they open. Discard any that remain closed. Strain, reserving the cooking liquid. Leave until cool enough to handle, reserving eight for the garnish.

2. Remove the clams from their shells, chopping them roughly if large, and reserve.

3. In a clean saucepan, fry the bacon with a little butter until browned and crisp. Drain on kitchen paper. Add the butter to the same saucepan, and when it has melted, add the onion. Pan-fry for 4–5 minutes until soft but not coloured. Add the thyme and cook briefly before adding the diced potato, reserved clam cooking liquid, milk and bay leaf. Bring to the boil, then reduce the heat and leave to simmer for 10 minutes, or until the potato is just tender.

4. Discard the bay leaf, then transfer to a food processor and process until smooth, or push through a sieve into a bowl.

5. Add the clams, bacon and cream. Simmer for a further 2–3 minutes until heated through. Season to taste with salt and pepper. Stir in the chopped parsley and serve, garnished with the reserved clams in their shells.

WINTER BEEF STEW WITH HERB DUMPLINGS

SERVES: 4   PREP TIME: 30 MINS   COOK TIME: 2 HRS 25 MINS

INGREDIENTS

3 tbsp plain flour

800 g/1 lb 12 oz braising steak, cubed

3 tbsp olive oil

12 shallots, peeled and halved

2 carrots, cut into batons

1 parsnip, sliced

2 bay leaves

1 tbsp chopped fresh rosemary

450 ml/16 fl oz cider

450 ml/16 fl oz beef stock

1 tbsp soy sauce

200 g/7 oz canned chestnuts, drained

salt and pepper

HERB DUMPLINGS

115 g/4 oz self-raising flour, plus extra for flouring

50 g/1¾ oz vegetable suet

2 tbsp chopped fresh thyme

1. Preheat the oven to 160°C/325°F/Gas Mark 3. Put the flour into a clean polythene bag or on a plate and season generously with salt and pepper. Toss the beef in the seasoned flour until coated.

2. Heat 1 tablespoon of the oil in a large, flameproof casserole over a medium–high heat. Add one third of the beef and cook for 5–6 minutes, turning occasionally, until browned all over – the meat may stick to the casserole until it is properly sealed. Remove the beef with a slotted spoon. Cook the remaining two batches, adding another tablespoon of oil as necessary. Set aside when all the beef has been sealed.

3. Add the remaining oil to the casserole with the shallots, carrots, parsnip and herbs and cook for 3 minutes, stirring occasionally. Pour in the cider and beef stock and bring to the boil. Cook over a high heat until the alcohol has evaporated and the liquid reduced. Add the soy sauce, then cook for a further 3 minutes.

4. Stir in the chestnuts and beef, cover and cook in the preheated oven for 1 hour 35 minutes.

5. Meanwhile, to make the herb dumplings, combine all the ingredients in a bowl and season to taste with salt and pepper. Mix in enough water to make a soft dough. Divide the dough into walnut-sized pieces and, using floured hands, roll each piece into a ball.

6. Add to the casserole, cover and cook for a further 25 minutes, or until the dumplings are cooked, the stock has formed a thick, rich gravy and the meat is tender. Remove the bay leaves and season to taste with salt and pepper before serving.

16 JANUARY

CHICKEN WITH TOMATO & CINNAMON SAUCE

SERVES: 4   PREP TIME: 15 MINS   COOK TIME: 1 HR

INGREDIENTS

55 g/2 oz butter

2 tbsp olive oil

4 chicken quarters

1 onion, finely chopped

2 garlic cloves, finely chopped

1 celery stick, finely chopped

400 g/14 oz canned chopped tomatoes

2 tbsp tomato purée

1 tsp Dijon mustard

brown sugar, to taste

2 tbsp lemon juice

3 tbsp chicken stock

1 tsp dried oregano

¾ tsp ground cinnamon

salt and pepper

1. Melt the butter with the oil in a flameproof casserole. Season the chicken well with salt and pepper to taste, add to the casserole and cook over a medium heat, turning frequently, for 8–10 minutes, until evenly browned. Remove from the casserole and set aside.

2. Add the onion, garlic and celery to the casserole and cook over a low heat, stirring occasionally, for 5 minutes, until softened. Stir in the tomatoes, tomato purée, mustard, sugar to taste, lemon juice, stock, oregano and cinnamon and season to taste with salt and pepper. Increase the heat to medium and bring to the boil, then reduce the heat and simmer, stirring occasionally, for 15 minutes.

3. Return the chicken to the casserole and spoon the sauce over it. Cover and simmer, stirring occasionally, for 30 minutes, until the chicken is tender and cooked through. Serve.

17 JANUARY

PRAWN STIR-FRY

SERVES: 4   PREP TIME: 10 MINS   COOK TIME: 5–6 MINS

INGREDIENTS

2 tbsp sunflower oil

1 garlic clove, thinly sliced

½ tsp crushed dried chillies

1 large red pepper, deseeded and thinly sliced

1 large yellow pepper, deseeded and thinly sliced

1 bunch spring onions, sliced diagonally

400 g/14 oz large cooked peeled prawns

4 tbsp oyster sauce

2 tbsp soy sauce

juice of 1 lime

cooked rice noodles or rice, to serve

1. Heat the oil in a wok, add the garlic and chillies and stir-fry for 30 seconds.

2. Add the red and yellow peppers and stir-fry for 2–3 minutes. Add the spring onions and prawns and stir-fry for a further 2–3 minutes.

3. Stir in the oyster sauce, soy sauce and lime juice and cook until heated through.

4. Serve with rice noodles.

CHICKEN POT PIE

SERVES: 4–6   PREP TIME: 30 MINS PLUS 15 MINS COOLING TIME   COOK TIME: 1 HR 15 MINS

INGREDIENTS

1 tbsp olive oil

225 g/8 oz button mushrooms, sliced

1 onion, finely chopped

350 g/12 oz carrots, sliced

115 g/4 oz celery, sliced

1 litre/1¾ pints chicken stock

85 g/3 oz butter

55 g/2 oz plain flour, plus extra for dusting

900 g/2 lb skinless, boneless chicken breasts, cut into 2.5-cm/1-inch cubes

115 g/4 oz frozen peas

1 tsp chopped fresh thyme

675 g/1 lb 8 oz shortcrust pastry, thawed, if frozen

1 egg, lightly beaten

salt and pepper

1. Heat the olive oil in a large saucepan over a medium heat. Add the mushrooms and onion and cook, stirring frequently, for about 8 minutes, until golden. Add the carrots, celery and half the stock and bring to the boil. Reduce the heat to low and simmer for 12–15 minutes, until the vegetables are almost tender.

2. Melt the butter in another large saucepan over a medium heat. Whisk in the flour and cook, stirring constantly, for 4 minutes, until the flour is light tan in colour. Gradually whisk in the remaining chicken stock. Reduce the heat to medium–low and simmer, stirring, until thickened.

3. Stir in the vegetable mixture, add the chicken, peas and thyme and season to taste with salt and pepper. Bring back to a simmer and cook, stirring constantly, for 5 minutes. Taste and adjust the seasoning, if necessary, and remove from the heat.

4. Preheat the oven to 200°C/400°F/Gas Mark 6.

5. Divide the filling between six large ramekins, filling them to within 1 cm/½ inch of the top. Roll out the pastry on a lightly floured work surface and cut out six rounds 2.5 cm/1 inch larger than the diameter of the ramekins.

6. Put the rounds on top of the filling, then fold over 1 cm/½ inch all the way around to make a rim. If you like, pinch with your fingertips to form a crimped edge. Cut a small cross in the centre of each crust.

7. Put the ramekins on a baking sheet and brush the tops with the beaten egg. Bake in the preheated oven for 35–40 minutes, until the pies are golden brown and bubbling. Remove from the oven and leave to cool for 15 minutes before serving.

19 JANUARY

PEAR & TOFFEE DESSERT

SERVES: 4   **PREP TIME: 15 MINS**   **COOK TIME: 50 MINS**

INGREDIENTS

1 tbsp unsalted butter, plus extra for greasing

4 large pears

ice cream, to serve

CRUMBLE TOPPING

115 g/4 oz self-raising flour

100 g/3½ oz unsalted butter, diced

5 tbsp demerara sugar

2 tbsp finely chopped hazelnuts

TOFFEE

3 tbsp golden syrup

3 tbsp demerara sugar

1 tbsp unsalted butter

2 tbsp single cream

½ tsp vanilla extract

1. Preheat the oven to 200°C/400°F/Gas Mark 6. Grease an ovenproof dish.

2. To make the crumble topping, put the flour in a large mixing bowl, then use your fingertips to rub in the unsalted butter until crumbly. Stir in 4 tablespoons of the sugar and the chopped hazelnuts, place in the prepared dish and cook in the preheated oven for 5–10 minutes until heated through.

3. To make the toffee, put the golden syrup into a saucepan over a low heat. Add the sugar, unsalted butter, cream and vanilla extract, and bring gently to the boil. Simmer for 3 minutes, stirring constantly, then remove from the heat and set aside.

4. Put the unsalted butter in a frying pan and melt over a low heat. Meanwhile, peel and roughly chop the pears, then add them to the pan and cook, stirring gently, for 3 minutes. Stir in the toffee and continue to cook, stirring, over a low heat for another 3 minutes.

5. Transfer the pear-and-toffee mixture to an ovenproof pie dish. Arrange the crumble evenly over the top, then sprinkle over the remaining sugar. Bake in the preheated oven for 25–30 minutes, or until the crumble is golden brown.

6. Serve hot with ice cream.

20 JANUARY

GOLDEN RAISIN CRUMBLE WITH MIXED SPICES

SERVES: 4   **PREP TIME: 15 MINS PLUS 8 HRS SOAKING TIME**   **COOK TIME: 35 MINS**

INGREDIENTS

225 g/8 oz prunes, chopped

225 g/8 oz golden raisins (sultanas)

700 ml/1¼ pints water

3 tbsp demerara sugar

1 tsp mixed spice

1 tbsp dark rum (optional)

ice cream, to serve

CRUMBLE TOPPING

115 g/4 oz self-raising flour

½ tsp mixed spice

100 g/3½ oz unsalted butter, diced

5 tbsp demerara sugar

1. Put the prunes and golden raisins in a large bowl, cover with the water and leave to soak overnight or for at least 8 hours.

2. Preheat the oven to 180°C/350°F/Gas Mark 4.

3. Drain the fruit, reserving the soaking liquid. Put the fruit in a large saucepan with the sugar and 600 ml/1 pint of the soaking liquid. Bring to the boil, then reduce the heat and simmer for about 10 minutes, or until the fruit has softened.

4. Meanwhile, to make the crumble topping, put the flour and mixed spice in a bowl, then use your fingertips to rub in the butter until crumbly. Stir in 4 tablespoons of the demerara sugar.

5. Remove the fruit from the heat, stir in the mixed spice, and the rum, if using, then pour into an ovenproof pie dish. Carefully arrange the crumble over the fruit in an even layer – keep your touch light or the crumble will sink into the filling and go mushy. Scatter the remaining sugar over the top, then transfer to the preheated oven and bake for 25 minutes, or until the crumble topping is golden brown.

6. Serve hot with ice cream.

PEAR & TOFFEE
DESSERT

MINCED BEEF & MASHED POTATOES

SERVES: 6 • PREP TIME: 20 MINS • COOK TIME: 55 MINS

INGREDIENTS

2 tbsp sunflower oil

1 onion, finely chopped

2 carrots, finely chopped

1 kg/2 lb 4 oz fresh beef mince

1 tbsp chopped fresh thyme

2 tbsp porridge oats

225 ml/8 fl oz beef stock

1 kg/2 lb 4 oz parsnips, finely chopped

1 kg/2 lb 4 oz potatoes, finely chopped

115 g/4 oz butter

6 tbsp double cream

salt and pepper

fresh flat-leaf parsley sprigs, to garnish

1. Heat the oil in a frying pan. Add the onion and carrots and cook over a low heat, stirring occasionally, for 5 minutes, until softened. Add the beef, increase the heat to medium and cook, stirring frequently and breaking it up with a wooden spoon, for 8–10 minutes, until evenly browned.

2. Stir in the thyme and oats, then pour in the stock. Season to taste with salt and pepper and bring to the boil. Reduce the heat, cover and simmer, stirring occasionally, for 25–30 minutes, until thickened.

3. Meanwhile, cook the parsnips and potatoes in a large saucepan of lightly salted boiling water for 10–15 minutes, until tender but not falling apart. Remove from the heat and drain. Return the vegetables to the pan and add the butter and cream. Season to taste with salt and pepper, then mash well until smooth.

4. Divide the mash among serving plates. Top with the beef mixture, garnish with parsley sprigs and serve.

GOLDEN CHICKEN CASSEROLE

SERVES: 4 • PREP TIME: 20 MINS • COOK TIME: 1 HR

INGREDIENTS

8 chicken joints (thighs and drumsticks)

2 tbsp olive oil

1 large onion, sliced

2.5-cm/1-inch piece fresh ginger, finely chopped

3 carrots, sliced

2 yellow peppers, deseeded and sliced

juice of 1 orange

150 ml/5 fl oz chicken stock

fresh thyme sprig

salt and pepper

1. Preheat the oven to 180°C/350°F/Gas Mark 4. Season the chicken pieces with salt and pepper to taste.

2. Heat the oil in a large saucepan or flameproof casserole, add the chicken pieces and fry, turning occasionally, for 4–5 minutes until golden brown. Remove from the pan and keep warm.

3. Add the onion to the pan and fry, stirring, for 2–3 minutes. Stir in the ginger, carrots and yellow peppers.

4. Return the chicken pieces to the pan and add the orange juice, stock and thyme. Bring to the boil, then cover and cook in the preheated oven for 40–45 minutes. Check the chicken is tender and the juices run clear when a skewer is inserted into the thickest part of the meat. Serve.

SILKY SMOOTH FISH PIE

SERVES: **6–8**   PREP TIME: **20 MINS**   COOK TIME: **1 HR 10 MINS**

INGREDIENTS

1 kg/2 lb 4 oz floury potatoes

150 g/5½ oz butter, plus extra for greasing

500 ml/18 fl oz milk

600 g/1 lb 5 oz firm white fish fillets, such as cod, haddock or pollock

400 g/14 oz undyed smoked haddock fillets

3 bay leaves

55 g/2 oz plain flour

handful of fresh parsley, chopped

250 g/9 oz cooked peeled prawns

4 hard-boiled eggs, shelled and quartered

4 tbsp melted butter

salt and pepper

minted peas, to serve

1. Peel and quarter the potatoes. Bring a large saucepan of lightly salted water to the boil, add the potatoes and cook for 15–20 minutes, or until tender. Drain and mash thoroughly with half of the butter and 2 tablespoons of the milk. Season to taste with salt and pepper and cover and keep warm.

2. Preheat the oven to 200°C/400°F/Gas Mark 6. Rinse the fish under cold running water and pat dry with kitchen paper. Place the fish fillets in a shallow saucepan and pour over the remaining milk. Add the bay leaves and place over a low heat. Bring the milk to a gentle simmer and poach the fish for 4 minutes (it shouldn't be fully cooked as it will be baked later). Remove from the saucepan and place on a plate, discard the bay leaves and reserve the milk. Remove any remaining bones and skin from the fish and flake into large chunks. Put in a bowl, cover and set aside.

3. Melt the remaining butter in a saucepan, then stir in the flour to make a roux and cook, stirring occasionally, for 3 minutes. Gradually add the reserved milk, a ladleful at a time, and mix into the roux. Add the parsley, the cooked fish, the prawns and eggs. Carefully fold together. Season to taste with salt and pepper.

4. Grease a pie dish with butter and fill it with the fish mixture. Spoon the mashed potatoes on top, smoothing the surface level. Drizzle the melted butter over the whole pie, place in the preheated oven and bake for 30–40 minutes, until the top is golden brown. Serve with minted peas.

24 JANUARY

SLOW-COOKED POTATO STEW

SERVES: 4 **PREP TIME: 20 MINS** **COOK TIME: 1 HR**

INGREDIENTS

700 g/1 lb 9 oz waxy potatoes, cut into 2.5-cm/1-inch cubes

25 g/1 oz butter

2 tbsp olive oil

55 g/2 oz pancetta or bacon, diced

1 onion, finely chopped

1 garlic clove, finely chopped

1 celery stick, finely chopped

400 g/14 oz canned chopped tomatoes

2 tbsp tomato purée

brown sugar, to taste

1 tbsp chopped fresh marjoram

100 ml/3½ fl oz vegetable stock

salt and pepper

1. Parboil the potatoes in a saucepan of lightly salted boiling water for 5 minutes. Drain and set aside.

2. Melt the butter with the oil in a saucepan. Add the pancetta, onion, garlic and celery and cook over a low heat, stirring occasionally, for 5 minutes, until softened. Stir in the tomatoes, tomato purée, sugar to taste, marjoram and stock and season to taste with salt and pepper. Increase the heat to medium and bring to the boil. Gently stir in the potatoes, reduce the heat to very low, cover and simmer, stirring occasionally, for 45–50 minutes, until the potatoes are tender and the sauce has thickened. (Use a fork to stir gently to avoid breaking up the potatoes.)

3. Taste and adjust the seasoning, adding salt and pepper if needed. Transfer the mixture to a serving dish and serve.

SLOW-COOKED
POTATO STEW

25 JANUARY

MAPLE-CREAM TART

SERVES: 6–8   PREP TIME: 15 MINS   COOK TIME: 55 MINS

INGREDIENTS

375 g/13 oz ready-made shortcrust pastry, thawed if frozen

60 g/2¼ oz plain flour, plus extra for dusting

3 tbsp soft light brown sugar

700 ml/1¼ pints double cream

250 ml/9 fl oz pure maple syrup

2 eggs

4 tsp lemon juice

½ tsp salt

½ tsp ground nutmeg

2 tbsp icing sugar

1. Preheat the oven to 200°C/400°F/Gas Mark 6. Roll out the pastry on a lightly floured surface and use to line a 23-cm/9-inch loose-based tart tin. Line the pastry with greaseproof paper and weigh down with dried beans. Place on a baking sheet and bake in the preheated oven for 15–20 minutes, until golden at the edges.

2. Meanwhile, combine the flour and sugar in a large bowl. Beat 450 ml/16 fl oz of the cream in another bowl with the maple syrup, eggs, lemon juice, salt and nutmeg. Slowly whisk this mixture into the flour, whisking until no lumps remain.

3. When the pastry case is golden, remove the paper and beans and reduce the oven temperature to 180°C/350°F/Gas Mark 4. Pour the filling into the pastry case, return to the oven and cook for 30–35 minutes, until set. Remove the tart from the oven and leave to cool completely on a wire rack.

4. Whip the remaining cream until soft peaks form. Sift over the icing sugar and continue whipping until stiff. Just before serving, spread the whipped cream over the surface of the tart. Cut into slices to serve.

26 JANUARY

CHURROS

SERVES: 4–6   PREP TIME: 15 MINS   COOK TIME: 15 MINS

INGREDIENTS

225 ml/8 fl oz water

85 g/3 oz butter or shortening, diced

2 tbsp brown sugar

finely grated rind of 1 small orange (optional)

pinch of salt

175 g/6 oz plain flour, well sifted

1 tsp ground cinnamon, plus extra for dusting

1 tsp vanilla essence

2 eggs

vegetable oil, for deep-frying

caster sugar, for dusting

1. Heat the water, butter, brown sugar, orange rind, if using, and salt in a heavy-based saucepan over a medium heat until the butter has melted.

2. Add the flour, all at once, the cinnamon and vanilla essence, then remove the pan from the heat and beat rapidly until the mixture pulls away from the side of the pan. Let cool slightly, then beat in the eggs, one at a time, beating well after each addition, until the mixture is thick and smooth. Spoon into a piping bag fitted with a wide star nozzle.

3. Heat the oil for deep-frying in a deep-fryer or deep saucepan to 180–190°C/350–375°F, or until a cube of bread browns in 30 seconds. Pipe 13-cm/5-inch lengths about 7.5 cm/3 inches apart into the oil. Deep-fry for 2 minutes on each side, or until golden brown. Remove with a slotted spoon and drain on kitchen paper.

4. Dust the churros with caster sugar and cinnamon and serve.

MAPLE-CREAM
TART

27 JANUARY

REAL HOT CHOCOLATE

SERVES: 1–2   **PREP TIME: 5 MINS**   **COOK TIME: 15 MINS**

INGREDIENTS

40 g/1½ oz plain chocolate, broken into pieces

300 ml/10 fl oz milk

chocolate curls, to decorate

1. Place the chocolate in a large, heatproof jug. Place the milk in a heavy-based saucepan and bring to the boil. Pour about one quarter of the milk on to the chocolate and leave until the chocolate has softened.

2. Whisk the milk and chocolate mixture until smooth. Return the remaining milk to the heat and return to the boil, then pour on to the chocolate, whisking constantly.

3. Pour into mugs or cups and decorate with chocolate curls.

28 JANUARY

CINNAMON MOCHA

SERVES: 6   **PREP TIME: 15 MINS**   **COOK TIME: 10 MINS**

INGREDIENTS

250 g/9 oz milk chocolate, broken into pieces

175 ml/6 fl oz single cream

1 litre/1¾ pints freshly brewed coffee

1 tsp ground cinnamon, plus extra to decorate

TO DECORATE

whipped cream

marbled chocolate caraque

1. Put the chocolate in a large heatproof bowl set over a saucepan of gently simmering water. Add the cream and stir until the chocolate has melted and the mixture is smooth.

2. Pour in the coffee, add the cinnamon and whisk until foamy. Pour into mugs or cups and decorate with the cream, caraque and cinnamon. If serving cold, remove the bowl from the heat and leave to cool. Chill in the refrigerator until required, then decorate with whipped cream, a sprinkling of ground cinnamon, and the caraque.

RICE PUDDING WITH CINNAMON-POACHED PLUMS

SERVES: 4   PREP TIME: 15 MINS   COOK TIME: 50–55 MINS

INGREDIENTS

85 g/3 oz pudding rice

25 g/1 oz caster sugar

15 g/½ oz unsalted butter

500 ml/18 fl oz milk

thinly pared strip of orange rind

shreds of orange zest, to decorate

COMPOTE

500 g/1 lb 2 oz red plums, halved and stoned

1 cinnamon stick

2 tbsp golden caster sugar

juice of 1 orange

1. Put the rice, sugar and butter into a saucepan and stir in the milk and orange rind. Heat gently, stirring occasionally, until almost boiling.

2. Reduce the heat to low, then cover and simmer gently for 40–45 minutes, stirring occasionally, until the rice is tender and most of the liquid has been absorbed.

3. Meanwhile, to make the compote, put the plums, cinnamon, sugar and orange juice into a large saucepan. Heat gently until just boiling, then reduce the heat, cover and simmer gently for about 10 minutes, or until the plums are tender.

4. Remove the plums with a slotted spoon and discard the cinnamon. Serve the rice pudding warm with the compote and sprinkled with orange zest.

30 JANUARY

CREAMY TURKEY & BROCCOLI GNOCCHI

SERVES: 4   **PREP TIME: 15 MINS**   **COOK TIME: 10 MINS**

INGREDIENTS

1 tbsp sunflower oil

500 g/1 lb 2 oz turkey stir-fry strips

2 small leeks, sliced diagonally

500 g/1 lb 2 oz ready-made fresh gnocchi

200 g/7 oz broccoli, cut into bite-sized pieces

85 g/3 oz crème fraîche

1 tbsp wholegrain mustard

3 tbsp orange juice

3 tbsp pine kernels

salt and pepper

1. Heat the oil in a wok or large frying pan, then add the turkey and leeks and stir-fry over a high heat for 5–6 minutes.

2. Meanwhile, bring a saucepan of lightly salted water to the boil. Add the gnocchi and broccoli, then cook for 3–4 minutes.

3. Drain the gnocchi and broccoli and stir into the turkey mixture.

4. Mix together the crème fraîche, mustard and orange juice in a small bowl. Season to taste with salt and pepper, then stir into the wok.

5. Sprinkle with pine kernels and serve.

31 JANUARY

TURKEY STEAKS WITH PROSCIUTTO & SAGE

SERVES: 4   **PREP TIME: 15 MINS**   **COOK TIME: 2 MINS**

INGREDIENTS

2 skinless, boneless turkey steaks

2 slices Parma ham, halved

4 fresh sage leaves

2 tbsp plain flour

2 tbsp olive oil

1 tbsp butter

salt and pepper

lemon wedges, to serve

1. Slice each turkey steak in half horizontally into two thinner escalopes.

2. Put each escalope between two sheets of clingfilm and pound lightly with a rolling pin. Season each escalope with salt and pepper to taste.

3. Lay half a slice of ham on each escalope, put a sage leaf on top and secure with a cocktail stick.

4. Mix the flour with salt and pepper to taste on a large plate. Dust both sides of each escalope with the seasoned flour.

5. Heat the oil in a large frying pan, add the butter and cook until foaming. Add the escalopes and fry over a medium heat for 1½ minutes, sage-side down.

6. Turn the escalopes over and fry for a further 30 seconds, or until golden brown and cooked through. Serve with lemon wedges.

CREAMY TURKEY &
BROCCOLI GNOCCHI

FEBRUARY

DOUGHNUTS WITH CINNAMON SUGAR

MAKES: 12–14   PREP TIME: 20 MINS PLUS RISING TIME   COOK TIME: 10–15 MINS

INGREDIENTS

500 g/1 lb 2 oz plain flour, plus extra for dusting

85 g/3 oz caster sugar

½ tsp salt

1 sachet easy-blend dried yeast

175 ml/6 fl oz lukewarm milk

70 g/2½ oz unsalted butter, melted

2 eggs, beaten

finely grated rind of 1 lemon

sunflower oil, for deep-frying

55 g/2 oz caster sugar and 1 tsp ground cinnamon, to coat

1. Sift together the flour, sugar and salt into a mixing bowl and stir in the yeast. Stir in the milk, butter, eggs and lemon rind, mixing to a soft, sticky dough.

2. Turn out the dough onto a lightly floured work surface and knead until smooth. Return to the bowl, cover and leave in a warm place for about 1 hour, or until doubled in size.

3. Turn out the dough onto a lightly floured work surface and knead again for 5 minutes until smooth and elastic. Roll out to a thickness of 1 cm/½ inch. Stamp out 7.5-cm/3-inch rounds with a cutter, then cut a 2.5-cm/1-inch round from the centre of each.

4. Place the rings on a baking sheet lined with greaseproof paper, cover and leave to rise in a warm place for about 1 hour until doubled in size.

5. Heat the oil for deep-frying in a deep-fryer or deep saucepan to 180–190°C/350–375°F, or until a cube of bread browns in 30 seconds. Add the doughnuts in small batches and fry, turning once, for 3–4 minutes until golden brown.

6. Remove the doughnuts with a slotted spoon and drain on absorbent kitchen paper. Mix together the caster sugar and cinnamon and toss the doughnuts in the mixture until lightly coated. Serve warm.

CHICKEN CHOW MEIN

SERVES: 4   PREP TIME: 20 MINS   COOK TIME: 10 MINS

INGREDIENTS

250 g/9 oz dried medium Chinese egg noodles

2 tbsp sunflower oil

280 g/10 oz cooked chicken breasts, shredded

1 garlic clove, finely chopped

1 red pepper, thinly sliced

100 g/3½ oz shiitake mushrooms, sliced

6 spring onions, sliced

100 g/3½ oz beansprouts

3 tbsp soy sauce

1 tbsp sesame oil

1. Place the noodles in a large bowl or dish and break them up slightly. Pour enough boiling water over the noodles to cover and set aside while preparing the other ingredients.

2. In a preheated wok or frying pan, heat the oil over a medium heat. Add the shredded chicken, garlic, red pepper, mushrooms, spring onions and beansprouts to the wok and stir-fry for about 5 minutes.

3. Drain the noodles thoroughly then add them to the wok, toss well and stir-fry for a further 5 minutes. Drizzle over the soy sauce and sesame oil and toss until thoroughly combined. Transfer to serving bowls and serve.

BAKED EGGS WITH TOMATO & SWEETCORN SAUCE

SERVES: 4 **PREP TIME: 20 MINS** **COOK TIME: 1 HR**

INGREDIENTS

25 g/1 oz butter

2 tbsp olive oil

1 onion, finely chopped

2 garlic cloves, finely chopped

1 celery stick, finely chopped

225 g/8 oz lean bacon, diced

1 red pepper, deseeded and diced

500 g/1 lb 2 oz plum tomatoes, peeled, cored and chopped

2 tbsp tomato purée

brown sugar, to taste

1 tbsp chopped fresh parsley

pinch of cayenne pepper

100 ml/3½ fl oz water

225 g/8 oz canned sweetcorn, drained

4 large eggs

salt and pepper

1. Melt the butter with the oil in a saucepan. Add the onion, garlic and celery and cook over a low heat, stirring occasionally, for 5 minutes, until softened. Add the bacon and red pepper and cook, stirring occasionally, for a further 10 minutes. Stir in the tomatoes, tomato purée, sugar to taste, parsley, cayenne and water and season to taste with salt and pepper. Increase the heat to medium and bring to the boil, then reduce the heat and simmer, stirring occasionally, for 15 minutes, until thickened. Meanwhile, preheat the oven to 180°C/350°F/Gas Mark 4.

2. Stir the sweetcorn into the sauce and transfer the mixture to an ovenproof dish. Make four small hollows with the back of a spoon and break an egg into each. Bake in the preheated oven for 25–30 minutes, until the eggs have set. Serve.

RICH ORANGE CRÊPES

SERVES: 4   PREP TIME: 15 MINS   COOK TIME: 10 MINS

INGREDIENTS

CRÊPES

150 g/5½ oz plain flour

200 ml/7 fl oz milk

3 tbsp fresh orange juice

1 large egg

2 tbsp melted butter, plus extra for frying

2 oranges, segmented, to serve

ORANGE BUTTER

55 g/2 oz unsalted butter

finely grated rind and juice of 1 orange

1 tbsp caster sugar

1. To make the crêpes, put all the ingredients (excluding the segmented oranges) into a mixing bowl and whisk until smooth. Alternatively, whizz in a food processor until smooth.

2. Heat a crêpe pan until hot, lightly brush with butter and pour in a small ladleful of batter, swirling to thinly coat the surface of the pan.

3. Cook the crêpes until golden underneath, then turn and cook the other side. Remove from the pan and keep warm while you cook the remaining batter. Keep warm.

4. To make the orange butter, melt the butter in a small saucepan, add the orange rind and juice and the sugar and stir until the sugar has dissolved. Simmer, stirring, for 30 seconds, then remove from the heat.

5. Serve the crêpes folded over, with the orange segments and the orange butter poured over.

BREAD & BUTTER PUDDING

SERVES: 4–6   PREP TIME: 15 MINS PLUS 15 MINS STANDING TIME   COOK TIME: 40 MINS

INGREDIENTS

85 g/3 oz butter, softened

6 slices of thick white bread

55 g/2 oz mixed dried fruit, such as sultanas, currants and raisins

25 g/1 oz mixed peel

3 large eggs

300 ml/10 fl oz milk

150 ml/5 fl oz double cream

55 g/2 oz caster sugar

whole nutmeg, for grating

1 tbsp demerara sugar

pouring cream, to serve (optional)

1. Preheat the oven to 180°C/350°F/Gas Mark 4.

2. Use a little of the butter to grease a 20 x 25-cm/8 x 10-inch baking dish. Butter the slices of bread, cut into quarters and arrange half of the slices overlapping in the prepared baking dish.

3. Scatter half the fruit and mixed peel over the bread, cover with the remaining bread slices, then add the remaining fruit and mixed peel.

4. In a mixing jug, whisk the eggs well and mix in the milk, cream and sugar. Pour over the pudding and leave to stand for 15 minutes to allow the bread to soak up some of the egg mixture. Tuck in most of the fruit as you don't want it to burn in the oven.

5. Grate nutmeg to taste over the top of the pudding, then sprinkle over the demerara sugar.

6. Place the pudding on a baking sheet and bake at the top of the preheated oven for 30–40 minutes, until just set and golden brown.

7. Remove from the oven and serve warm with a little cream, if using.

RICH ORANGE
CRÊPES

CHICKEN CASSEROLE PROVENÇAL

SERVES: 4 | **PREP TIME: 15 MINS** | **COOK TIME: 1 HR 10 MINS**

INGREDIENTS

4 chicken leg joints

2 tbsp olive oil

1 large red onion, cut into 8 wedges

1 large green pepper, deseeded and thickly sliced

1 aubergine, cubed

2 garlic cloves, crushed

400 g/14 oz canned plum tomatoes

8 black olives, stoned

salt and pepper

crusty bread or cooked polenta, to serve

1. Trim any excess fat from the chicken and season well with salt and pepper. Heat half the oil in a flameproof casserole or wide saucepan. Add the chicken and fry over a fairly high heat, turning occasionally, for 5–6 minutes until golden brown. Remove from the casserole and keep warm.

2. Add the remaining oil, the onion, green pepper and aubergine to the casserole and fry, stirring frequently, for 4–5 minutes until lightly browned. Stir in the garlic. Return the chicken to the casserole and add the tomatoes and olives.

3. Bring to the boil, then reduce the heat to low, cover and simmer very gently for 45–50 minutes until the vegetables and chicken are tender and the juices run clear when a skewer is inserted into the thickest part of the meat.

4. Adjust the seasoning to taste and serve the casserole hot, with crusty bread.

CHILLI, HAM & SPINACH PASTA

SERVES: 4 | **PREP TIME: 10 MINS** | **COOK TIME: 20 MINS**

INGREDIENTS

250 g/9 oz dried penne pasta

2 tbsp olive oil

1 onion, thinly sliced

1 dried red chilli, chopped

2 plum tomatoes, diced

200 g/7 oz cooked ham, sliced into strips

200 g/7 oz baby spinach leaves

salt and pepper

1. Bring a large, heavy-based saucepan of lightly salted water to the boil. Add the penne, bring back to the boil and cook for 8–10 minutes, or until just tender but still firm to the bite. Drain.

2. Meanwhile, heat the oil in a large frying pan over a medium heat, add the onion and fry, stirring, for 2–3 minutes until soft.

3. Add the chilli and tomatoes and cook, stirring, for 2 minutes, then add the ham and cook, stirring, for 2–3 minutes until heated through.

4. Add the spinach and stir until the leaves are just wilted, then stir in the pasta. Season to taste with salt and pepper and serve.

TAMALE PIE

SERVES: 6   **PREP TIME: 15 MINS**   **COOK TIME: 50 MINS**

INGREDIENTS

2 tbsp corn oil

1 onion, finely chopped

350 g/12 oz fresh beef mince

1½ tsp chilli powder

200 g/7 oz canned chopped tomatoes

140 g/5 oz canned sweetcorn, drained

2 tbsp chopped stoned black olives

100 ml/3½ fl oz soured cream

125 g/4½ oz cornmeal or coarse polenta

½ tsp baking powder

55 g/2 oz butter, cut into pieces

3 tbsp milk

about 225 ml/8 fl oz hot chicken stock

85 g/3 oz Cheddar cheese, grated

salt

1. Preheat the oven to 190°C/375°F/Gas Mark 5. Heat the oil in a large frying pan. Add the onion and cook over a low heat, stirring occasionally, for 5 minutes, until softened.

2. Add the beef, increase the heat to medium and cook, stirring frequently and breaking it up with a wooden spoon, for 8–10 minutes, until evenly browned. Stir in the chilli powder, tomatoes, sweetcorn, olives and soured cream and season to taste with salt. Transfer the mixture to an ovenproof dish.

3. Put the cornmeal, baking powder, butter and milk in a food processor and process until combined. With the motor running, gradually add enough of the hot stock through the feeder tube to make a thick, smooth mixture.

4. Pour the cornmeal mixture over the beef mixture and smooth the surface with a palette knife. Bake in the preheated oven for 20 minutes, until the topping is just beginning to brown. Sprinkle with the cheese, return to the oven and bake for a further 15 minutes, until golden and bubbling. Serve.

WILD MUSHROOM RISOTTO

SERVES: 6   PREP TIME: 20 MINS PLUS 30 MINS SOAKING TIME   COOK TIME: 15–20 MINS

INGREDIENTS

55 g/2 oz dried porcini or morel mushrooms

about 500 g/1 lb 2 oz mixed fresh wild mushrooms, such as porcini, field mushrooms and chanterelles, halved if large

4 tbsp olive oil

3–4 garlic cloves, finely chopped

55 g/2 oz butter

1 onion, finely chopped

350 g/12 oz risotto rice

50 ml/2 fl oz dry white vermouth

1.2 litres/2 pints simmering chicken or vegetable stock

115 g/4 oz freshly grated Parmesan cheese

4 tbsp chopped fresh flat-leaf parsley

salt and pepper

1. Place the dried mushrooms in a heatproof bowl and add boiling water to cover. Set aside to soak for 30 minutes, then carefully lift out and pat dry. Strain the soaking liquid through a sieve lined with kitchen paper and set aside.

2. Trim the fresh mushrooms and gently brush clean. Heat 3 tablespoons of the oil in a large frying pan. Add the fresh mushrooms and stir-fry for 1–2 minutes. Add the garlic and the soaked mushrooms and cook, stirring frequently, for 2 minutes. Transfer to a plate.

3. Heat the remaining oil and half the butter in a large heavy-based saucepan. Add the onion and cook over a medium heat, stirring occasionally, for 2 minutes, until softened.

4. Reduce the heat, stir in the rice and cook, stirring constantly, for 2–3 minutes, until the grains are translucent. Add the vermouth and cook, stirring, for 1 minute until reduced.

5. Gradually add the hot stock, a ladleful at a time, until all the liquid is absorbed and the rice is creamy. Add half the reserved mushroom soaking liquid to the risotto and stir in the mushrooms. Season to taste and add more mushroom liquid, if necessary.

6. Remove the pan from the heat and stir in the remaining butter, grated Parmesan and chopped parsley. Serve.

LAMB STEW

SERVES: 4   PREP TIME: **10 MINS**   COOK TIME: **40 MINS**

INGREDIENTS

1 tbsp sunflower oil

4 lamb chump chops

1 garlic clove, crushed

2 small onions, quartered

300 g/10½ oz small whole carrots

2 small turnips, quartered

1 tbsp plain flour

300 ml/10 fl oz lamb stock or beef stock

1 tbsp wholegrain mustard

salt and pepper

chopped fresh flat-leaf parsley, to garnish

1. Heat the oil in a flameproof casserole, add the lamb chops and fry until golden brown, turning once. Remove from the pan and keep warm.

2. Add the garlic and onions to the pan and fry, stirring, for 2–3 minutes. Stir in the carrots and turnips.

3. Stir the flour into the vegetables and add the stock. Cook, stirring, until boiling, then add the chops. Season to taste with salt and pepper, then cover and simmer gently for 35 minutes, stirring occasionally.

4. Stir in the mustard and adjust the seasoning to taste. Sprinkle with the parsley and serve.

CAULIFLOWER CHEESE

SERVES: 4–6   PREP TIME: 15 MINS   COOK TIME: 10 MINS

INGREDIENTS

1 cauliflower, trimmed and cut into florets (675 g/1 lb 8 oz prepared weight)

40 g/1½ oz butter

40 g/1½ oz plain flour

450 ml/16 fl oz milk

115 g/4 oz Cheddar cheese, finely grated

whole nutmeg, for grating

1 tbsp freshly grated Parmesan cheese

salt and pepper

1. Bring a saucepan of lightly salted water to the boil, add the cauliflower, bring back to the boil and cook for 4–5 minutes. It should still be firm. Drain, place in a warmed 1.4-litre/2½-pint gratin dish and keep warm.

2. Melt the butter in the rinsed-out pan over a medium heat and stir in the flour. Cook for 1 minute, stirring constantly.

3. Remove the pan from the heat and gradually stir in the milk until you have a smooth consistency.

4. Return the pan to a low heat and continue to stir while the sauce comes to the boil and thickens. Reduce the heat and simmer gently, stirring constantly, for about 3 minutes, until the sauce is creamy and smooth.

5. Remove from the heat and stir in the Cheddar cheese and a good grating of the nutmeg. Taste and season well with salt and pepper. Meanwhile, preheat the grill to high.

6. Pour the hot sauce over the cauliflower, top with the Parmesan cheese and place under the preheated grill to brown. Serve.

ROAST POTATOES

SERVES: 4–6   PREP TIME: 10 MINS   COOK TIME: 1 HR 5 MINS

INGREDIENTS

1.3 kg/3 lb large floury potatoes, such as King Edward, Maris Piper or Desirée, peeled and cut into even-sized chunks

3 tbsp dripping, goose fat, duck fat or olive oil

salt

1. Preheat the oven to 220°C/425°F/Gas Mark 7.

2. Bring a large saucepan of lightly salted water to the boil, add the potatoes, bring back to the boil and cook for 5–7 minutes. The potatoes should still be firm. Remove from the heat.

3. Meanwhile, add the dripping to a roasting tin and place the tin in the preheated oven.

4. Drain the potatoes well and return them to the saucepan. Cover with the lid and firmly shake the pan so that the surface of the potatoes is roughened to help give a much crisper texture.

5. Remove the roasting tin from the oven and carefully tip the potatoes into the hot oil. Baste them to ensure they are all coated with the oil.

6. Roast at the top of the oven for 45–50 minutes until they are browned all over and thoroughly crisp. Turn the potatoes and baste again only once during the process or the crunchy edges will be destroyed.

7. Carefully transfer the potatoes from the roasting tin into a serving dish. Sprinkle with a little salt and serve.

CAULIFLOWER
CHEESE

WALNUT & PECORINO SCONES

MAKES: **ABOUT 10**   PREP TIME: **20 MINS**   COOK TIME: **15 MINS**

INGREDIENTS

450 g/1 lb self-raising flour, plus extra for dusting

pinch of salt

85 g/3 oz butter, diced, plus extra for greasing

50 g/1¾ oz caster sugar

50 g/1¾ pecorino cheese

100 g/3½ oz walnut pieces

about 300 ml/10 fl oz milk

1. Preheat the oven to 200°C/400°F/Gas Mark 6. Grease a baking sheet.

2. Sift the flour and salt into a large bowl. Add the butter and rub in with your fingertips until the mixture resembles fine breadcrumbs. Stir in the sugar, pecorino cheese and walnuts. Add enough of the milk to bring the mixture together into a soft but not sticky dough.

3. Gently roll the dough out on a lightly floured work surface to a thickness of 2.5–3 cm/1–1¼ inches. Use a 6-cm/2½-inch round biscuit cutter to cut into rounds (make the scones smaller or larger if you prefer).

4. Put the rounds on the prepared baking sheet and bake in the preheated oven for 15 minutes, or until golden and firm. Remove from the oven and leave to cool on a wire rack.

BE MY VALENTINE WHOOPIE PIES

MAKES: 14   PREP TIME: **20 MINS**   COOK TIME: **30–35 MINS**

INGREDIENTS

250 g/9 oz plain flour

1 tsp bicarbonate of soda

large pinch of salt

115 g/4 oz butter, softened

150 g/5½ oz caster sugar

1 large egg, beaten

1 tsp vanilla extract

150 ml/5 fl oz buttermilk

¼ tsp edible red liquid food colouring

2 tbsp pink heart-shaped sugar sprinkles

VANILLA BUTTERCREAM

150 g/5½ oz unsalted butter, softened

1 tsp vanilla extract

4 tbsp double cream

280 g/10 oz icing sugar, sifted

ICING

150 g/5½ oz icing sugar

1–2 tbsp warm water

few drops edible red liquid food colouring

1. Preheat the oven to 180°C/350°F/Gas Mark 4. Line two to three large baking sheets with greaseproof paper. Sift together the plain flour, bicarbonate of soda and salt.

2. Place the butter and sugar in a large bowl and beat with an electric whisk until pale and fluffy. Beat in the egg and vanilla extract followed by half of the flour mixture then the buttermilk and food colouring. Stir in the rest of the flour mixture and mix until thoroughly incorporated.

3. Pipe or spoon 28 mounds of the mixture onto the prepared baking sheets, spaced well apart to allow for spreading. Bake in the preheated oven, one sheet at a time, for 9–11 minutes until risen and just firm to the touch. Cool for 5 minutes then using a palette knife transfer to a wire rack and leave to cool completely.

4. For the vanilla buttercream, place the butter and vanilla extract in a bowl and beat with an electric whisk for 2–3 minutes until pale and creamy. Beat in the cream then gradually beat in the icing sugar and continue beating for 2–3 minutes.

5. For the icing, sift the icing sugar into a bowl and stir in enough water to make a smooth icing that is thick enough to coat the back of a wooden spoon. Beat in a few drops of food colouring to colour the icing pale pink.

6. To assemble, spread or pipe the vanilla buttercream on the flat side of half of the cakes. Top with the rest of the cakes. Spoon the icing over the whoopie pies and decorate with the heart-shaped sugar sprinkles. Leave to set.

ROASTED SALMON WITH LEMON & HERBS

SERVES: 4–6   PREP TIME: 20 MINS   COOK TIME: 15 MINS

INGREDIENTS

6 tbsp extra virgin olive oil

1 onion, sliced

1 leek, trimmed and sliced

juice of ½ lemon

2 tbsp chopped fresh parsley

2 tbsp chopped fresh dill

500 g/1 lb 2 oz salmon fillets

salt and pepper

cooked baby spinach leaves and lemon wedges, to serve

1. Preheat the oven to 200°C/400°F/Gas Mark 6. Heat 1 tablespoon of the oil in a frying pan over a medium heat. Add the onion and leek and cook, stirring, for about 4 minutes, until slightly soft.

2. Meanwhile, put the remaining oil in a small bowl with the lemon juice, herbs and salt and pepper to taste. Stir together well. Rinse the fish under cold running water, then pat dry with kitchen paper. Arrange the fish in an ovenproof baking dish.

3. Remove the frying pan from the heat and spread the onion and leek over the fish. Pour the oil mixture over the top, ensuring that everything is well coated. Bake in the preheated oven for about 10 minutes, or until the fish is cooked through.

4. Arrange the cooked spinach on serving plates. Remove the fish and vegetables from the oven and arrange on top of the spinach. Serve with the lemon wedges.

CARAMELIZED ONION TART

SERVES: 4–6   PREP TIME: 10 MINS   COOK TIME: 1 HR

INGREDIENTS

100 g/3½ oz unsalted butter

600 g/1 lb 5 oz onions, thinly sliced

2 eggs

100 ml/3½ fl oz double cream

100 g/3½ oz grated Gruyère cheese

20-cm/8-inch ready-baked pastry case

100 g/3½ oz Parmesan cheese, coarsely grated

salt and pepper

1. Melt the butter in a heavy-based frying pan over a medium heat. Add the onions and cook, stirring frequently to avoid burning, for 30 minutes, or until well-browned and caramelized. Remove the onions from the pan and set aside.

2. Preheat the oven to 190°C/375°F/Gas Mark 5. Beat the eggs in a large bowl, stir in the cream and season to taste with salt and pepper. Add the Gruyère cheese and mix well. Stir in the cooked onions.

3. Pour the egg and onion mixture into the baked pastry case and sprinkle with the Parmesan cheese. Place on a baking sheet and bake in the preheated oven for 15–20 minutes until the filling has set and is beginning to brown.

4. Remove from the oven and leave to rest for at least 10 minutes. The tart can be served hot or left to cool to room temperature.

BROCCOLI & STILTON SOUP

SERVES: 4–6   PREP TIME: 15 MINS   COOK TIME: 35 MINS

INGREDIENTS

40 g/1½ oz butter

2 onions, chopped

1 large potato, chopped

750 g/1 lb 10 oz broccoli florets

1.5 litres/2¾ pints vegetable stock

150 g/5½ oz Stilton cheese, diced

pinch of ground mace

salt and pepper

croûtons, to garnish

1. Melt the butter in a large saucepan. Add the onions and potato and stir well. Cover and cook over a low heat for 7 minutes. Add the broccoli and stir well, then re-cover the pan and cook for a further 5 minutes.

2. Increase the heat to medium, pour in the stock and bring to the boil. Reduce the heat, season to taste with salt and pepper and re-cover. Simmer for 15–20 minutes, until the vegetables are tender.

3. Remove the pan from the heat, strain into a bowl, reserving the vegetables, and leave to cool slightly. Put the vegetables into a food processor, add 1 ladleful of the stock and process to a smooth purée. With the motor running, gradually add the remaining stock.

4. Return the soup to the rinsed-out pan and reheat gently, but do not allow the soup to boil. Remove from the heat and stir in the cheese until melted and thoroughly combined. Stir in the mace and taste and adjust the seasoning, if necessary. Ladle into serving bowls, sprinkle with the croûtons and serve.

FISH WITH WHITE WINE, CHILLI & TAPENADE

SERVES: 4   PREP TIME: 5 MINS   COOK TIME: 20 MINS

INGREDIENTS

1 tbsp olive oil

4 white fish fillets

4 tbsp tapenade

1 small red finger chilli, finely diced

4 tbsp freshly grated Parmesan cheese

4 tbsp dry white wine

salt and pepper

cooked rice, to serve

1. Preheat the oven to 220°C/425°F/Gas Mark 7. Brush a wide, ovenproof dish with the oil.

2. Season the fish with salt and pepper to taste and place in the prepared dish in a single layer.

3. Mix together the tapenade and chilli and spread over the fish, then sprinkle with the cheese.

4. Pour the wine around the fish and bake in the preheated oven for about 15 minutes, or until the flesh flakes easily. Serve with rice.

APPLE & SPICE PORRIDGE

SERVES: 4   PREP TIME: 5 MINS   COOK TIME: 10 MINS

INGREDIENTS

600 ml/1 pint milk or water

1 tsp salt

115 g/4 oz medium rolled porridge oats

2 large apples

½ tsp ground mixed spice

honey, to serve (optional)

1. Put the milk in a saucepan and bring to the boil. Add the salt and sprinkle in the oats, stirring constantly.

2. Place over a low heat and leave the oats to simmer for 10 minutes, stirring occasionally.

3. Meanwhile, peel, halve, core and grate the apples. When the porridge is creamy and most of the liquid has evaporated, stir in the grated apple and mixed spice. Spoon into serving bowls and drizzle with the honey, if using.

SLOPPY JOES

SERVES: 4   PREP TIME: 15 MINS   COOK TIME: 40 MINS

INGREDIENTS

450 g/1 lb fresh beef mince

1 onion, chopped

1 garlic clove, chopped

1 green pepper, deseeded and chopped

1 tbsp American mustard

175 ml/6 fl oz tomato ketchup

1 tsp white vinegar

1 tbsp brown sugar

pinch of chilli powder, ground cloves or paprika (optional)

4 burger buns, split

salt and pepper

1. Put the beef, onion, garlic and green pepper into a non-stick frying pan and cook over a medium heat, stirring frequently and breaking up the beef with a wooden spoon, for 8–10 minutes, until the beef is evenly browned. Carefully drain off the fat.

2. Stir in the mustard, tomato ketchup, vinegar, brown sugar and chilli powder, if using. Season to taste with salt and pepper. Reduce the heat and simmer, stirring occasionally, for 30 minutes.

3. Divide the mixture among the burger buns and serve.

APPLE & SPICE
PORRIDGE

SPAGHETTI BOLOGNESE

SERVES: 4   PREP TIME: 25 MINS   COOK TIME: 1 HR

INGREDIENTS

1 tbsp olive oil

1 onion, finely chopped

2 garlic cloves, chopped

1 carrot, chopped

1 celery stick, chopped

50 g/1¾ oz pancetta or streaky bacon, diced

350 g/12 oz fresh beef mince

400 g/14 oz canned chopped tomatoes

2 tsp dried oregano

125 ml/4 fl oz red wine

2 tbsp tomato purée

350 g/12 oz dried spaghetti

salt and pepper

chopped fresh flat-leaf parsley, to garnish

1. Heat the oil in a large frying pan. Add the onion and cook for 3 minutes. Add the garlic, carrot, celery and pancetta and sauté for 3–4 minutes, or until just beginning to brown.

2. Add the beef and cook over a high heat for another 3 minutes or until all of the meat is brown. Stir in the tomatoes, oregano and red wine and bring to the boil. Reduce the heat and leave to simmer for about 45 minutes.

3. Stir in the tomato purée and season to taste with salt and pepper.

4. Bring a large, heavy-based saucepan of lightly salted water to the boil. Add the spaghetti, bring back to the boil and cook for 8–10 minutes, or until just tender but still firm to the bite. Drain.

5. Transfer the spaghetti to serving plates and pour over the bolognese sauce. Toss to mix well, garnish with parsley and serve hot.

ROAST CHICKEN

SERVES: 6   PREP TIME: 10 MINS   COOK TIME: 2 HRS 10 MINS

INGREDIENTS

1 chicken, weighing 2.25 kg/5 lb

55 g/2 oz soft butter

2 tbsp chopped fresh lemon thyme, plus extra sprigs to garnish

1 lemon, quartered

125 ml/4 fl oz white wine, plus extra if needed

salt and pepper

1. Preheat the oven to 220°C/425°F/Gas Mark 7. Place the chicken in a roasting tin.

2. Place the butter in a bowl, mix in the chopped thyme and season well with salt and pepper. Butter the chicken all over with the herb butter, inside and out, and place the lemon quarters inside the cavity. Pour the wine over the chicken.

3. Roast the chicken in the centre of the preheated oven for 15 minutes. Reduce the temperature to 190°C/375°F/Gas Mark 5 and continue to roast, basting frequently, for a further 1¾ hours. Cover with foil if the skin begins to brown too much. If the tin dries out, add a little more wine or water.

4. Test that the chicken is cooked by inserting a skewer into the thickest part of the meat and making sure the juices run clear. Remove from the oven.

5. Remove the chicken from the roasting tin and place on a warmed serving plate. Cover with foil and leave to rest for 10 minutes before carving.

6. Place the roasting tin on the top of the hob and simmer the pan juices gently over a low heat until they have reduced and are thick and glossy. Season to taste with salt and pepper. Serve the chicken with the pan juices and garnish with thyme sprigs.

23 FEBRUARY

CHICKEN & BROCCOLI CASSEROLE

SERVES: 4   PREP TIME: 10 MINS   COOK TIME: 35 MINS

INGREDIENTS

400 g/14 oz broccoli florets

40 g/1½ oz butter

1 onion, thinly sliced

350 g/12 oz cooked chicken, cut into bite-sized chunks

100 g/3½ oz crème fraîche

200 ml/7 fl oz chicken stock

25 g/1 oz fresh white breadcrumbs

55 g/2 oz Gruyère or Emmenthal cheese, grated

salt and pepper

1. Preheat the oven to 200°C/400°F/Gas Mark 6. Bring a saucepan of lightly salted water to the boil, add the broccoli and cook for 5 minutes until tender. Drain well.

2. Meanwhile, melt 25g/1 oz of the butter in a frying pan, add the onion and stir-fry over a medium heat for 3–4 minutes until soft.

3. Layer the broccoli, onion and chicken in a 1.5-litre/2¾-pint ovenproof dish and season well with salt and pepper. Pour over the crème fraîche and stock.

4. Melt the remaining butter in a small saucepan and stir in the breadcrumbs. Mix with the cheese and sprinkle over the dish.

5. Place the dish on a baking sheet in the preheated oven and bake for 20–25 minutes until golden brown and bubbling. Serve hot.

PAPRIKA TURKEY STRIPS

SERVES: 4   PREP TIME: 10 MINS   COOK TIME: 7–10 MINS

INGREDIENTS

500 g/1 lb 2 oz turkey breast steaks

1 tbsp paprika

1 tsp crushed coriander seeds

½ tsp garlic salt

¼ tsp pepper

2 tbsp olive oil

1 red onion, sliced

3 tbsp chopped fresh coriander

cooked rice, to serve

1. Cut the turkey into long strips, about 1-cm/½-inch thick.

2. Put the paprika, coriander seeds, garlic salt and pepper into a large bowl and mix together. Stir in 1 tablespoon of the oil. Add the turkey strips and turn to coat evenly in the mixture.

3. Heat the remaining oil in a large frying pan or wok, add the onion and stir-fry for 1 minute. Add the turkey strips and stir-fry over a fairly high heat for 6–8 minutes until cooked through.

4. Sprinkle over the chopped coriander and serve with rice.

WARM BULGAR WHEAT SALAD

SERVES: 4   PREP TIME: 10 MINS PLUS 10 MINS SOAKING TIME   COOK TIME: 2 MINS

INGREDIENTS

200 g/7 oz bulgar wheat

1 litre/1¾ pints boiling water

4 tbsp extra virgin olive oil

1 bunch spring onions, sliced

100 g/3½ oz ready-to-eat dried apricots, chopped

40 g/1½ oz blanched almonds, toasted

2 tbsp chopped fresh parsley

2 tbsp chopped fresh coriander

juice of 1 lime

1 garlic clove, crushed

salt and pepper

1. Place the bulgar wheat in a bowl and pour over the boiling water. Cover and leave to stand for 10 minutes or until the grains have swelled and softened. Drain off any excess liquid.

2. Heat 1 tablespoon of the oil in a frying pan, add the spring onions and stir-fry for 1 minute until soft. Add the apricots and almonds and stir for 30 seconds until heated through.

3. Stir in the bulgar wheat, parsley and coriander, then tip into a large salad bowl.

4. Put the remaining oil, the lime juice and garlic into a screw-top jar and shake well. Season to taste with salt and pepper.

5. Stir the dressing into the warm salad, tossing to coat all the ingredients evenly. Serve warm or cold.

PAN-FRIED PRAWNS

SERVES: 4   PREP TIME: 5 MINS   COOK TIME: 5 MINS

INGREDIENTS

4 garlic cloves

20–24 large raw prawns, shell on

125 g/4½ oz butter

4 tbsp olive oil

6 tbsp brandy

salt and pepper

chopped fresh parsley, to garnish

lemon wedges, to serve

1. Using a sharp knife, peel and slice the garlic.

2. Wash the prawns and pat dry using kitchen paper.

3. Melt the butter with the oil in a large frying pan, add the garlic and prawns, and fry over a high heat, stirring, for 3–4 minutes until the prawns are pink.

4. Sprinkle with brandy and season to taste with salt and pepper. Sprinkle with parsley and serve with lemon wedges.

MACARONI CHEESE

SERVES: 4 **PREP TIME: 10 MINS** **COOK TIME: 35 MINS**

INGREDIENTS

250 g/9 oz dried macaroni pasta

600 ml/1 pint milk

½ tsp grated nutmeg

55 g/2 oz butter, plus extra for cooking the pasta

55 g/2 oz plain flour

200 g/7 oz mature Cheddar cheese, grated

55 g/2 oz freshly grated Parmesan cheese

200 g/7 oz baby spinach

salt and pepper

1. Cook the macaroni according to the instructions on the packet. Remove from the heat, drain and add a small knob of butter to keep it soft. Return to the saucepan and cover to keep warm.

2. Put the milk and nutmeg into a saucepan over a low heat and heat until warm, but do not boil. Put the butter into a heavy-based saucepan over a low heat, melt the butter, add the flour and stir to make a roux. Cook gently for 2 minutes. Add the milk a little at a time, whisking it into the roux, then cook for about 10–15 minutes to make a loose, custard-style sauce.

3. Add three quarters of the Cheddar cheese and Parmesan cheese and stir through until they have melted in, then add the spinach, season to taste with salt and pepper and remove from the heat.

4. Preheat the grill to high. Put the macaroni into a shallow heatproof dish, then pour the sauce over. Scatter the remaining cheese over the top and place the dish under the preheated grill. Grill until the cheese begins to brown, then serve.

FISH STEW WITH CIDER

SERVES: 4　　**PREP TIME: 25 MINS**　　**COOK TIME: 35 MINS**

INGREDIENTS

2 tsp butter

1 large leek, thinly sliced

2 shallots, finely chopped

125 ml/4 fl oz dry cider

300 ml/10 fl oz fish stock

250 g/9 oz potatoes, diced

1 bay leaf

4 tbsp plain flour

200 ml/7 fl oz milk

200 ml/7 fl oz double cream

55 g/2 oz fresh sorrel leaves, chopped

350 g/12 oz skinless monkfish or cod fillet, cut into 2.5-cm/1-inch pieces

salt and pepper

1. Melt the butter in a large saucepan over a medium–low heat. Add the leek and shallots and cook for about 5 minutes, stirring frequently, until they start to soften. Add the cider and bring to the boil.

2. Stir in the stock, potatoes and bay leaf with a large pinch of salt (unless the stock is salty) and bring back to the boil. Reduce the heat, cover and cook gently for 10 minutes.

3. Put the flour in a small bowl and very slowly whisk in a few tablespoons of the milk to make a thick paste. Stir in a little more milk to make a smooth liquid.

4. Adjust the heat so the stew bubbles gently. Stir in the flour mixture and cook, stirring frequently, for 5 minutes. Add the remaining milk and half the cream. Continue cooking for about 10 minutes until the potatoes are tender. Remove and discard the bay leaf.

5. Combine the sorrel with the remaining cream. Stir the sorrel cream into the stew and add the fish. Continue cooking, stirring occasionally, for about 3 minutes, until the monkfish stiffens. Taste the stew and adjust the seasoning, if needed. Ladle into serving bowls and serve.

PORK CHOPS BRAISED WITH SHALLOTS

SERVES: 4　　**PREP TIME: 15 MINS**　　**COOK TIME: 1 HR 10 MINS**

INGREDIENTS

2 tbsp olive oil

4 lean pork chops

12 small shallots, peeled

3 celery sticks, sliced

2 eating apples, cored and sliced

200 ml/7 fl oz chicken stock

2 tbsp Worcestershire sauce

1 tbsp finely chopped fresh rosemary

fresh rosemary sprigs, to garnish

1. Heat the oil in a large, wide saucepan or flameproof casserole, add the pork chops and fry, turning once, for 2–3 minutes until lightly browned.

2. Add the shallots and celery and fry for a further 2 minutes until lightly browned.

3. Stir in the apples, then add the stock, Worcestershire sauce and chopped rosemary and bring to the boil. Reduce the heat to very low, cover and simmer very gently for about 1 hour until the meat is tender.

4. Garnish with rosemary sprigs and serve.

FISH STEW
WITH CIDER

MARCH

LEEK & GOAT'S CHEESE TARTLETS

SERVES: 4   PREP TIME: 15 MINS   COOK TIME: 20 MINS

INGREDIENTS

375 g/13 oz (1 rectangular sheet, 35 x 23 cm/14 x 9 inches) ready-rolled puff pastry

40 g/1½ oz butter

350 g/12 oz baby leeks, thickly sliced diagonally

1 tbsp chopped fresh oregano

125 g/4½ oz goat's cheese, sliced or crumbled

milk, for brushing

salt and pepper

1. Preheat the oven to 220°C/425°F/Gas Mark 7. Cut the pastry into six 12-cm/4½-inch squares.

2. Place the pastry squares on a baking sheet and use the tip of a sharp knife to score each one about 1-cm/½-inch from the edge all around.

3. Melt the butter in a frying pan, add the leeks and fry gently, stirring frequently, for 4–5 minutes until soft. Add the oregano, season with salt and pepper and divide the leek mixture between the pastry squares, placing it inside the scored lines.

4. Top each tartlet with cheese and brush the pastry with milk. Bake in the preheated oven for 12–15 minutes until risen and golden brown. Serve warm.

MINI CAKE POPS

MAKES: 24　　**PREP TIME: 40 MINS PLUS 1–2 HRS CHILLING TIME**　　**COOK TIME: 10 MINS**

INGREDIENTS

450 g/1 lb cooked vanilla or almond sponge or shop-bought

85 g/3 oz mascarpone cheese

70 g/2½ oz icing sugar

½ tsp vanilla or almond extract

DECORATION

225 g/8 oz milk chocolate, roughly chopped

24 lolly sticks

150 g/5½ oz fondant icing sugar

edible pink food colouring

4 tsp cold water

24 small sweets

sugar sprinkles

1. Line a baking sheet with greaseproof paper. Crumble the sponge into a mixing bowl. Add the mascarpone cheese, icing sugar and vanilla extract and mix together until you have a thick paste.

2. Roll a 25 g/1 oz piece of the paste into a ball. Push this ball into a mini paper case, pressing it down so that when it is removed from the case you have a mini cupcake shape. Shape the remaining 23 cake pops in the same way. Place on the baking sheet and chill for 1–2 hours to firm up.

3. To make the decoration, put the chocolate in a heatproof bowl. Set the bowl over a saucepan of gently simmering water and heat until melted. Remove from the heat. Push a lolly stick into each cake pop. Dip a cake pop into the chocolate, turning it until coated. Lift it from the bowl, letting the excess drip back into the bowl, then place it in a cup or tumbler. Repeat with the remaining cake pops. Chill or leave in a cool place until the chocolate has set.

4. Put the fondant icing sugar in a mixing bowl and beat in a dash of pink food colouring and the water until smooth. The icing should almost hold its shape. Spoon a little onto a cake pop, easing it slightly down the sides with the side of a teaspoon. If the icing is too firm you might need to add a dash more water. Before the icing sets, place a small sweet in the centre of each cake pop and scatter with sugar sprinkles.

CHOCOLATE & NUT OAT BARS

MAKES: 15   PREP TIME: 5 MINS   COOK TIME: 15 MINS

INGREDIENTS

85 g/3 oz unsalted butter, plus extra for greasing

175 g/6 oz chocolate hazelnut spread

175 g/6 oz porridge oats

70 g/2½ oz blanched hazelnuts, chopped

1. Preheat the oven to 200°C/400°F/Gas Mark 6. Grease a baking sheet.

2. Place the butter and chocolate hazelnut spread in a saucepan and heat gently until just melted.

3. Add the porridge oats and hazelnuts to the chocolate mixture and stir to combine thoroughly.

4. Shape the mixture into 15 equal-sized balls, then press onto the prepared baking sheet. Bake in the preheated oven for 10–12 minutes. Remove from the oven and leave until firm before transferring the cookies to a wire rack to finish cooling.

FIERY BEEF TACOS

| SERVES: 4 | PREP TIME: 25 MINS | COOK TIME: 25 MINS |

INGREDIENTS

2 tbsp corn oil

1 small onion, finely chopped

2 garlic cloves, finely chopped

280 g/10 oz fresh beef mince

1½ tsp hot chilli powder

1 tsp ground cumin

8 taco shells

1 avocado

2 tbsp lemon juice

¼ head of lettuce, shredded

4 spring onions, thinly sliced

2 tomatoes, peeled and diced

125 ml/4 fl oz soured cream

115 g/4 oz Cheddar cheese, grated

salt and pepper

1. Heat the oil in a frying pan. Add the onion and garlic and cook over a low heat, stirring occasionally, for 5 minutes, until softened. Add the beef, increase the heat to medium and cook, stirring frequently and breaking it up with a wooden spoon, for 8–10 minutes, until evenly browned. Drain off as much fat as possible.

2. Stir in the chilli powder and cumin, season to taste with salt and pepper and cook over a low heat, stirring frequently for a further 8 minutes, then remove from the heat.

3. Heat the taco shells according to the packet instructions. Meanwhile, peel, stone and slice the avocado and gently toss with the lemon juice in a bowl.

4. Divide the lettuce, spring onions, tomatoes and avocado slices among the taco shells. Add a tablespoon of soured cream to each, then divide the beef mixture among them. Sprinkle with the cheese and serve immediately.

CHILLI CON CARNE

| SERVES: 4 | PREP TIME: 25 MINS | COOK TIME: 2 HRS 20 MINS |

INGREDIENTS

750 g/1 lb 10 oz lean stewing steak

2 tbsp vegetable oil

1 large onion, sliced

2–4 garlic cloves, crushed

1 tbsp plain flour

425 ml/15 fl oz tomato juice

400 g/14 oz canned chopped tomatoes

1–2 tbsp sweet chilli sauce

1 tsp ground cumin

425 g/15 oz canned red kidney beans, drained and rinsed

½ teaspoon dried oregano

1–2 tbsp chopped fresh parsley

salt and pepper

sprigs of fresh herbs, to garnish

cooked rice and tortilla chips, to serve

1. Preheat the oven to 160°C/325°F/Gas Mark 3. Using a sharp knife, cut the beef into 2-cm/¾-inch cubes. Heat the vegetable oil in a large flameproof casserole dish and fry the beef over a medium heat until well sealed on all sides. Remove the beef from the casserole with a slotted spoon and reserve until required.

2. Add the onion and garlic to the casserole and fry until lightly browned. Stir in the flour and cook for 1–2 minutes.

3. Stir in the tomato juice and tomatoes and bring to the boil. Return the beef to the casserole and add the chilli sauce, cumin and salt and pepper to taste. Cover and cook in the preheated oven for 1½ hours, or until the beef is almost tender.

4. Stir in the kidney beans, oregano and parsley, and adjust the seasoning to taste, if necessary. Cover the casserole and return to the oven for 45 minutes. Garnish with sprigs of fresh herbs and serve with rice, accompanied by tortilla chips.

FIERY BEEF
TACOS

06 MARCH

PASTA WITH PESTO

SERVES: 4　　**PREP TIME: 10 MINS**　　**COOK TIME: 10 MINS**

INGREDIENTS

450 g/1 lb dried tagliatelle

sprigs of fresh basil, to garnish

PESTO

2 garlic cloves

25 g/1 oz pine kernels

115 g/4 oz fresh basil leaves

125 ml/4 fl oz olive oil

55 g/2 oz freshly grated Parmesan cheese

salt

1. To make the pesto, put the garlic, pine kernels and a large pinch of salt into a food processor and process briefly. Add the basil leaves and process to a paste. With the motor still running, gradually add the oil. Scrape into a bowl and beat in the Parmesan cheese. Season to taste with salt.

2. Bring a large saucepan of lightly salted water to the boil. Add the tagliatelle, bring back to the boil and cook for 8–10 minutes, or until tender but still firm to the bite. Drain well, return to the saucepan and toss with half the pesto, then divide between serving dishes and top with the remaining pesto. Garnish with sprigs of basil and serve.

07 MARCH

CARROT & CORIANDER SOUP

SERVES: 6　　**PREP TIME: 15 MINS**　　**COOK TIME: 40 MINS**

INGREDIENTS

3 tbsp olive oil

1 red onion, chopped

1 large potato, chopped

1 celery stick, chopped

500 g/1 lb 2 oz carrots, chopped

1 litre/1¾ pints vegetable stock

1 tbsp butter

2 tsp coriander seeds, crushed

1½ tbsp chopped fresh coriander, plus extra to garnish

225 ml/8 fl oz milk

salt and pepper

1. Heat the oil in a large saucepan. Add the onion and cook over a low heat, stirring occasionally, for 5 minutes, until softened.

2. Add the potato and celery and cook, stirring occasionally, for a further 5 minutes, then add the carrots and cook, stirring occasionally, for 5 minutes more. Cover the pan, reduce the heat to very low and cook, shaking the pan occasionally, for 10 minutes.

3. Pour in the stock and bring to the boil, then cover and simmer for 10 minutes, until the vegetables are tender.

4. Meanwhile, melt the butter in a frying pan. Add the coriander seeds and cook, stirring constantly, for 1 minute. Add the chopped coriander and cook, stirring constantly, for 1 minute, then remove from the heat.

5. Remove the soup from the heat and leave to cool slightly. Transfer to a food processor, in batches if necessary, and process to a purée. Return the soup to the rinsed-out pan, stir in the coriander mixture and milk and season to taste with salt and pepper. Reheat gently, then serve, sprinkled with chopped coriander.

BAKED CHEESE & AUBERGINE LAYERS

SERVES: 4–6   PREP TIME: 25 MINS   COOK TIME: 1 HR

INGREDIENTS

55 g/2 oz plain flour

2 large aubergines, sliced

6 tbsp olive oil

225 g/8 oz mozzarella cheese, thinly sliced

55 g/2 oz freshly grated Parmesan cheese

TOMATO SAUCE

15 g/½ oz butter

1 tbsp olive oil

1 shallot, finely chopped

1 garlic clove, finely chopped

1 small celery stick, finely chopped

200 g/7 oz canned chopped tomatoes

1 tbsp tomato purée

brown sugar, to taste

½ tsp dried oregano

50 ml/2 fl oz water

salt and pepper

1. First, make the tomato sauce. Melt the butter with the oil in a saucepan. Add the shallot, garlic and celery and cook over a low heat, stirring occasionally, for 5 minutes, until softened. Stir in the tomatoes, tomato purée, sugar to taste, oregano and water and season to taste with salt and pepper. Increase the heat to medium and bring to the boil, then reduce the heat and simmer, stirring occasionally, for 15–20 minutes, until thickened.

2. Meanwhile, preheat the oven to 180°C/350°F/Gas Mark 4. Spread out the flour on a shallow dish and season to taste with salt and pepper. Dip the aubergine slices in the flour to coat and shake off any excess. Heat the oil in a frying pan, add the aubergine slices, in batches, and cook for 2 minutes on each side, until lightly browned. Remove and drain on kitchen paper.

3. Make alternating layers of aubergine slices, mozzarella slices and tomato sauce in an ovenproof dish. Sprinkle with the Parmesan cheese and bake in the preheated oven for 25 minutes, until the topping is golden and bubbling. Serve.

09 MARCH

TURKEY STEAKS WITH TARRAGON SAUCE

SERVES: 4   **PREP TIME: 10 MINS**   **COOK TIME: 15–20 MINS**

INGREDIENTS

1 tbsp plain flour

4 turkey breast steaks

1 tbsp olive oil

25 g/1 oz butter

2 shallots, finely chopped

150 ml/5 fl oz dry white wine

thinly pared rind and juice of ½ lemon

2 tbsp chopped fresh tarragon

75 ml/2½ fl oz double cream

salt and pepper

1. Put the flour into a shallow bowl and season to taste with salt and pepper. Add the turkey steaks and turn in the flour until lightly coated.

2. Heat the oil with half the butter in a frying pan, add the turkey steaks and fry over a medium heat, turning once, for 8–10 minutes until golden brown and cooked through. Remove from the pan and keep warm.

3. Add the remaining butter to the pan, then add the shallots and fry, stirring, for 3–4 minutes until soft. Add the wine, lemon rind and juice and half the tarragon. Bring to the boil and boil for 2–3 minutes until reduced by about half.

4. Strain the sauce into a clean saucepan, add the cream and the remaining tarragon and cook, stirring, until boiling. Adjust the seasoning to taste, then spoon the sauce over the turkey steaks and serve.

10 MARCH

TURKEY CASSEROLE WITH CABBAGE & DILL

SERVES: 4   **PREP TIME: 10 MINS**   **COOK TIME: 35 MINS**

INGREDIENTS

2 tbsp olive oil

450 g/1 lb turkey breast, cubed

1 large onion, thinly sliced

1 garlic clove, chopped

200 ml/7 fl oz chicken stock

400 g/14 oz firm cabbage, sliced

2 tomatoes, diced

1 tbsp chopped fresh dill, plus extra to garnish

salt and pepper

1. Heat the oil in a large, flameproof casserole, add the turkey and fry over a fairly high heat for 2–3 minutes until lightly browned.

2. Add the onion and stir-fry for a further 2 minutes. Stir in the garlic, then add the stock and bring to the boil. Add the cabbage, tomatoes and dill and season to taste with salt and pepper.

3. Return to the boil, then reduce the heat, cover and simmer gently for 20–25 minutes until tender. Adjust the seasoning to taste, then sprinkle with fresh dill and serve.

SPRING STEW

SERVES: 4 　 PREP TIME: 25 MINS 　 COOK TIME: 35 MINS

INGREDIENTS

2 tbsp olive oil

4–8 baby onions, halved

1 celery sticks, sliced

225 g/8 oz baby carrots, scrubbed, and halved if large

300 g/10½ oz new potatoes, scrubbed and halved, or quartered if large

850 ml–1.2 litres/1½–2 pints vegetable stock

400 g/14 oz canned haricot beans, drained and rinsed

1 fresh bouquet garni

1½–2 tbsp light soy sauce

85 g/3 oz baby sweetcorn

115 g/4 oz frozen or shelled fresh broad beans, thawed if frozen

½–1 Savoy or spring cabbage, about 225 g/8 oz

1½ tbsp cornflour

2 tbsp cold water

salt and pepper

freshly grated Parmesan cheese, to serve

1. Heat the oil in a large, heavy-based saucepan with a tight-fitting lid. Add the onions, celery, carrots and potatoes and cook, stirring frequently, for 5 minutes, or until softened. Add the stock, drained beans, bouquet garni and soy sauce, then bring to the boil. Reduce the heat, cover and simmer for 12 minutes.

2. Add the baby sweetcorn and broad beans and season to taste with salt and pepper. Simmer for a further 3 minutes.

3. Meanwhile, discard the outer leaves and hard central core from the cabbage and shred the leaves. Add to the saucepan and simmer for a further 3–5 minutes, or until all the vegetables are tender.

4. Blend the cornflour with the water, stir into the saucepan and cook, stirring, for 4–6 minutes, or until the liquid has thickened. Serve with a bowl of Parmesan cheese for stirring into the stew.

CHOCOLATE FUDGE CAKE

SERVES: 8   PREP TIME: 20 MINS PLUS 1 HR COOLING TIME   COOK TIME: 40 MINS

INGREDIENTS

175 g/6 oz unsalted butter, softened, plus extra for greasing

175 g/6 oz golden caster sugar

3 eggs, beaten

3 tbsp golden syrup

40 g/1½ oz ground almonds

175 g/6 oz self-raising flour

pinch of salt

40 g/1½ oz cocoa powder

ICING

225 g/8 oz plain chocolate, broken into pieces

55 g/2 oz dark muscovado sugar

225 g/8 oz unsalted butter, diced

5 tbsp evaporated milk

½ tsp vanilla extract

1. Preheat the oven to 180°C/350°F/Gas Mark 4. Grease and line two 20-cm/8-inch sandwich tins.

2. For the icing, place the ingredients in a heavy-based saucepan. Heat gently, stirring constantly, until melted.

3. Pour into a bowl and leave to cool. Cover and chill for 1 hour, or until spreadable.

4. For the cake, place the butter and sugar in a bowl and beat together until light and fluffy. Gradually beat in the eggs. Stir in the golden syrup and almonds.

5. Sift the flour, salt and cocoa powder into a separate bowl, then fold into the mixture. Add a little water, if necessary, to make a dropping consistency.

6. Spoon the mixture into the prepared tins and bake in the preheated oven for 30–35 minutes, or until springy to the touch and a skewer inserted in the centre comes out clean.

7. Cool in the tins for 5 minutes, then turn out onto a wire rack to cool completely.

8. When the cakes are cold, sandwich them together with half the icing. Spread the remaining icing over the top and sides of the cake, swirling it to give a frosted appearance.

KEY LIME PIE

SERVES: 4–6   PREP TIME: 20 MINS PLUS 2 HRS CHILLING TIME   COOK TIME: 20 MINS

INGREDIENTS

CRUMB BASE

175 g/6 oz digestive or ginger biscuits

2 tbsp caster sugar

½ tsp ground cinnamon

70 g/2½ oz butter, melted, plus extra for greasing

FILLING

400 ml/14 fl oz canned condensed milk

125 ml/4 fl oz freshly squeezed lime juice

finely grated rind of 3 limes

4 egg yolks

whipped cream, to serve

1. Preheat the oven to 160°C/325°F/Gas Mark 3. Lightly grease a 23-cm/9-inch round tart tin, about 4 cm/1½ inches deep.

2. To make the crumb crust, put the biscuits, sugar and cinnamon in a food processor and process until fine crumbs form – do not overprocess to a powder. Add the melted butter and process again until moistened.

3. Tip the crumb mixture into the prepared tart tin and press over the base and up the side. Place the tart tin on a baking sheet and bake in the preheated oven for 5 minutes.

4. Meanwhile, to make the filling, beat together the condensed milk, lime juice, lime rind and egg yolks in a bowl until well blended.

5. Remove the tart tin from the oven, pour the filling into the crumb crust and spread out to the edges. Return to the oven for a further 15 minutes, or until the filling is set around the edges but still wobbly in the centre.

6. Leave to cool completely on a wire rack, then cover and chill for at least 2 hours. Spread thickly with whipped cream and serve.

CHOCOLATE
FUDGE CAKE

RHUBARB & ORANGE CRUMBLE

| SERVES: 4 | PREP TIME: 15 MINS | COOK TIME: 30–35 MINS |

INGREDIENTS

500 g/1 lb 2 oz rhubarb, chopped

55 g/2 oz caster sugar

finely grated rind and juice of
1 orange

custard or pouring cream, to serve

CRUMBLE

55 g/2 oz plain flour

55 g/2 oz light muscovado sugar

55 g/2 oz unsalted butter

40 g/1½ oz porridge oats

40 g/1½ oz ground almonds

1. Preheat the oven to 200°C/400°F/Gas Mark 6. Put the rhubarb, sugar and orange rind and juice into a saucepan and heat until boiling. Reduce the heat, cover and simmer for about 5 minutes until the rhubarb is just tender.

2. Tip into a 1.3-litre/2¼-pint ovenproof dish and place on a baking sheet.

3. To make the crumble, put the flour and sugar into a bowl and mix together. Add the butter and rub it in with your fingertips to make a crumbly mixture. Stir in the oats and almonds.

4. Sprinkle the crumble evenly over the fruit and bake in the preheated oven for 25–30 minutes until golden brown. Serve warm with custard.

ALL-IN-ONE VANILLA SPONGE CAKE

SERVES: 8   **PREP TIME: 20 MINS**   **COOK TIME: 20–25 MINS**

INGREDIENTS

225 g/8 oz plain flour

2 tsp baking powder

225 g/8 oz unsalted butter, softened, plus extra for greasing

225 g/8 oz caster sugar

4 eggs, beaten

1 tsp vanilla extract

FROSTING

140 g/5 oz unsalted butter

200 g/7 oz icing sugar

1 tsp vanilla extract

coloured flower sprinkles, to decorate

1. Preheat the oven to 180°C/350°F/Gas Mark 4. Grease and line two 20-cm/8-inch sandwich tins.

2. Sift together the flour and baking powder into a mixing bowl and add the butter, sugar, eggs and vanilla extract. Beat with an electric whisk until just smooth.

3. Spoon the mixture into the prepared tins and level the tops. Bake in the preheated oven for 20–25 minutes until risen, golden brown and firm to the touch.

4. Cool in the tins for 5 minutes, then turn out onto a wire rack to cool completely.

5. To make the frosting, put the butter, sugar and vanilla extract into a bowl and beat until smooth and spreadable. Use half the frosting to sandwich the two cakes together.

6. Spread the remaining frosting over the top of the cake and decorate with flower sprinkles.

16 MARCH

IRISH STEW

SERVES: 4	PREP TIME: 20 MINS	COOK TIME: 2½ HRS

INGREDIENTS

4 tbsp plain flour

1.3 kg/3 lb middle neck of lamb, trimmed of visible fat

3 large onions, chopped

3 carrots, sliced

450 g/1 lb potatoes, peeled and cut into wedges

½ tsp dried thyme

850 ml/1½ pints hot beef stock

salt and pepper

chopped fresh parsley, to garnish

1. Preheat the oven to 160°C/325°F/Gas Mark 3. Spread the flour on a plate and season with salt and pepper to taste. Roll the pieces of lamb in the flour to coat, shaking off any excess, and arrange in the base of a casserole.

2. Layer the onions, carrots and potatoes on top of the lamb.

3. Sprinkle in the thyme and pour in the stock, then cover and cook in the preheated oven for 2½ hours. Serve garnished with the parsley.

17 MARCH

CHAMP

SERVES: 4	PREP TIME: 10 MINS	COOK TIME: 25 MINS

INGREDIENTS

900 g/2 lb potatoes

55 g/2 oz butter, plus extra for serving

2 bunches of spring onions, cut into 1-cm/½-inch slices

200 ml/7 fl oz milk or single cream

salt and pepper

chopped fresh chives and chopped fresh parsley, to garnish

1. Peel the potatoes and cut into large chunks. Bring a large saucepan of water to the boil, add the potatoes and cook for 15–20 minutes until tender.

2. Drain the potatoes well and mash with a potato masher. If you want very smooth champ you could press them through a sieve. Keep warm.

3. Melt the butter in a medium-sized saucepan and add the spring onions. Sweat for 3–4 minutes until soft. Add the milk and bring to a simmer. Season well and allow to thicken slightly.

4. Stir the onion mixture into the warm potatoes and adjust the seasoning, if necessary. Scatter over the chopped herbs and serve with extra butter.

BEEF ENCHILADAS

MAKES: 18   **PREP TIME: 35 MINS**   **COOK TIME: ABOUT 1 HR**

INGREDIENTS

1 tbsp corn oil, plus extra for brushing

1 onion, finely chopped

2 fresh green chillies, deseeded and chopped

280 g/10 oz fresh beef mince

115 g/4 oz Cheddar cheese, grated

18 tortillas

chopped fresh coriander, to garnish

PIQUANT TOMATO SAUCE

25 g/1 oz butter

2 tbsp olive oil

1 onion, finely chopped

2 garlic cloves, finely chopped

1 fresh green chilli, deseeded and chopped

400 g/14 oz canned chopped tomatoes

2 tbsp tomato purée

brown sugar, to taste

1 tsp dried oregano

½ tsp cayenne pepper

125 ml/4 fl oz double cream

salt and pepper

1. Heat the corn oil in a frying pan. Add the onion and chillies and cook over a low heat, stirring occasionally, for 5 minutes. Add the beef, increase the heat to medium and cook, stirring frequently and breaking it up with the spoon, for 8–10 minutes, until evenly browned. Remove the pan from the heat and stir in half the cheese.

2. To make the piquant tomato sauce, melt the butter with the olive oil in a saucepan. Add the onion, garlic and chilli and cook over a medium heat, stirring occasionally, for 5–8 minutes, until the onion is golden brown. Stir in the tomatoes, tomato purée, sugar to taste, oregano and cayenne pepper and season to taste with salt and pepper. Increase the heat to medium and bring to the boil. Reduce the heat, stir in the cream and simmer, stirring occasionally, for 15–20 minutes, until thickened. Remove from the heat and leave to cool slightly.

3. Meanwhile, preheat the oven to 180°C/350°F/Gas Mark 4. Heat a frying pan and brush with corn oil. One at a time, dip the tortillas in the sauce, shake off any excess and cook in the frying pan for 30 seconds on each side. Transfer to a large plate, put a tablespoon of the meat mixture in the centre and roll up. Put the filled tortillas, seam-side down, in a large ovenproof dish and pour the remaining sauce over them. Sprinkle with the remaining cheese and bake in the preheated oven for 15–20 minutes. Garnish with coriander and serve.

19 MARCH

CHICKEN FRIED RICE

SERVES: 4 | PREP TIME: 25 MINS | COOK TIME: 10–12 MINS

INGREDIENTS

½ tbsp sesame oil

6 shallots, quartered

450 g/1 lb cooked chicken, diced

3 tbsp soy sauce

2 carrots, diced

1 celery stick, diced

1 red pepper, deseeded and diced

175 g/6 oz fresh peas

100 g/3½ oz canned sweetcorn, drained

275 g/9¾ oz cooked long-grain rice

2 large eggs, scrambled

1. Heat the oil in a large frying pan or wok over a medium heat. Add the shallots and cook until soft, then add the chicken and 2 tablespoons of the soy sauce and stir-fry for 5–6 minutes.

2. Stir in the carrots, celery, red pepper, peas and sweetcorn and stir-fry for a further 5 minutes. Add the rice and stir thoroughly.

3. Finally, stir in the scrambled eggs and the remaining soy sauce. Serve.

20 MARCH

PENNE WITH TURKEY MEATBALLS

SERVES: 4 | PREP TIME: 25 MINS | COOK TIME: 1 HR 10 MINS

INGREDIENTS

350 g/12 oz fresh turkey mince

1 small garlic clove, finely chopped

2 tbsp finely chopped fresh parsley

1 egg, lightly beaten

plain flour, for dusting

3 tbsp olive oil

1 onion, finely chopped

1 celery stick, finely chopped

1 carrot, finely chopped

400 ml/14 fl oz passata

1 fresh rosemary sprig

1 bay leaf

350 g/12 oz dried penne

salt and pepper

freshly grated Parmesan cheese, to serve

1. Put the turkey, garlic and parsley in a bowl and mix well. Stir in the egg and season to taste with salt and pepper. Dust your hands lightly with flour and shape the mixture into walnut-sized balls between your palms. Lightly dust each meatball with flour.

2. Heat the olive oil in a saucepan. Add the onion, celery and carrot and cook over a low heat, stirring occasionally, for 5 minutes, until softened. Increase the heat to medium, add the meatballs and cook, turning frequently, for 8–10 minutes, until golden brown all over.

3. Pour in the passata, add the rosemary and bay leaf, season to taste with salt and pepper and bring to the boil. Lower the heat, cover and simmer gently, stirring occasionally, for 40–45 minutes. Remove and discard the herbs.

4. Shortly before the meatballs are ready, bring a large saucepan of lightly salted water to the boil. Add the penne, bring back to the boil and cook for 8–10 minutes, or until tender but still firm to the bite. Drain and add to the pan with the meatballs. Stir gently and heat through briefly, then spoon into serving dishes. Sprinkle generously with Parmesan cheese and serve.

CHICKEN
FRIED RICE

21 MARCH
SWORDFISH STEAKS WITH LIME BUTTER

SERVES: 4   PREP TIME: 20 MINS PLUS 30 MINS MARINATING TIME   COOK TIME: 10 MINS

INGREDIENTS

4 swordfish steaks, about 175 g/6 oz each

3 tbsp olive oil, plus extra for brushing

6 tbsp lime juice

1 tsp sweet paprika

125 g/4½ oz unsalted butter, cut into pieces

grated rind of 1 lime

4-cm/1½-inch piece of fresh ginger, chopped

1 tbsp chopped fresh coriander

pinch of cayenne pepper

salt and pepper

lime wedges, to serve

1. Place the swordfish steaks in a shallow, non-metallic dish. Mix together the olive oil, 2 tablespoons of the lime juice and the paprika in a jug and season to taste with salt and pepper. Pour the mixture over the fish steaks and turn to coat. Cover with clingfilm and set aside in a cool place to marinate for 30 minutes.

2. Meanwhile, put the remaining lime juice in a blender with the butter, lime rind, ginger and coriander. Season to taste with salt and cayenne pepper. Process until thoroughly combined, scraping down the sides if necessary.

3. Scrape the lime butter onto a piece of foil and roll into a sausage shape. Chill in the refrigerator until ready to serve.

4. Meanwhile, place a ridged cast-iron frying pan over a high heat until you can feel the heat rising from the surface. When the fish is thoroughly marinated, lift out of the marinade, place on the hot pan and chargrill for 4 minutes. Turn the fish over, brush with more marinade and chargrill on the other side for another 4 minutes, or until cooked through.

5. Transfer the swordfish steaks to serving plates. Unwrap the lime butter and cut it into slices. Top each fish steak with 1–2 slices of the butter and serve with lime wedges.

22 MARCH
TUNA STEAKS WITH CATALAN SAUCE

SERVES: 4   PREP TIME: 20 MINS   COOK TIME: ABOUT 30 MINS

INGREDIENTS

2 tbsp olive oil, plus extra for brushing

1 onion, chopped

2 red peppers, deseeded and chopped

1 red chilli, deseeded and chopped

1 garlic clove, chopped

400 g/14 oz canned chopped tomatoes

dash of white wine vinegar

50 g/1¾ oz ground almonds

4 tuna steaks, about 125 g/4½ oz each

salt and pepper

1. Heat the oil in a non-stick frying pan over a medium–high heat, add the onion and red peppers and cook, stirring frequently, for 10 minutes, or until soft. Add the chilli and garlic and cook, stirring, for 1 minute. Add the tomatoes and their juices, bring to a simmer and cook for 15 minutes. Stir in the vinegar.

2. Transfer the tomato mixture to a food processor. Add the ground almonds and process for 20 seconds, or until smooth. Season to taste with a little salt and pepper, and add a little water if the mixture is too thick to pour.

3. Preheat the grill to high, or heat a frying pan over a high heat. Pat the tuna steaks dry with kitchen paper and lightly brush with oil on both sides. Cook under the preheated grill or in the very hot frying pan for 1½ minutes on each side to sear, or until cooked to your liking.

4. Serve the tuna steaks with the sauce spooned around.

FRIED CHICKEN WITH TOMATO & BACON SAUCE

SERVES: 4   PREP TIME: 20 MINS   COOK TIME: 45 MINS

INGREDIENTS

25 g/1 oz butter

2 tbsp olive oil

4 skinless, boneless chicken breasts or 8 skinless, boneless chicken thighs

TOMATO & BACON SAUCE

25 g/1 oz butter

2 tbsp olive oil

1 large onion, finely chopped

2 garlic cloves, finely chopped

1 celery stick, finely chopped

4 rashers bacon, diced

400 g/14 oz canned chopped tomatoes

2 tbsp tomato purée

brown sugar, to taste

100 ml/3½ fl oz water

1 tbsp chopped fresh basil

1 tbsp chopped fresh flat-leaf parsley, plus extra to garnish

salt and pepper

1. First, make the tomato and bacon sauce. Melt the butter with the oil in a large saucepan. Add the onion, garlic, celery and bacon and cook over a low heat, stirring occasionally, for 5 minutes, until softened. Stir in the tomatoes, tomato purée, sugar to taste and water and season to taste with salt and pepper. Increase the heat to medium and bring to the boil, then reduce the heat and simmer, stirring occasionally, for 15–20 minutes, until thickened.

2. Meanwhile, melt the butter with the oil in a large frying pan. Add the chicken and cook over a medium–high heat for 4–5 minutes on each side, until evenly browned.

3. Stir the basil and parsley into the sauce. Add the chicken and spoon the sauce over it. Cover and simmer for 10–15 minutes. Check the chicken is tender and the juices run clear when a skewer is inserted into the thickest part of the meat. Garnish with parsley and serve.

NEW POTATOES WITH GARLIC & CHILLI BUTTER

SERVES: 4   PREP TIME: 10 MINS   COOK TIME: 15 MINS

INGREDIENTS

700 g/1 lb 9 oz baby new potatoes

40 g/1½ oz butter

1 garlic clove, finely chopped

1 red chilli, deseeded and finely chopped

salt and pepper

chopped fresh coriander leaves, to garnish

1. Bring a large saucepan of lightly salted water to the boil, add the potatoes, bring back to the boil and cook for 15 minutes, or until tender. Drain well.

2. Melt the butter in a large saucepan, add the garlic and chilli and gently stir-fry for 30 seconds, without browning.

3. Add the potatoes and stir to coat in the butter, then season to taste with salt and pepper. Sprinkle with the coriander and serve hot.

CHICKEN WITH CREAMY PENNE

SERVES: 2   PREP TIME: 5 MINS   COOK TIME: 15–18 MINS

INGREDIENTS

200 g/7 oz dried penne

1 tbsp olive oil

2 skinless, boneless chicken breasts

4 tbsp dry white wine

115 g/4 oz frozen peas

5 tbsp double cream

salt

chopped fresh flat-leaf parsley,
to garnish

1. Bring a large, heavy-based saucepan of lightly salted water to the boil. Add the penne, bring back to the boil and cook for 8–10 minutes, or until just tender but still firm to the bite.

2. Meanwhile, heat the oil in a frying pan, add the chicken and cook over a medium heat for about 4 minutes on each side.

3. Pour in the wine and cook over a high heat until it has almost evaporated.

4. Drain the pasta. Add the peas, cream and pasta to the frying pan and stir well. Cover and simmer for 2 minutes. Check the chicken is tender and the juices run clear when a skewer is inserted into the thickest part of the meat.

5. Garnish with parsley and serve.

CHORIZO, CHILLI & CHICKPEA CASSEROLE

SERVES: 4 • PREP TIME: 15 MINS • COOK TIME: 30 MINS

INGREDIENTS

2 tbsp olive oil

1 onion, sliced

1 large yellow pepper, deseeded and sliced

1 garlic clove, crushed

1 tsp chilli flakes

225 g/8 oz chorizo sausage

400 g/14 oz canned chopped tomatoes

400 g/14 oz canned chickpeas, drained and rinsed

200 g/7 oz basmati rice

handful of rocket leaves

salt and pepper

chopped fresh basil, to garnish

1. Heat the oil in a flameproof casserole and fry the onion over a medium heat, stirring occasionally, for 5 minutes.

2. Add the yellow pepper, garlic and chilli flakes and cook for 2 minutes, stirring. Chop the chorizo into bite-sized chunks and stir into the casserole.

3. Add the tomatoes and chickpeas and season to taste with salt and pepper. Bring to the boil, cover and simmer for 10 minutes.

4. Meanwhile, cook the rice in a saucepan of lightly salted boiling water for 10–12 minutes, until tender. Drain.

5. Stir the rocket into the casserole. Serve spooned over the rice, garnished with fresh basil.

TARTIFLETTE

SERVES: 4   PREP TIME: 10 MINS   COOK TIME: 45 MINS

INGREDIENTS

1 kg/2 lb 4 oz small waxy potatoes, sliced

2 tbsp olive oil

3 garlic cloves, peeled but kept whole

150 g/5½ oz bacon lardons

600 ml/1 pint double cream

2 tbsp fresh thyme leaves

200 g/7 oz Reblochon cheese or any other good melting cheese, sliced

salt

1. Preheat the oven to 180°C/350°F/Gas Mark 4.

2. Cook the potato slices in a large saucepan of lightly salted boiling water for 10–15 minutes until just tender. Drain.

3. Heat the oil in a large frying pan over a medium heat. Hit the garlic cloves with the back of a sturdy knife to split them and add to the frying pan. Add the bacon lardons and cook for 3–4 minutes until just cooked. Add the potato slices and cook for 3–4 minutes. Pour in the cream, add the thyme leaves and stir well.

4. Transfer the mixture to a gratin dish and top with the cheese slices. Bake in the preheated oven for 20 minutes, or until golden and bubbling.

MACARONI & SEAFOOD BAKE

SERVES: 4   PREP TIME: 20 MINS   COOK TIME: 40 MINS

INGREDIENTS

350 g/12 oz dried macaroni

85 g/3 oz butter, plus extra for greasing

2 small fennel bulbs, trimmed and thinly sliced

175 g/6 oz mushrooms, thinly sliced

175 g/6 oz cooked peeled prawns

pinch of cayenne pepper

600 ml/1 pint shop-bought béchamel, or white sauce

55 g/2 oz freshly grated Parmesan cheese

2 large tomatoes, halved and sliced

olive oil, for brushing

1 tsp dried oregano

salt

1. Preheat the oven to 180°C/350°F/Gas Mark 4. Bring a large saucepan of lightly salted water to the boil. Add the pasta, bring back to the boil and cook for 8–10 minutes, or until just tender but still firm to the bite. Drain and return to the saucepan. Add 25 g/1 oz of the butter to the pasta, cover, shake the saucepan and keep warm.

2. Melt the remaining butter in a separate saucepan. Add the fennel and cook for 3–4 minutes. Stir in the mushrooms and cook for a further 2 minutes. Stir in the prawns, then remove the saucepan from the heat. Stir the cooked pasta, cayenne pepper and prawn mixture into the béchamel sauce.

3. Grease a large ovenproof dish, then pour the mixture into the dish and spread evenly. Sprinkle over the Parmesan cheese and arrange the tomato slices in a ring around the edge. Brush the tomatoes with oil, then sprinkle over the oregano. Bake in the preheated oven for 25 minutes, or until golden brown. Serve.

TARTIFLETTE

BEEF MEDALLIONS WITH ORANGE, LIME & HONEY

SERVES: 4 | PREP TIME: 10 MINS PLUS 20 MINS STANDING TIME | COOK TIME: 8–10 MINS

INGREDIENTS

4 fillet steaks

2 oranges

juice of 1 lime

1 tbsp olive oil

15 g/½ oz butter

1 sprig of fresh thyme

2 tbsp clear honey

salt and pepper

1. Place the steaks in a wide, non-metallic dish. Squeeze the juice from 1 orange and pour over the steak with the lime juice. Cover and leave to stand in a cool place for 20 minutes. Drain, reserving the juices.

2. Cut all the peel and white pith from the remaining orange and remove the segments, catching any juice in a bowl.

3. Heat a heavy-based frying pan over a medium–high heat. Brush the steaks with oil and season to taste with salt and pepper. Place in the hot pan and cook for 2–2½ minutes on each side, for medium rare to medium. Remove, cover and keep warm.

4. Melt the butter in the pan, then stir in the marinade and reserved citrus juice, thyme and honey. Bring to the boil and stir for 1 minute. Season to taste with salt and pepper and add the orange segments.

5. Arrange the steaks on serving plates, spoon over the juices and the orange segments and serve.

RASPBERRY CRUMBLE MUFFINS

MAKES: 12   PREP TIME: 20 MINS   COOK TIME: 20 MINS

INGREDIENTS

oil or melted butter, for greasing (if using)

280 g/10 oz plain flour

1 tbsp baking powder

½ tsp bicarbonate of soda

pinch of salt

115 g/4 oz caster sugar

2 eggs

250 ml/9 fl oz natural yogurt

85 g/3 oz butter, melted and cooled

1 tsp vanilla extract

150 g/5½ oz frozen raspberries

CRUMBLE TOPPING

50 g/1¾ oz plain flour

35 g/1¼ oz butter

25 g/1 oz caster sugar

1. Preheat the oven to 200°C/400°F/Gas Mark 6. Grease a 12-cup muffin tin or line with 12 paper cases.

2. To make the crumble topping, sift the flour into a bowl. Cut the butter into small pieces, add to the bowl with the flour and rub it in with your fingertips until the mixture resembles fine breadcrumbs. Stir in the sugar and set aside.

3. To make the muffins, sift together the flour, baking powder, bicarbonate of soda and salt into a large bowl. Stir in the sugar.

4. Lightly beat the eggs in a large bowl then beat in the yogurt, butter and vanilla extract. Make a well in the centre of the dry ingredients, pour in the beaten liquid ingredients and add the raspberries. Stir gently until just combined; do not over-mix.

5. Spoon the mixture into the prepared muffin tin. Scatter the crumble topping over each muffin and press down lightly. Bake in the preheated oven for about 20 minutes until well risen, golden brown and firm to the touch.

6. Leave the muffins in the tin for 5 minutes then serve warm or transfer to a wire rack and leave to cool.

EASTER CUPCAKES

MAKES: 12   PREP TIME: 20 MINS   COOK TIME: 20 MINS

INGREDIENTS

115 g/4 oz butter, softened, plus extra for greasing (if using)

115 g/4 oz caster sugar

2 eggs, lightly beaten

85 g/3 oz self-raising flour

25 g/1 oz cocoa powder

two 125 g/4½ oz packets mini chocolate candy shell eggs, to decorate

FROSTING

85 g/3 oz butter, softened

175 g/6 oz icing sugar

1 tbsp milk

2–3 drops of vanilla extract

1. Preheat the oven to 180°C/350°F/Gas Mark 4. Grease a 12-cup bun tray or line with 12 double-layer paper cases.

2. Put the butter and sugar in a bowl and beat together until light and fluffy. Gradually add the eggs, beating well after each addition. Sift in the flour and cocoa powder and, using a large metal spoon, fold into the mixture. Spoon the mixture into the prepared bun tray.

3. Bake the cupcakes in the preheated oven for 15–20 minutes, or until well risen and firm to the touch. Transfer to a wire rack and leave to cool.

4. To make the frosting, put the butter in a bowl and beat until fluffy. Sift in the icing sugar and beat together until well mixed, adding the milk and vanilla extract. Put the frosting in a piping bag fitted with a large star-shaped nozzle. When the cupcakes are cold, pipe circles of frosting on top of the cupcakes to form nests. Decorate with chocolate eggs.

RASPBERRY
CRUMBLE MUFFINS

APRIL

01 APRIL

MANGO & PASSION FRUIT FOOL

SERVES: 4   **PREP TIME: 10 MINS**   **COOK TIME: NO COOKING**

INGREDIENTS

1 mango

2 passion fruit

40 g/1½ oz caster sugar

4 tbsp sweet white wine

300 ml/10 fl oz double cream

1. Halve, stone and thinly peel the mango. Place the flesh in a food processor or blender and whizz to a smooth purée.

2. Scoop out the flesh from the passion fruit and add half to the mango purée.

3. Put the sugar, wine and cream into a bowl and whip until it holds its shape.

4. Fold the fruit purée lightly into the cream, then spoon into four serving bowls.

5. Spoon the remaining passion fruit on top of each and serve.

DEEP SOUTH CHERRY PIES

MAKES: 24 | PREP TIME: 25 MINS | COOK TIME: 15 MINS

INGREDIENTS

butter, for greasing

350 g/12 oz cherries

2 tsp cornflour

2 tbsp cherry jam

grated rind of 2 limes

450 g/1 lb ready-made sweet shortcrust pastry, chilled

plain flour, for dusting

1 egg yolk mixed with 1 tbsp water, to glaze

caster sugar, for sprinkling

TO SERVE

225 ml/8 fl oz double cream

grated rind of 2 limes

2 tbsp icing sugar

1. Preheat the oven to 180°C/350°F/Gas Mark 4. Grease 2 x 12-cup muffin tins.

2. Roughly chop the cherries. Put them in a mixing bowl and stir in the cornflour, jam and lime rind.

3. Roll half the pastry out thinly on a lightly floured surface. Using a fluted cookie cutter, stamp out 24 circles, each 6 cm/2½ inches in diameter. Press these gently into the prepared tins, re-rolling the trimmings as needed.

4. Brush the top edges of the pie cases with a little of the egg glaze, then spoon in the filling.

5. Roll the reserved pastry out thinly on a lightly floured surface. Stamp out 24 circles, each 5 cm/2 inches in diameter, re-rolling the trimmings as needed. Attach the rounds as lids to the base of the pies with water, pressing the edges together. Use a cookie cutter to cut out mini hearts from the pastry and attach them to the lids with water. Brush egg glaze over the pastry and sprinkle with caster sugar.

6. Bake in the preheated oven for 15 minutes, or until golden. Leave to cool in the tins for 10 minutes, then loosen with a round-bladed knife and transfer to a wire rack to cool. Whip the cream until it forms soft swirls, then fold in half the lime rind and all the icing sugar. Sprinkle with the rest of the lime rind. Serve spoonfuls of the cream with the pies.

RISOTTO PRIMAVERA

SERVES: 4   PREP TIME: 25 MINS   COOK TIME: 20 MINS

INGREDIENTS

200 g/7 oz fresh or frozen peas

200 g/7 oz asparagus

200 g/7 oz courgettes

200 g/7 oz French beans

2 tbsp olive oil

1 large onion, finely chopped

250 g/9 oz risotto rice

700 ml/1¼ pints warm chicken stock

3½ tbsp Vermouth or white wine

handful chopped parsley

1 tbsp fresh thyme leaves

75 g/2½ oz butter

125 g/4½ oz freshly grated Parmesan cheese, plus extra to serve

salt and pepper

1. Prepare the green vegetables: pod the peas if using fresh ones, chop the asparagus into bite-sized portions, cut the courgettes diagonally into finger-thick slices, and top and tail the beans.

2. Bring a large saucepan of lightly salted water to the boil, add the prepared vegetables and blanch for 1 minute, then remove and drain.

3. Place a large heavy-based saucepan over a medium heat, add the olive oil and the onion and cook gently for about 10 minutes until soft. Add the rice and fry, stirring it into the oil for 2 minutes. Reduce the heat, add a ladleful of stock and stir it into the rice. Gradually add more stock as each ladleful is absorbed. Check the rice, it should be slightly hard in the middle (you may need a little more or less of the liquid). Add the last ladle of stock, the Vermouth and the herbs and cook for another 5 minutes.

4. Add the butter, Parmesan cheese and blanched vegetables. Check for seasoning and heat through, stirring gently.

5. Serve in serving bowls, with Parmesan cheese to sprinkle on top.

GRILLED HALIBUT WITH CARAMELIZED ONION

SERVES: 2   PREP TIME: 20 MINS   COOK TIME: 25 MINS

INGREDIENTS

1 tbsp vegetable oil

1 small onion, thinly sliced

1 tsp balsamic vinegar

2 halibut fillets or steaks, each about 115 g/4 oz

2 tbsp melted butter

fresh flat-leaf parsley sprigs, to garnish

cooked new potatoes, to serve

1. Heat the oil in a large frying pan over a medium heat. Add the onion, stir well and reduce the heat. Cook over a very low heat, stirring occasionally, for 15–20 minutes, until the onion is very soft and brown.

2. Add the vinegar to the pan and cook, stirring constantly to prevent sticking, for 2 minutes.

3. Rinse the fish under cold running water and pat dry with kitchen paper. Brush the melted butter over the fish.

4. Preheat the grill to hot. Sear the fish, then reduce the heat and cook for about 10 minutes, turning once. The cooking time will depend on the thickness of the fillets, but the fish should be firm and tender when done.

5. Remove the fish from the heat, transfer to serving plates and top with the caramelized onion. Garnish with parsley and serve with new potatoes.

RISOTTO
PRIMAVERA

DARK CHOCOLATE ROULADE

SERVES: 6–8   PREP TIME: 45 MINS   COOK TIME: 15–20 MINS

INGREDIENTS

butter, for greasing

175 g/6 oz plain chocolate, broken into squares

4 large eggs, separated

115 g/4 oz caster sugar

cocoa powder, sifted, for dusting

225 g/8 oz white chocolate, broken into squares

225 g/8 oz mascarpone cheese or double cream

icing sugar, for sprinkling

RASPBERRY COULIS

300 g/10½ oz raspberries

2 tbsp icing sugar

1. Preheat the oven to 180°C/350°F/Gas Mark 4. Grease a 33 x 23-cm/13 x 9-inch Swiss roll tin and line with greaseproof paper.

2. Melt the plain chocolate in a heatproof bowl set over a saucepan of simmering water, taking care that the bowl does not touch the water. Remove from the heat and leave to cool slightly.

3. Put the egg yolks and sugar into a bowl and whisk until pale and thick. Whisk the egg whites in a separate grease-free bowl until they hold soft peaks. Quickly stir the melted plain chocolate into the egg yolk mixture, then fold in the whisked egg whites.

4. Spread the mixture into the prepared tin. Bake in the preheated oven for 15–20 minutes, until risen and firm. Dust a sheet of greaseproof paper with cocoa powder. Turn out the roulade onto the paper, cover with a clean tea towel and leave to cool.

5. Meanwhile, melt the white chocolate in a heatproof bowl set over a saucepan of simmering water, taking care that the bowl does not touch the water. Remove from the heat and leave to cool slightly. Stir into the mascarpone cheese, mixing until it reaches a spreadable consistency.

6. Uncover the roulade, remove the greaseproof paper and spread with the white chocolate cream. Use the paper to roll up the roulade to enclose the filling (do not worry if it cracks).

7. To make the raspberry coulis, put the raspberries and sugar into a food processor and process to a smooth purée. Press through a sieve to remove the pips.

8. Sprinkle the roulade with icing sugar and serve in slices with the raspberry coulis poured over.

06 APRIL
MUSTARD & HONEY DRUMSTICKS

SERVES: 4 PREP TIME: 10 MINS PLUS 1 HR MARINATING TIME COOK TIME: 30 MINS

INGREDIENTS

8 chicken drumsticks

fresh flat-leaf parsley sprigs, to garnish

GLAZE

125 ml/4 fl oz clear honey

4 tbsp Dijon mustard

4 tbsp wholegrain mustard

4 tbsp white wine vinegar

2 tbsp sunflower oil

salt and pepper

1. Using a sharp knife, make a few diagonal slashes in the chicken drumsticks and place them in a large non-metallic dish.

2. Mix together all the ingredients for the glaze in a jug. Pour the glaze over the drumsticks, turning until the drumsticks are well coated. Cover with clingfilm and leave to marinate in the refrigerator for at least 1 hour.

3. Preheat the grill to high. Drain the chicken drumsticks, reserving the marinade. Cook the chicken under the preheated grill, turning frequently and basting with the reserved marinade, for 25–30 minutes, or until the chicken is tender and the juices run clear when a skewer is inserted into the thickest part of the meat. Transfer to serving plates, garnish with parsley sprigs and serve.

07 APRIL
ASPARAGUS WITH LEMON BUTTER SAUCE

SERVES: 4 PREP TIME: 10 MINS COOK TIME: 15 MINS

INGREDIENTS

800 g/1 lb 12 oz asparagus spears, trimmed

1 tbsp olive oil

salt and pepper

LEMON BUTTER SAUCE

juice of ½ lemon

2 tbsp water

100 g/3½ oz butter, cut into cubes

1. Preheat the oven to 200°C/400°F/Gas Mark 6. Lay the asparagus spears out in a single layer on a large baking sheet. Drizzle over the oil and season to taste with salt and pepper. Roast in the preheated oven for 10 minutes, or until just tender.

2. Meanwhile, make the lemon butter sauce. Pour the lemon juice into a saucepan and add the water. Heat for about 1 minute, then slowly add the butter, cube by cube, stirring constantly until it has all been incorporated. Season to taste with pepper and serve drizzled over the asparagus.

PEPPERED LAMB FILLET

SERVES: 4   PREP TIME: 20 MINS   COOK TIME: 45 MINS

INGREDIENTS

900 g/2 lb lamb fillet

3 tbsp olive oil

2–3 tbsp black peppercorns, coarsely ground

cooked broccoli, to serve

ONION GRATIN

butter, for greasing

6 onions, sliced

3–4 tbsp dry sherry or white wine

1 tbsp fresh thyme leaves

3–4 tbsp mascarpone cheese

150 g/5½ oz Gorgonzola cheese, crumbled

salt and pepper

1. Preheat the oven to 180°C/350°F/Gas Mark 4. Lightly grease a gratin dish.

2. To make the onion gratin, lay the onions out in an even layer in the prepared gratin dish. Pour over the sherry, scatter over the thyme leaves and season to taste with salt and pepper. Dot the mascarpone cheese evenly over the onions and scatter over the Gorgonzola cheese. Bake in the preheated oven for 30–40 minutes until the onions are soft and the gratin is golden and bubbling.

3. Meanwhile, brush the lamb with 1 tablespoon of the oil and season to taste with a little salt. Roll in the ground peppercorns. Heat the remaining oil in a frying pan over a high heat, add the lamb fillet and cook for 3–4 minutes on each side. Leave to rest for 5 minutes, then slice and serve immediately with the onion gratin and broccoli.

POACHED EGGS 'FLORENTINE' WITH SPINACH & CHEDDAR

SERVES: 4   PREP TIME: 10 MINS   COOK TIME: 6–8 MINS

INGREDIENTS

1 tbsp olive oil

200 g/7 oz young spinach leaves

4 thick slices ciabatta bread

25 g/1 oz butter

4 large eggs

100 g/3½ oz Cheddar cheese, grated

salt and pepper

freshly grated nutmeg, to serve

1. Preheat the grill to high. Heat the oil in a wok or large saucepan, add the spinach and stir-fry for 2–3 minutes until the leaves are wilted. Drain in a colander, season to taste with salt and pepper and keep warm.

2. Toast the bread on both sides until golden. Spread one side of each slice with butter and place buttered side up in a baking sheet.

3. Bring a small saucepan of lightly salted water to the boil, crack the eggs into the water and poach for about 3 minutes until the whites are set but the yolks still runny. Remove from the pan with a draining spoon.

4. Arrange the spinach on the toast and top each slice with a poached egg. Sprinkle with the grated cheese. Cook under the preheated grill for 1–2 minutes until the cheese has melted. Sprinkle with nutmeg and serve.

SNICKERDOODLES

MAKES: 40   **PREP TIME:** 15 MINS PLUS 1 HR CHILLING TIME   **COOK TIME:** 12 MINS

INGREDIENTS

225 g/8 oz butter, softened

140 g/5 oz caster sugar

2 large eggs, lightly beaten

1 tsp vanilla extract

400 g/14 oz plain flour

1 tsp bicarbonate of soda

½ tsp freshly grated nutmeg

55 g/2 oz pecan nuts, finely chopped

salt

CINNAMON COATING

1 tbsp caster sugar

2 tbsp ground cinnamon

1. Put the butter and sugar into a bowl and mix well with a wooden spoon, then beat in the eggs and vanilla extract. Sift together the flour, bicarbonate of soda, nutmeg and a pinch of salt into the mixture, add the pecan nuts and stir until thoroughly combined. Shape the dough into a ball, wrap in clingfilm and chill in the refrigerator for 30–60 minutes.

2. Preheat the oven to 190°C/375°F/Gas Mark 5. Line two to three baking sheets with greaseproof paper.

3. For the cinnamon coating, mix together the caster sugar and cinnamon in a shallow dish. Scoop up tablespoons of the cookie dough and roll into balls. Roll each ball in the cinnamon mixture to coat and place on the prepared baking sheets spaced well apart.

4. Bake in the preheated oven for 10–12 minutes, until golden brown. Leave to cool on the baking sheets for 5–10 minutes, then using a palette knife, carefully transfer to wire racks to cool completely.

11 APRIL

PEPPERONI PASTA

SERVES: 4 | **PREP TIME: 10 MINS** | **COOK TIME: 45 MINS**

INGREDIENTS

3 tbsp olive oil

1 onion, chopped

1 red pepper, deseeded and diced

1 orange pepper, deseeded and diced

800 g/1 lb 12 oz canned chopped tomatoes

1 tbsp sun-dried tomato paste

1 tsp paprika

225 g/8 oz pepperoni sausage, sliced

2 tbsp chopped fresh flat-leaf parsley, plus extra to garnish

450 g/1 lb dried penne

salt and pepper

1. Heat 2 tablespoons of the olive oil in a large, heavy-based frying pan. Add the onion and cook over a low heat, stirring occasionally, for 5 minutes, or until softened. Add the red and orange peppers, tomatoes and their can juices, sun-dried tomato paste and paprika and bring to the boil.

2. Add the pepperoni and parsley and season to taste with salt and pepper. Stir well, bring to the boil, then reduce the heat and simmer for 10–15 minutes.

3. Meanwhile, bring a large, heavy-based saucepan of lightly salted water to the boil. Add the penne, bring back to the boil and cook for 8–10 minutes, or until just tender but still firm to the bite. Drain well and transfer to a serving dish. Add the remaining olive oil and toss. Add the sauce and toss again. Sprinkle with parsley and serve.

12 APRIL

QUICK PAN BRAISE OF HAM CHUNKS

SERVES: 4 | **PREP TIME: 10 MINS** | **COOK TIME: ABOUT 5 MINS**

INGREDIENTS

2 tbsp olive oil

1 bunch spring onions, cut into 1-cm/½-inch pieces

2.5-cm/1-inch piece fresh ginger, finely chopped

350 g/12 oz cooked ham, cut into bite-sized chunks

225 g/8 oz canned pineapple chunks in natural juice, drained and juice reserved

2 tbsp chopped fresh mint

2 tbsp balsamic vinegar

cooked rice or couscous, to serve

1. Heat the oil in a frying pan or wok, add the spring onions and ginger and fry, stirring, for 1 minute.

2. Add the ham and cook, stirring, for a further 2 minutes. Add the pineapple with 2 tablespoons of the can juices and stir over a medium heat for 2–3 minutes.

3. Stir in the mint and vinegar and bring to the boil. Remove from the heat and serve with rice.

LEMON TURKEY WITH SPINACH

SERVES: 4   PREP TIME: 30 MINS PLUS 30 MINS MARINATING TIME   COOK TIME: 10 MINS

INGREDIENTS

450 g/1 lb turkey breast, skinned and cut into strips

1 tbsp vegetable oil

6 spring onions, finely sliced

½ lemon, peeled and thinly sliced

1 garlic clove, finely chopped

300 g/10½ oz spinach, washed, drained and roughly chopped

3 tbsp chopped fresh flat-leaf parsley

sprigs of flat-leaf parsley, to garnish

cooked pasta, to serve

MARINADE

1 tbsp soy sauce

1 tbsp white wine vinegar

1 tsp cornflour

1 tsp finely grated lemon zest

½ tsp finely ground black pepper

1. To make the marinade, put the soy sauce, vinegar, cornflour, lemon zest and black pepper in a bowl and mix thoroughly. Add the turkey and stir to coat. Cover with clingfilm and marinate in the refrigerator for 30 minutes.

2. Heat the oil in a large preheated wok or frying pan. Add the turkey and the marinade and cook over a medium heat for 2–3 minutes or until the turkey is opaque.

3. Add the spring onions, lemon slices and garlic and cook for another 2–3 minutes. Stir in the spinach and parsley and cook until the spinach is just wilted.

4. Remove from the heat and spoon over pasta. Garnish with sprigs of parsley and serve.

SWEETCORN & CHIVE FRITTERS

MAKES: 16 | **PREP TIME: 10 MINS** | **COOK TIME: 6–8 MINS**

INGREDIENTS

150 g/5½ oz plain flour

1½ tsp baking powder

200 ml/7 fl oz milk

2 eggs, separated

2 tbsp melted butter

200 g/7 oz canned or frozen sweetcorn

2 tbsp chopped chives, plus extra for sprinkling

oil, for frying

salt and pepper

1. Sift together the flour, baking powder, and salt and pepper to taste into a mixing bowl. Add the milk, egg yolks and butter and whisk to a smooth batter. Stir in the sweetcorn and chives.

2. Put the egg whites into a separate grease-free bowl and whisk until they hold soft peaks. Fold lightly and evenly into the batter.

3. Pour a shallow depth of oil into a large frying pan and heat until hot. Drop large spoonfuls of batter into the pan and cook for 3–4 minutes, turning once, until golden brown. Cook in batches, keeping the cooked fritters warm, until you have made about 16 fritters, draining on absorbent kitchen paper.

4. Serve hot, sprinkled with chives.

MOROCCAN LAMB STEW

SERVES: 8 | **PREP TIME: 25 MINS PLUS 4 HRS MARINATING TIME** | **COOK TIME: 2½ HRS**

INGREDIENTS

1.5–2 kg/3 lb 5 oz–4 lb 8 oz boned lamb shoulder, cut into cubes

4 tbsp olive oil

250 g/9 oz stoned dates

250 g/9 oz stoned olives

700 ml/1¼ pints red wine

10 whole garlic cloves, peeled

large handful of fresh coriander

couscous, to serve

DRY MARINADE

2 large onions, grated

4 garlic cloves, crushed

1 red chilli, finely chopped

1 tsp paprika

2 tsp ground cumin

1 tsp ground ginger

1 tsp pepper

1. Combine all the dry marinade ingredients in a flameproof casserole, add the lamb and leave to marinate in the refrigerator for 4 hours or overnight.

2. Preheat the oven to 150°C/300°F/Gas Mark 2. Remove the lamb from the refrigerator. Add the oil, dates, olives, wine and garlic to the casserole and cover. Transfer to the preheated oven and cook for 2½ hours, removing the lid for the last 30 minutes. Check that the lamb is meltingly tender, stir in the coriander and serve with couscous.

SWEETCORN &
CHIVE FRITTERS

TURBOT STEAKS WITH PARSLEY, LEMON & GARLIC

SERVES: 4 PREP TIME: **10 MINS** COOK TIME: **20 MINS**

INGREDIENTS

2 tbsp olive oil, for brushing

4 turbot steaks

juice and finely grated rind of 1 lemon

2 garlic cloves, finely chopped

4 tbsp finely chopped fresh flat-leaf parsley

40 g/1½ oz pine kernels, toasted

salt and pepper

cooked seasonal vegetables, to serve

1. Preheat the oven to 220°C/425°F/Gas Mark 7. Brush a wide, ovenproof dish with oil.

2. Place the turbot steaks in the dish, brush with oil, season with salt and pepper and pour over the lemon juice.

3. Mix together the lemon rind, garlic, parsley and pine kernels and spoon over the fish. Drizzle with the remaining oil.

4. Bake in the preheated oven for 15–20 minutes until the fish flakes easily with a fork.

5. Serve hot with vegetables.

CHOCOLATE PRETZELS

MAKES: 30   PREP TIME: 30 MINS PLUS 15 MINS CHILLING TIME   COOK TIME: 12 MINS

INGREDIENTS

100 g/3½ oz unsalted butter, plus extra for greasing

100 g/3½ oz caster sugar

1 egg

225 g/8 oz plain flour

2 tbsp cocoa powder

TO DECORATE

15 g/½ oz butter

100 g/3½ oz plain chocolate

icing sugar, for dusting

1. Preheat the oven to 190°C/375°F/Gas Mark 5. Lightly grease a baking sheet with a little butter. Beat together the butter and sugar in a large mixing bowl until light and fluffy. Beat in the egg, ensuring all the ingredients are well combined.

2. Sift together the flour and cocoa powder and gradually beat into the egg mixture to form a soft dough. Use your fingers to incorporate the last of the flour and bring the dough together. Chill for 15 minutes.

3. Break pieces from the dough and roll into thin sausage shapes about 10 cm/4 inches long and 5 mm/¼ inch thick. Carefully twist into pretzel shapes by making a circle, then twist the ends through each other to form a letter 'B'.

4. Place the pretzels on the prepared baking sheet, spaced slightly apart to allow for expansion during cooking. Bake in the preheated oven for 8–12 minutes. Leave the pretzels to cool slightly on the baking sheet, then transfer to a wire rack to cool completely.

5. Melt the butter and chocolate in a bowl set over a saucepan of gently simmering water, stirring. Dip half of each pretzel into the chocolate and allow the excess chocolate to drip back into the bowl. Place the pretzels on a sheet of greaseproof paper and leave to set. When set, dust the uncoated side of each pretzel with icing sugar before serving.

CREAMY MANGO BRÛLÉE

SERVES: 4   PREP TIME: 30 MINS PLUS 2 HRS CHILLING TIME   COOK TIME: 3 MINS

INGREDIENTS

2 mangoes, stoned, peeled and chopped

250 g/9 oz mascarpone cheese

200 ml/7 fl oz Greek-style yogurt

1 tsp ground ginger

grated rind and juice of 1 lime

2 tbsp soft light brown sugar

8 tbsp demerara sugar

1. Divide the mango between four ramekins.

2. Beat the mascarpone cheese with the yogurt. Fold in the ginger, lime rind and juice and soft brown sugar. Divide the mixture between the ramekins and level off the tops. Chill for 2 hours.

3. Sprinkle 2 tablespoons of demerara sugar over the top of each dish, covering the creamy mixture. Place under a hot grill for 2–3 minutes, until melted and browned. Let cool, then chill until needed.

LEMON MERINGUE PIE

SERVES: 6–8 PREP TIME: 20 MINS PLUS 30 MINS CHILLING TIME COOK TIME: 1 HR

INGREDIENTS

PASTRY

150 g/5½ oz plain flour, plus extra for dusting

85 g/3 oz butter, cut into small pieces, plus extra for greasing

35 g/1¼ oz icing sugar, sifted

finely grated rind of ½ lemon

½ egg yolk, beaten

1½ tbsp milk

FILLING

3 tbsp cornflour

300 ml/10 fl oz water

juice and grated rind of 2 lemons

175 g/6 oz caster sugar

2 eggs, separated

1. To make the pastry, sift the flour into a bowl. Rub in the butter with your fingertips until the mixture resembles fine breadcrumbs. Mix in the remaining ingredients. Turn out onto a lightly floured work surface and knead briefly. Wrap in clingfilm and chill in the refrigerator for 30 minutes. Meanwhile, preheat the oven to 180°C/350°F/Gas Mark 4.

2. Grease a 20-cm/8-inch round tart tin. Roll out the pastry to a thickness of 5 mm/¼ inch, then use it to line the base and side of the tin. Prick all over with a fork, line with baking paper and fill with baking beans. Bake in the preheated oven for 15 minutes. Remove the pastry case from the oven and take out the paper and beans. Reduce the oven temperature to 150°C/300°F/Gas Mark 2.

3. To make the filling, mix the cornflour with a little of the water to form a paste. Put the remaining water in a saucepan. Stir in the lemon juice, lemon rind and cornflour paste. Bring to the boil, stirring. Cook for 2 minutes. Leave to cool slightly. Stir in 5 tablespoons of the caster sugar and the egg yolks, then pour into the pastry case.

4. Whisk the egg whites in a clean, grease-free bowl until stiff. Gradually whisk in the remaining caster sugar and spread over the pie. Bake for a further 40 minutes. Remove from the oven, cool and serve.

VEGETABLE COUSCOUS

SERVES: 4   PREP TIME: 10 MINS PLUS 20 MINS SOAKING TIME   COOK TIME: 25–30 MINS

INGREDIENTS

200 g/7 oz couscous

1 red pepper, halved and deseeded

1 green pepper, halved and deseeded

1 yellow pepper, halved and deseeded

1 red onion

1 garlic clove, sliced

2 tbsp olive oil

2 tomatoes, quartered

2 tbsp lemon juice

55 g/2 oz toasted cashew nuts

salt and pepper

paprika, to garnish

1. Preheat the oven to 200°C/400°F/Gas Mark 6. Put the couscous into a bowl and pour over boiling water to just cover. Leave to stand for 20 minutes until the grains are swollen. Drain well.

2. Meanwhile, cut the red, green and yellow peppers into bite-size chunks and slice the onion into thick wedges. Place the peppers, onion and garlic in a roasting tin, sprinkle with salt and pepper and drizzle over the oil.

3. Bake in the preheated oven for 20 minutes, then add the tomatoes and cook for a further 5–10 minutes until tender.

4. Stir in the couscous and lemon juice, add the cashew nuts and season to taste with salt and pepper. Serve hot, sprinkled with paprika.

TURKEY STEAKS WITH BUTTER BEANS

SERVES: 4   PREP TIME: 10 MINS   COOK TIME: 20 MINS

INGREDIENTS

1 tbsp plain flour

1 tsp dried thyme

4 turkey breast steaks

2 tbsp olive oil

1 red onion, thinly sliced

1 garlic clove, crushed

300 g/10½ oz canned butter beans, drained and rinsed

400 g/14 oz canned plum tomatoes, chopped

salt and pepper

1. Put the flour, thyme and salt and pepper to taste into a shallow bowl and mix. Add the turkey steaks and turn in the mixture until lightly coated.

2. Heat the oil in a wide saucepan, add the turkey steaks and fry over a fairly high heat, turning once, for 2–3 minutes until golden.

3. Add the onion and garlic and cook for a further minute, then stir in the beans and tomatoes.

4. Bring to the boil, then reduce the heat, cover the pan and simmer gently, stirring occasionally, for 10–15 minutes until the turkey is tender. Season to taste with salt and pepper and serve hot.

SPRING ONION & RICOTTA TARTS

MAKES: 12   PREP TIME: 40 MINS PLUS 30 MINS CHILLING TIME   COOK TIME: 15 MINS

INGREDIENTS

PASTRY

200 g/7 oz plain flour, plus extra for dusting

pinch of salt

125 g/4½ oz butter, diced, plus extra for greasing

1 egg yolk

FILLING

250 g/9 oz ricotta cheese

100 g/3½ oz freshly grated pecorino cheese

1 egg, beaten

12 spring onions, finely chopped

2 tbsp fresh shelled peas, lightly cooked and cooled

1 tsp green peppercorns in brine, drained

salt and pepper

1. To make the pastry, sift together the flour and salt into a bowl, add the butter and rub in with your fingertips until the mixture resembles fine breadcrumbs. Add the egg and enough cold water to form a smooth dough. Cover and refrigerate for 30 minutes.

2. Preheat the oven to 190°C/375°F/Gas Mark 5. Lightly grease a 12-cup muffin tin.

3. Roll the pastry out on a floured work surface to a thickness of 3–4 mm/about ¼ inch. Using a round pastry cutter or a glass, cut out rounds large enough to line the cups of the muffin tin. Gently press the pastry cases into the cups. Line each pastry case with a small piece of greaseproof paper and fill with baking beans.

4. Bake the pastry cases in the preheated oven for 4–5 minutes until golden and crisp. Remove the paper and beans.

5. Meanwhile, to make the filling, mix together the ricotta and pecorino cheeses in a large bowl. Add the egg, spring onions and peas. Chop the peppercorns very finely, then add to the mixture. Season to taste with salt and a good grinding of pepper.

6. Spoon the filling into the pastry cases and bake for 10 minutes, or until golden. Serve warm.

FISH & CHIPS

SERVES: 2   PREP TIME: 20 MINS   COOK TIME: 25 MINS

INGREDIENTS

vegetable oil, for deep-frying

3 large potatoes, such as Cara or Desirée

2 thick cod or haddock fillets, 175 g/6 oz each

175 g/6 oz self-raising flour, plus extra for dusting

200 ml/7 fl oz cold lager

salt and pepper

tartare sauce, to serve

1. Heat enough oil for deep-frying in a large frying pan or deep-fryer to 120°C/250°F, checking the temperature with a thermometer, to blanch the chips. Preheat the oven to 150°C/300°F/Gas Mark 2.

2. Peel the potatoes and cut into even-sized chips. Fry for about 8–10 minutes, depending on size, until soft but not coloured. Remove from the oil, drain on kitchen paper and place in a warmed dish in the preheated oven. Increase the temperature of the oil to 180–190°C/ 350–375°F, or until a cube of bread browns in 30 seconds.

3. Meanwhile, season the fish with salt and pepper to taste and dust lightly with flour.

4. Make a thick batter by sifting the flour into a bowl with a little salt and whisking in most of the lager. Check the consistency of the batter before adding the remaining lager: it should be very thick like double cream.

5. Dip one fillet into the batter and allow the batter to coat it thickly. Carefully place the fish in the hot oil, then repeat with the other fillet.

6. Cook for 8–10 minutes, depending on the thickness of the fish. Turn over the fillets halfway through the cooking time. Remove the fish from the fryer, drain and keep warm.

7. Return the chips to the fryer at the increased temperature and cook for a further 2–3 minutes until they are golden brown and crisp. Drain and season to taste with salt and pepper before serving with the battered fish and tartare sauce.

MINI CHICKEN POT PIES

MAKES: 12   **PREP TIME: 30 MINS**   **COOK TIME: 45 MINS**

INGREDIENTS

25 g/1 oz salted butter, plus extra for greasing

1 tbsp olive oil

500 g/1 lb 2 oz boneless, skinless chicken breasts, cut into 1-cm/½-inch cubes

1 leek, about 175 g/6 oz, thinly sliced, white and green slices kept separate

2 tbsp plain flour, plus extra for dusting

450 ml/16 fl oz chicken stock

4 tbsp dry white wine

2 tbsp roughly chopped fresh tarragon

2 tbsp roughly chopped fresh parsley

1 tbsp chopped capers

650 g/1 lb 7 oz ready-made plain shortcrust pastry, chilled

1 egg yolk mixed with 1 tbsp water, to glaze

1. Preheat the oven to 180°C/350°F/Gas Mark 4. Lightly grease a 12-cup muffin tin.

2. Heat the butter and oil in a frying pan over a medium heat. Add the chicken and white leek slices and fry, stirring, for 10 minutes, or until the chicken is golden brown and the leeks are softened. Sprinkle the flour over the top, mix together, then add the stock and wine. Simmer for 5 minutes, stirring from time to time, until the sauce has thickened and the chicken is tender and cooked through. Add the green leek slices and cook for 2 minutes, or until the leeks are just soft. Sprinkle over the tarragon, parsley and capers and leave to cool.

3. Roll two thirds of the pastry out thinly on a lightly floured surface. Using a plain cookie cutter, stamp out 12 circles each 10 cm/4 inches in diameter. Press these gently into the prepared muffin tin, re-rolling the trimmings as needed. Brush the top edges of the pie cases with a little of the egg glaze, then spoon in the filling.

4. Roll out the reserved pastry and any trimmings on a lightly floured surface. Using a plain cookie cutter, stamp out 12 circles each 7cm/ 2¾ inches in diameter. Arrange these on top of the pies, pressing the edges together well to seal. Brush the pastry with egg glaze; add leaves cut out from rolled pastry trimmings using a sharp knife, then brush these with egg too.

5. Bake in the preheated oven for 25 minutes, or until golden brown. Leave to cool in the tin for 5 minutes then transfer to serving plates. Serve hot or cold.

CHILLI BEEF STIR-FRY SALAD

SERVES: 4 | PREP TIME: 30 MINS | COOK TIME: ABOUT 10 MINS

INGREDIENTS

450 g/1 lb rump steak, cut into thin strips

1 ripe avocado

2 tbsp sunflower oil

425 g/15 oz canned red kidney beans, drained and rinsed

175 g/6 oz cherry tomatoes, halved

1 large packet tortilla chips

iceberg lettuce, shredded

chopped fresh coriander, to garnish

MARINADE

2 garlic cloves, crushed

1 tsp chilli powder

½ tsp salt

1 tsp ground coriander

1. To make the marinade, place all the marinade ingredients in a large bowl and stir until well mixed.

2. Add the strips of beef to the marinade and toss thoroughly to coat all over.

3. Using a sharp knife, peel the avocado. Slice the avocado lengthways in half and remove and discard the stone, then slice crossways to form small dice.

4. Heat the oil in a large preheated wok. Add the beef and stir-fry for 5 minutes, tossing frequently. Add the kidney beans, tomatoes and avocado and cook for 2 minutes.

5. Arrange the tortilla chips and iceberg lettuce around the edge of a serving plate and spoon the beef into the centre. Alternatively, serve the tortilla chips and lettuce separately. Garnish with fresh coriander and serve immediately.

SPAGHETTI WITH MEATBALLS

SERVES: 6 | PREP TIME: 10 MINS | COOK TIME: 45 MINS

INGREDIENTS

1 potato, diced

400 g/14 oz fresh beef mince

1 onion, finely chopped

1 egg

4 tbsp chopped fresh flat-leaf parsley

plain flour, for dusting

5 tbsp olive oil

400 ml/14 fl oz passata

2 tbsp tomato purée

400 g/14 oz dried spaghetti

salt and pepper

1. Place the potato in a small saucepan, add cold water to cover and a pinch of salt and bring to the boil. Cook for 10–15 minutes, until tender, then drain. Either mash thoroughly with a potato masher or fork or pass through a potato ricer.

2. Combine the potato, beef, onion, egg and parsley in a bowl and season to taste with salt and pepper. Spread out the flour on a plate. With dampened hands, shape the meat mixture into walnut-sized balls and roll in the flour. Shake off any excess.

3. Heat the oil in a heavy-based frying pan, add the meatballs and cook over a medium heat, stirring and turning frequently, for 8–10 minutes, until golden all over.

4. Add the passata and tomato purée and cook for a further 10 minutes, until the sauce is reduced and thickened.

5. Meanwhile, bring a large saucepan of lightly salted water to the boil. Add the spaghetti, bring back to the boil and cook for 8–10 minutes, or until just tender but still firm to the bite.

6. Drain well and add to the meatball sauce, tossing well to coat. Serve.

**CHILLI BEEF
STIR-FRY SALAD**

27 APRIL

COOKIES & CREAM SANDWICHES

MAKES: 15 | PREP TIME: 20 MINS PLUS 2 HRS CHILLING TIME | COOK TIME: 20 MINS

INGREDIENTS

125 g/4½ oz butter, softened

75 g/2¾ oz icing sugar

115 g/4 oz plain flour

40 g/1½ oz cocoa powder

½ tsp ground cinnamon

FILLING

125 g/4½ oz plain chocolate, broken into pieces

50 ml/2 fl oz double cream

1. Preheat the oven to 160°C/325°F/Gas Mark 3. Line a baking sheet with greaseproof paper. Place the butter and sugar in a large bowl and beat together until light and fluffy. Sift the flour, cocoa and ground cinnamon into the bowl and mix to form a dough.

2. Place the dough between 2 sheets of greaseproof paper and roll out to 3-mm/⅛-inch thick. Cut out 6-cm/2½-inch circles and place on the prepared baking sheet. Bake in the preheated oven for 15 minutes, or until firm to the touch. Leave to cool for 2 minutes, then transfer to wire racks to cool completely.

3. Meanwhile, make the filling. Place the chocolate and cream in a saucepan and heat gently until the chocolate has melted. Stir until smooth. Leave to cool, then leave to chill in the refrigerator for 2 hours, or until firm. Sandwich the biscuits together in pairs with a spoonful of chocolate cream and serve.

28 APRIL

QUICK TIRAMISÙ

SERVES: 4 | PREP TIME: 30 MINS | COOK TIME: NO COOKING

INGREDIENTS

225 g/8 oz mascarpone or full-fat soft cheese

1 egg, separated

2 tbsp natural yogurt

2 tbsp caster sugar

2 tbsp dark rum

2 tbsp strong black coffee

8 sponge finger biscuits

1. Put the mascarpone cheese in a large bowl, add the egg yolk and yogurt and beat until smooth.

2. Whisk the egg white until stiff but not dry, then whisk in the sugar and fold into the mascarpone mixture. Spoon half of the mixture into 4 glasses.

3. Mix together the rum and coffee in a shallow dish. Dip the sponge fingers into the rum mixture, break them in half, or into smaller pieces if necessary, and divide between the glasses.

4. Stir any remaining coffee mixture into the remaining cheese and spoon over the top. Serve.

NEW YORK CHEESECAKE

SERVES: 4   PREP TIME: 20 MINS PLUS 2 HRS COOLING TIME   COOK TIME: 55 MINS

INGREDIENTS

100 g/3½ oz butter, plus extra for greasing

150 g/5½ oz digestive biscuits, finely crushed

1 tbsp granulated sugar

900 g/2 lb cream cheese

250 g/9 oz caster sugar

2 tbsp plain flour

1 tsp vanilla extract

finely grated zest of 1 orange

finely grated zest of 1 lemon

3 eggs

2 egg yolks

300 ml/10 fl oz double cream

1. Preheat the oven to 180°C/350°F/Gas Mark 4. Place a small saucepan over a low heat, add the butter and heat until it melts. Remove from the heat, stir in the biscuits and granulated sugar and mix.

2. Press the biscuit mixture tightly into the base of a 23-cm/9-inch springform cake tin. Place in the preheated oven and bake for 10 minutes. Remove from the oven and leave to cool on a wire rack.

3. Increase the oven temperature to 200°C/400°F/Gas Mark 6. Use an electric mixer to beat the cheese until creamy, then gradually add the caster sugar and flour and beat until smooth. Increase the speed and beat in the vanilla extract, orange zest and lemon zest, then beat in the eggs and egg yolks one at a time. Finally, beat in the cream. Scrape any excess from the sides and paddles of the beater into the mixture. It should be light and fluffy – beat on a faster setting if you need to.

4. Grease the side of the cake tin and pour in the filling. Smooth the top, transfer to the oven and bake for 15 minutes. Reduce the temperature to 110°C/225°F/Gas Mark ¼ and bake for a further 30 minutes. Turn off the oven and leave the cheesecake in it for 2 hours to cool and set. Cover and chill in the refrigerator overnight.

5. Slide a knife around the edge of the cake then unfasten the tin, cut the cheesecake into slices and serve.

DEVILLED CRAB RAMEKINS

SERVES: 4   PREP TIME: 10 MINS   COOK TIME: 15 MINS

INGREDIENTS

melted butter, for greasing

175 g/6 oz crabmeat, light and dark meat

1 large egg, beaten

4 tbsp crème fraîche

juice of 1 lime

1 tsp hot chilli sauce

85 g/3 oz fresh white breadcrumbs

4 tbsp Parmesan cheese, finely grated

salt and pepper

paprika, to garnish

TO SERVE

lime wedges

salad leaves

toasted wholemeal bread

1. Preheat the oven to 200°C/400°F/Gas Mark 6. Brush four 150-ml/5-fl oz ramekin dishes with butter and place on a baking sheet.

2. Mix the crabmeat with the egg, crème fraîche, lime juice and chilli sauce. Stir in the breadcrumbs and season to taste with salt and pepper.

3. Spoon the mixture into the prepared ramekins and sprinkle with the cheese. Bake in the preheated oven for about 15 minutes until golden and bubbling.

4. Sprinkle with paprika and serve hot, with lime wedges, salad leaves and toast.

MINI PEACH CHEESECAKE CRUMBLES

SERVES: 4   **PREP TIME: 15 MINS PLUS AT LEAST 1 HR CHILLING TIME**   **COOK TIME: NO COOKING**

INGREDIENTS

3 ripe peaches, halved and stoned

3 tbsp peach liqueur or orange juice

200 g/7 oz mascarpone cheese

25 g/1 oz caster sugar

½ tsp almond extract

40 g/1½ oz digestive biscuits, crushed

40 g/1½ oz ground almonds

25 g/1 oz unsalted butter, melted

1. Reserve eight small slices of peach and roughly chop the remainder. Divide between four 150-ml/5-fl oz ramekins and spoon over the liqueur.

2. Put the mascarpone cheese, sugar and almond extract into a bowl and beat together. Spoon the mixture over the peaches, covering completely.

3. Mix together the biscuits and ground almonds, then stir in the butter. Spoon the biscuit mixture over the mascarpone mixture and top with the reserved peach slices. Chill in the refrigerator for at least 1 hour before serving.

FUSILLI WITH COURGETTES & LEMON

SERVES: 4   PREP TIME: 20 MINS   COOK TIME: 30 MINS

INGREDIENTS

6 tbsp olive oil

1 small onion, very thinly sliced

2 garlic cloves, very finely chopped

2 tbsp chopped fresh rosemary

1 tbsp chopped fresh flat-leaf parsley

450 g/1 lb small courgettes, cut into 4-cm/1½ -inch strips

finely grated rind of 1 lemon

450 g/1 lb dried fusilli

salt and pepper

freshly grated Parmesan cheese, to serve

1. Heat the oil in a large frying pan over a medium–low heat. Add the onion and cook gently, stirring occasionally, for about 10 minutes, until golden.

2. Increase the heat to medium–high. Add the garlic, rosemary and parsley. Cook for a few seconds, stirring.

3. Add the courgettes and lemon rind. Cook for 5–7 minutes, stirring occasionally, until just tender. Season to taste with salt and pepper. Remove from the heat.

4. Bring a large saucepan of lightly salted water to the boil. Add the fusilli, bring back to the boil and cook for 8–10 minutes, or until just tender but still firm to the bite.

5. Drain the pasta and transfer to a serving dish.

6. Briefly reheat the courgette sauce. Pour over the pasta and toss well to mix.

7. Sprinkle with the Parmesan cheese and serve.

FISH GOUJONS WITH CHILLI MAYONNAISE

SERVES: 4 **PREP TIME: 20 MINS** **COOK TIME: 15 MINS**

INGREDIENTS

200 g/7 oz plain flour

3 eggs

140 g/5 oz matzo meal

450 g/1 lb firm white fish fillets, cut into strips

sunflower or groundnut oil, for shallow-frying

salt and pepper

CHILLI MAYONNAISE

2 tbsp sweet chilli sauce

4–5 tbsp mayonnaise

1. Mix the flour with plenty of salt and pepper on a large flat plate.

2. Beat the eggs in a bowl.

3. Spread out the matzo meal on another flat plate.

4. Dip the fish pieces into the seasoned flour, then into the beaten egg, then into the matzo meal, ensuring a generous coating.

5. Pour the oil into a non-stick frying pan to a depth of 1 cm/½ inch and heat. Cook the fish pieces in batches for a few minutes, turning once, until golden and cooked through.

6. To make the chilli mayonnaise, put the chilli sauce and mayonnaise in a bowl and beat together until combined.

7. Transfer the fish to serving plates and serve with the chilli mayonnaise on the side.

ASPARAGUS & TOMATO TART

SERVES: 4 | PREP TIME: 35 MINS | COOK TIME: 1 HR 10 MINS

INGREDIENTS

butter, for greasing

375 g/13 oz ready-made shortcrust pastry, thawed, if frozen

1 bunch thin asparagus spears

250 g/9 oz spinach leaves

3 large eggs, beaten

150 ml/5 fl oz double cream

1 garlic clove, crushed

10 small cherry tomatoes, halved

handful fresh basil, chopped

25 g/1 oz freshly grated Parmesan cheese

salt and pepper

1. Preheat the oven to 190°C/375°F/Gas Mark 5. Grease a 25–30-cm/10–12-inch tart tin with butter, then roll out the pastry and use to line the tin.

2. Cut off any excess pastry and prick the base with a fork. Cover with a piece of greaseproof paper and fill with baking beans. Blind-bake the base in the preheated oven for 20–30 minutes until lightly browned. Remove from the oven and take out the greaseproof paper and beans. Reduce the oven temperature to 180°C/350°F/Gas Mark 4.

3. Meanwhile, bend the asparagus spears until they snap, and discard the woody bases. Bring a large saucepan of lightly salted water to the boil. Add the asparagus and blanch for 1 minute, then remove and drain. Add the spinach to the boiling water, then remove immediately and drain very well.

4. Mix together the eggs, cream and garlic and season to taste with salt and pepper. Lay the blanched spinach at the bottom of the pastry base. Add the asparagus and tomatoes, cut side up, in any arrangement you like. Scatter over the basil, then pour the egg mixture on top.

5. Transfer to the oven and bake for about 35 minutes, or until the filling has set. Sprinkle the cheese on top and leave to cool to room temperature before serving.

TOMATO & MOZZARELLA STACKS

SERVES: 4 | PREP TIME: 25 MINS | COOK TIME: 10 MINS

INGREDIENTS

4 large tomatoes, about 200 g/7 oz each

225 g/8 oz buffalo mozzarella

24 fresh basil leaves

olive oil, for brushing

salt and pepper

1. Preheat the barbecue. Using a sharp serrated knife, cut a thin slice from the top and bottom of each tomato, and discard. Slice the rest of the tomato horizontally into three. Slice the mozzarella into thin rounds. Slice the basil leaves into thin ribbons, reserving a few whole leaves.

2. Brush a piece of double-thickness foil with oil. Place a tomato slice on the foil, brush with oil and season to taste with salt and pepper. Add a few basil shreds and a slice of cheese. Continue layering using the second and third tomato slices, seasoning each layer, and finishing with a layer of mozzarella. Top each stack with the reserved basil leaves. Fold up the edges of the foil to make a bowl shape. Repeat with the three remaining tomatoes and mozzarella.

3. Arrange on the grill rack and cook over medium–hot coals, covered, for 8–10 minutes until the top tomato slice is heated through and the mozzarella is melted. Transfer to serving plates and serve.

ASPARAGUS &
TOMATO TART

SALAD NIÇOISE

SERVES: 4–6   PREP TIME: 35 MINS   COOK TIME: 10 MINS

INGREDIENTS

2 tuna steaks, about 2 cm/¾ inch thick

olive oil, for brushing

250 g/9 oz French beans, topped and tailed

shop-bought garlic vinaigrette, to taste

2 hearts of lettuce, leaves separated

3 large hard-boiled eggs, halved

2 tomatoes, cut into wedges

50 g/1¾ oz anchovy fillets in oil, drained

55 g/2 oz Niçoise olives

salt and pepper

1. Heat a ridged cast-iron griddle pan over a high heat. Brush the tuna steaks with oil on one side, place oiled-side down on the hot pan and chargrill for 2 minutes.

2. Lightly brush the top side of the tuna steaks with a little more oil. Turn the tuna steaks over, then season to taste. Continue chargrilling for a further 2 minutes for rare or up to 4 minutes for well done. Leave to cool.

3. Meanwhile, bring a saucepan of lightly salted water to the boil. Add the beans to the pan and bring back to the boil, then boil for 3 minutes. Drain the beans and immediately transfer them to a large bowl. Pour over the garlic vinaigrette and stir together.

4. To serve, line a serving dish with lettuce leaves. Lift the beans out of the bowl, leaving the excess dressing behind, and pile them in the centre of the platter. Break the tuna into large flakes and arrange it over the beans.

5. Arrange the hard-boiled eggs, tomatoes, anchovy fillets and olives on the platter. Drizzle over more vinaigrette, if required, and serve.

CALAMARI WITH PRAWNS & BROAD BEANS

SERVES: 4–6   PREP TIME: 10 MINS   COOK TIME: 20 MINS

INGREDIENTS

2 tbsp olive oil

4 spring onions, thinly sliced

2 garlic cloves, finely chopped

500 g/1 lb 2 oz cleaned squid bodies, thickly sliced

100 ml/3½ fl oz dry white wine

225 g/8 oz fresh or frozen baby broad beans

250 g/9 oz raw king prawns, peeled and deveined

4 tbsp chopped fresh flat-leaf parsley

salt and pepper

crusty bread, to serve

1. Heat the oil in a large frying pan with a lid, add the spring onions and cook over a medium heat, stirring occasionally, for 4–5 minutes, until soft.

2. Add the garlic and cook, stirring, for 30 seconds, until soft.

3. Add the squid and cook over a high heat, stirring occasionally, for 2 minutes, or until golden brown.

4. Stir in the wine and bring to the boil. Add the beans, reduce the heat, cover and simmer for 5–8 minutes, if using fresh beans, or 4–5 minutes, if using frozen beans, until tender.

5. Add the prawns, re-cover and simmer for a further 2–3 minutes, until the prawns turn pink and start to curl.

6. Stir in the parsley and season to taste with salt and pepper. Serve with crusty bread.

TUNA & CHEESE QUICHE

SERVES: 4   **PREP TIME: 25 MINS**   **COOK TIME: ABOUT 1 HR**

INGREDIENTS

FLAN CASE

450 g/1 lb floury potatoes, diced

2 tbsp butter

6 tbsp plain flour, plus extra for dusting

FILLING

1 tbsp vegetable oil

1 shallot, chopped

1 garlic clove, crushed

1 red pepper, deseeded and diced

175 g/6 oz canned tuna in brine, drained

50 g/1¾ oz canned sweetcorn, drained

150 ml/5 fl oz skimmed milk

3 eggs, beaten

1 tbsp chopped fresh dill

50 g/1¾ oz Cheddar cheese, grated

salt and pepper

1. Preheat the oven to 200°C/400°F/Gas Mark 6. Cook the potatoes in a saucepan of lightly salted boiling water for 10 minutes, or until tender. Drain and mash the potatoes. Add the butter and flour and mix to form a dough.

2. Knead the potato dough on a lightly floured surface and press the mixture into a 20-cm/8-inch tart tin. Prick the base with a fork, cover with a piece of greaseproof paper and fill with baking beans, then blind-bake the base in the preheated oven for 20–30 minutes until lightly browned. Remove from the oven and take out the greaseproof paper and beans.

3. Heat the oil in a frying pan. Cook the shallot, garlic and red pepper for 5 minutes. Spoon the mixture into the flan case. Flake the tuna and arrange it on top with the sweetcorn.

4. In a bowl, combine the milk, eggs and dill and season to taste with salt and pepper. Pour the mixture into the flan case and sprinkle the grated cheese on top. Bake in the preheated oven for 20 minutes, until the filling has set. Serve.

09 MAY

SCALLOPS IN BLACK BEAN SAUCE

SERVES: 4   PREP TIME: 10 MINS   COOK TIME: 5 MINS

INGREDIENTS

2 tbsp vegetable or groundnut oil

1 tbsp finely chopped garlic

1 tbsp finely chopped fresh ginger

1 tbsp fermented black beans, rinsed and lightly mashed

400 g/14 oz scallops

½ tbsp light soy sauce

1 tbsp Chinese rice wine

1 tbsp sugar

3–4 red bird's-eye chillies, finely chopped

1–2 tbsp chicken stock

1 tbsp finely chopped spring onion

1. Heat the oil in a preheated wok. Add the garlic and stir, then add the ginger and stir-fry together for about 1 minute until fragrant.

2. Mix in the black beans, add the scallops and stir-fry for 1 minute. Add the light soy sauce, rice wine, sugar and chillies.

3. Lower the heat and simmer for 2 minutes, then add the stock. Finally add the spring onion, stir and serve.

10 MAY

NACHOS

SERVES: 6   PREP TIME: 20 MINS   COOK TIME: 8 MINS

INGREDIENTS

175 g/6 oz tortilla chips

400 g/14 oz canned refried beans, warmed

2 tbsp finely chopped bottled jalapeño chillies

200 g/7 oz canned or bottled pimientos or roasted peppers, drained and finely sliced

115 g/4 oz Gruyère cheese, grated

115 g/4 oz Cheddar cheese, grated

salt and pepper

1. Preheat the oven to 200°C/400°F/Gas Mark 6. Spread the tortilla chips out over the bottom of a large, shallow, ovenproof dish or roasting pan. Cover with the warmed refried beans. Sprinkle over the chillies and pimientos and season to taste with salt and pepper.

2. Mix together the cheeses in a bowl and sprinkle on top.

3. Bake in the preheated oven for 5–8 minutes, or until the cheese is bubbling and melted. Serve.

FRESH POTATO SALAD

SERVES: 4–6 PREP TIME: 20 MINS COOK TIME: 12 MINS

INGREDIENTS

900 g/2 lb small red-skinned salad potatoes, unpeeled

16–18 cornichons, halved diagonally

2 tbsp finely chopped red onion

3 tbsp snipped chives

¼ tsp pepper

salt

MUSTARD VINAIGRETTE

2 tsp Dijon mustard

1 tbsp red wine vinegar

¼ tsp pepper

4 tbsp extra virgin olive oil

sea salt flakes

1. Put the potatoes in a saucepan of lightly salted water and bring to the boil. Reduce the heat to medium and cook for 10–12 minutes until tender. Drain, then return to the pan and leave for a few minutes.

2. To make the mustard vinaigrette, combine the mustard, vinegar, pepper and a pinch of sea salt flakes in a bowl, mixing well. Add the olive oil and whisk until smooth and thickened.

3. Put the potatoes in a serving bowl and pour over the dressing. Add the remaining ingredients and toss gently to mix. Leave to stand at room temperature for at least 30 minutes before serving.

12 MAY

PIRI PIRI CHICKEN

SERVES: 4–6 • **PREP TIME: 15 MINS** • **COOK TIME: 25 MINS**

INGREDIENTS

8 chicken drumsticks

1½ tsp crushed dried red chillies

2 garlic cloves, crushed

1 tsp dried oregano

2 tsp smoked paprika

juice of ½ lemon

salt and pepper

TO SERVE

lemon wedges

mixed salad leaves

tortillas

1. Preheat the oven to 220°C/425°F/Gas Mark 7. Cut deep slashes into the thickest parts of the meat.

2. Place the chillies, garlic, oregano, paprika and lemon juice in a large mixing bowl. Season to taste with salt and pepper and mix together. Add the chicken and turn to coat evenly.

3. Arrange the chicken in a single layer in a large, shallow roasting tin. Bake in the preheated oven for 20–25 minutes, turning occasionally. Check the chicken is tender and the juices run clear when a skewer is inserted into the thickest part of the meat.

4. Transfer to serving plates. Serve with lemon wedges, mixed salad leaves and tortillas.

13 MAY

PIZZA MARGHERITA

MAKES: 2 • **PREP TIME: 40 MINS PLUS 1 HR RISING TIME** • **COOK TIME: 20 MINS**

INGREDIENTS

PIZZA DOUGH

225 g/8 oz plain flour, plus extra for dusting

1 tsp salt

1 tsp easy-blend dried yeast

1 tbsp olive oil, plus extra for brushing

6 tbsp lukewarm water

TOPPING

6 tomatoes, thinly sliced

175 g/6 oz mozzarella cheese, drained and thinly sliced

2 tbsp shredded fresh basil leaves

2 tbsp olive oil

salt and pepper

1. To make the pizza dough, sift the flour and salt into a bowl and stir in the yeast. Make a well in the centre and pour in the oil and water. Gradually incorporate the dry ingredients into the liquid, using a wooden spoon or floured hands.

2. Turn out the dough onto a lightly floured surface and knead well for 5 minutes, or until smooth and elastic. Return to the clean bowl, cover with lightly oiled clingfilm and set aside to rise in a warm place for 1 hour, or until doubled in size.

3. Preheat the oven to 230°C/450°F/Gas Mark 8. Turn out the dough onto a lightly floured surface and knock back. Knead briefly, then cut it in half and roll out each piece into a round about 5 mm/¼ inch thick. Transfer to a lightly oiled baking sheet and push up the edges with your fingers to form a small rim.

4. To make the topping, arrange the tomato and mozzarella slices alternately over the pizza bases. Season to taste with salt and pepper, sprinkle with the basil and drizzle with the olive oil.

5. Bake in the preheated oven for 15–20 minutes, or until the crust is crisp and the cheese has melted. Serve.

PIRI PIRI
CHICKEN

CHICKEN BREASTS BRAISED WITH BABY VEGETABLES

SERVES: 4 **PREP TIME: 10 MINS** **COOK TIME: 25–30 MINS**

INGREDIENTS

4 skinless chicken breasts

15 g/½ oz butter

1 tbsp olive oil

8 shallots

250 ml/9 fl oz chicken stock

12 baby carrots

8 baby turnips

2 bay leaves

140 g/5 oz fresh or frozen peas

salt and pepper

boiled new potatoes, to serve

1. Cut deep slashes through the chicken at intervals and sprinkle with salt and pepper.

2. Heat the butter and oil in a wide, flameproof casserole or saucepan, add the chicken breasts and shallots and fry, turning, for 3–4 minutes until golden brown.

3. Add the stock and bring to the boil, then add the carrots, turnips and bay leaves. Reduce the heat, cover and simmer gently for 20 minutes.

4. Stir in the peas and cook for a further 5 minutes. Check the chicken and vegetables are tender and the juices run clear when a skewer is inserted into the thickest part of the meat.

5. Adjust the seasoning to taste and serve with new potatoes.

ROASTED PEPPER & GARLIC FOCACCIA

SERVES: 6–8 **PREP TIME: 30 MINS PLUS 1½ HRS RISING TIME** **COOK TIME: 45 MINS**

INGREDIENTS

500 g/1 lb 2 oz strong white flour, plus extra for dusting

1½ tsp salt

1 sachet easy-blend dried yeast

350 ml/12 fl oz lukewarm water

4 tbsp olive oil, plus extra for greasing

1 red pepper, halved and deseeded

3 garlic cloves

1. Preheat the oven to 240°C/475°F/Gas Mark 9. Grease a baking sheet.

2. Put the flour and salt into a mixing bowl and stir in the yeast. Add the water and 3 tablespoons of the oil and mix to a soft dough.

3. Turn out the dough onto a lightly floured work surface and knead until smooth. Return to the bowl, cover and leave to rest in a warm place for 30 minutes.

4. Meanwhile, place the red pepper cut side down on a baking sheet, add the unpeeled garlic cloves and roast in the preheated oven for 20 minutes, until the skins are charred. Remove from the oven (do not turn off the oven), peel the pepper and cut it into strips, then squeeze the flesh from the garlic and chop.

5. Turn out the dough onto a lightly floured work surface and lightly knead the dough until smooth. Roll out to a rectangle and press into the prepared sheet with your knuckles. Scatter the dough with the red peppers and garlic, pressing them into the dough.

6. Cover and leave to rise in a warm place for about 1 hour until doubled in size.

7. Drizzle the remaining oil over the dough and bake for 20–25 minutes, until golden brown and firm. Turn out and leave to cool on a wire rack.

16 MAY

RASPBERRY MACAROON BOMBE

SERVES: 6   PREP TIME: 30 MINS PLUS SOAKING AND FREEZING TIME   COOK TIME: NO COOKING

INGREDIENTS

125 g/4½ oz amaretti biscuits

2 tbsp cherry brandy

300 g/10½ oz fresh raspberries

50 g/1¾ oz caster sugar

300 ml/10 fl oz double cream

150 ml/5 fl oz single cream

3 tbsp cocoa powder

2 tbsp icing sugar

1. Put the biscuits in a food processor and process to form coarse crumbs. Alternatively, put the biscuits in a strong polythene bag and crush with a rolling pin. Put the crumbs in a bowl, add the cherry brandy and leave to soak for 30 minutes.

2. Meanwhile, put the raspberries in a food processor and process to form a purée. Add the caster sugar and mix well together. Pour the raspberry mixture into a bowl.

3. Pour the double cream and single cream into a large bowl and whip together until the mixture holds its shape. Add a third of the whipped cream to the biscuit mixture and fold in until well blended. Add another third of the cream to the raspberry mixture and fold in. Sift the cocoa powder and icing sugar over the remaining third of the cream, then fold into the cream until thoroughly incorporated.

4. Put the macaroon mixture in the bottom of a 1.4-litre/2½ -pint pudding bowl. Add the chocolate cream and spread over to form a layer, then add the raspberry mixture. Cover the bowl and freeze for 5 hours, or until firm or required.

5. Take the ice cream out of the freezer about 30 minutes before you are ready to serve it. Uncover, place a serving plate over the bowl, invert it and leave at room temperature.

17 MAY

RED VELVET CAKE

SERVES: 12   PREP TIME: 20 MINS   COOK TIME: 30 MINS

INGREDIENTS

225 g/8 oz unsalted butter, plus extra for greasing

4 tbsp water

55 g/2 oz cocoa powder

3 eggs

250 ml/9 fl oz buttermilk

2 tsp vanilla extract

2 tbsp edible red food colouring

280 g/10 oz plain flour

55 g/2 oz cornflour

1½ tsp baking powder

280 g/10 oz caster sugar

FROSTING

250 g/9 oz full-fat soft cheese

40 g/1½ oz unsalted butter

3 tbsp caster sugar

1 tsp vanilla extract

1. Preheat the oven to 190°C/375°F/Gas Mark 5. Grease 2 x 23-cm/ 9-inch sandwich tins and line the bases with greaseproof paper.

2. Place the butter, water and cocoa powder in a small saucepan and heat gently, without boiling, stirring until melted and smooth. Remove from the heat and leave to cool slightly.

3. Beat together the eggs, buttermilk, vanilla extract and food colouring until frothy. Beat in the butter mixture. Sift in the flour, cornflour and baking powder, then stir quickly and evenly into the mixture with the caster sugar.

4. Divide the mixture between the prepared tins and bake in the preheated oven for 25–30 minutes, or until risen and firm to the touch. Leave to cool in the tins for 3–4 minutes, then turn out and finish cooling on a wire rack.

5. To make the frosting, beat together all the ingredients until smooth. Use about half of the frosting to sandwich the cakes together, then spread the remainder over the top, swirling with a palette knife.

APRICOT ALMOND TART

SERVES: 6–8   PREP TIME: 30 MINS   COOK TIME: 45–50 MINS

INGREDIENTS

85 g/3 oz unsalted butter, softened

85 g/3 oz caster sugar

1 large egg, beaten

140 g/5 oz ground almonds

40 g/1½ oz plain flour

½ tsp almond extract

10–12 apricots, stoned and quartered

4 tbsp apricot jam

1 tbsp water

PASTRY

175 g/6 oz plain flour, plus extra for dusting

100 g/3½ oz cold unsalted butter

2 tbsp icing sugar

1 egg yolk

2 tbsp orange juice

1. Preheat the oven to 190°C/375°F/Gas Mark 5. To make the pastry, put the flour, butter and icing sugar into a food processor and process to fine crumbs. Mix the egg yolk and orange juice and stir into the flour mixture to make a soft dough.

2. Turn out the pastry onto a lightly floured work surface and roll out to a round large enough to line a 23-cm/9-inch loose-based flan tin. Prick the base with a fork, cover with a piece of greaseproof paper and fill with baking beans. Blind-bake the base in the preheated oven for 10 minutes. Remove from the oven and take out the greaseproof paper and beans.

3. Put the butter, sugar, egg, almonds, flour and almond extract into a food processor and process to a smooth paste.

4. Spread the almond filling over the base of the pastry case and arrange the apricots cut side up on top.

5. Reduce the oven temperature to 180°C/350°F/Gas Mark 4 and bake the tart for 35–40 minutes until the filling is set and golden brown.

6. Put the apricot jam into a small saucepan with the water and heat gently until melted. Brush over the apricots and serve.

19 MAY

SPAGHETTI WITH FRESH PEA PESTO

SERVES: 4   PREP TIME: 10 MINS   COOK TIME: ABOUT 15 MINS

INGREDIENTS

250 g/9 oz shelled broad beans

500 g/1 lb 2 oz dried spaghetti

salt and pepper

PEA PESTO

300 g/10½ oz fresh shelled peas

75 ml/2½ fl oz extra virgin olive oil

2 garlic cloves, crushed

100 g/3½ oz freshly grated Parmesan cheese, plus extra, shaved, to serve

100 g/3½ oz blanched almonds, chopped

pinch of sugar

1. To make the pea pesto, cook the peas in a saucepan of boiling water for 2–3 minutes until just tender. Drain and transfer to a food processor. Add the oil, garlic and grated Parmesan cheese and process to a coarse paste. Add the almonds and process again. Add the sugar and season to taste with salt and pepper. Set aside.

2. Blanch the broad beans in a saucepan of lightly salted boiling water until just tender. Drain and leave to cool. Peel off the dull skins.

3. Bring a large, heavy-based saucepan of lightly salted water to the boil. Add the spaghetti, bring back to the boil and cook for 8–10 minutes, or until just tender but still firm to the bite. Drain, stir in the broad beans and toss with the pesto. Add a good coarse grinding of pepper and serve with Parmesan cheese shavings.

20 MAY

QUICK CHICKEN STEW

SERVES: 4   PREP TIME: 10 MINS   COOK TIME: ABOUT 20 MINS

INGREDIENTS

850 ml/1½ pints canned coconut milk

200 ml/7 fl oz chicken stock

2–3 tbsp laksa paste

3 skinless, boneless chicken breasts, about 175 g/6 oz each, sliced into strips

250 g/9 oz cherry tomatoes, halved

250 g/9 oz sugar snap peas, diagonally halved

200 g/7 oz dried rice noodles

1 bunch fresh coriander, roughly chopped

1. Pour the coconut milk and stock into a saucepan and stir in the laksa paste. Add the chicken strips and simmer for 10–15 minutes over a low heat. Check the chicken is tender and cooked through.

2. Stir in the tomatoes, sugar snap peas and noodles. Simmer for a further 2–3 minutes. Stir in the coriander and serve.

SPAGHETTI WITH
FRESH PEA PESTO

21 MAY

RED SALAD WITH BEETROOT & RADISH

SERVES: 4   **PREP TIME: 10 MINS**   **COOK TIME: NO COOKING**

INGREDIENTS

400 g/14 oz small cooked beetroot, quartered

1 small red onion, cut into thin wedges

1 bunch radishes, sliced

2 tbsp chopped fresh mint

flatbread, to serve

DRESSING

5 tbsp extra virgin olive oil

1 tbsp wholegrain mustard

1 tbsp balsamic vinegar

1 tbsp lemon juice

2 tsp clear honey

salt and pepper

1. Toss together the beetroot, onion and radishes and stir in half the mint. Arrange on four serving plates.

2. To make the dressing, put the oil, mustard, vinegar, lemon juice and honey into a screw-top jar and shake well to mix. Season to taste with salt and pepper.

3. Spoon the dressing over the salad and scatter the remaining mint on top. Serve immediately with flatbread.

22 MAY

CHICKEN SATAY SKEWERS WITH PEANUT SAUCE

SERVES: 4–6   **PREP TIME: 35 MINS PLUS 2 HRS MARINATING TIME**   **COOK TIME: 20 MINS**

INGREDIENTS

4 skinless, boneless chicken breasts, about 115 g/4 oz each, cut into 2-cm/¾ -inch cubes

4 tbsp soy sauce

1 tbsp cornflour

2 garlic cloves, finely chopped

2.5-cm/1-inch piece fresh ginger, peeled and finely chopped

cucumber cubes, to serve

PEANUT SAUCE

2 tbsp groundnut or vegetable oil

½ onion, finely chopped

1 garlic clove, finely chopped

4 tbsp crunchy peanut butter

4–5 tbsp water

½ tsp chilli powder

1. Put the chicken in a shallow dish. Mix the soy sauce, cornflour, garlic and ginger together in a small bowl and pour over the chicken. Cover and leave to marinate in the refrigerator for at least 2 hours.

2. Preheat the oven to 190°C/375°F/Gas Mark 5. Divide the chicken cubes between presoaked wooden skewers or metal skewers. Heat a ridged griddle pan until hot, add the skewers and cook over a high heat for 3–4 minutes, turning occasionally, until browned all over. Transfer the skewers to a baking sheet and cook in the preheated oven for 5–8 minutes, until cooked through.

3. Meanwhile, to make the peanut sauce, heat the oil in a saucepan, add the onion and garlic and cook over a medium heat, stirring frequently, for 3–4 minutes, until softened. Add the peanut butter, water and chilli powder and simmer for 2–3 minutes, until softened and thinned.

4. Serve the skewers with the peanut sauce and the cucumber.

HONEY & MUSTARD CHICKEN PASTA SALAD

SERVES: 4   PREP TIME: 25 MINS   COOK TIME: 20 MINS

INGREDIENTS

250 g/9 oz dried fusilli

2 tbsp olive oil

1 onion, thinly sliced

1 garlic clove, crushed

4 skinless, boneless chicken breasts, about 115 g/4 oz each, thinly sliced

2 tbsp wholegrain mustard

2 tbsp clear honey

175 g/6 oz cherry tomatoes, halved

handful of mizuna or rocket leaves

fresh thyme leaves, to garnish

DRESSING

3 tbsp olive oil

1 tbsp sherry vinegar

2 tsp clear honey

1 tbsp fresh thyme leaves

salt and pepper

1. To make the dressing, place all the ingredients in a small bowl and whisk together until well blended.

2. Bring a large, heavy-based saucepan of lightly salted water to the boil. Add the fusilli, bring back to the boil and cook for 8–10 minutes, or until just tender but still firm to the bite.

3. Meanwhile, heat the oil in a large frying pan. Add the onion and garlic and fry for 5 minutes. Add the chicken and cook, stirring frequently, for 3–4 minutes. Stir the mustard and honey into the pan and cook for a further 2–3 minutes until the chicken and onion are golden brown and sticky. Check the chicken is tender and cooked through.

4. Drain the pasta and transfer to a serving bowl. Pour over the dressing and toss well. Stir in the chicken and onion and leave to cool.

5. Gently stir the tomatoes and mizuna into the pasta. Serve garnished with thyme leaves.

GRILLED MONKISH WITH HERB POLENTA SLICES

SERVES: 4   PREP TIME: 10 MINS PLUS CHILLING TIME   COOK TIME: 12–15 MINS

INGREDIENTS

1 litre/1¾ pints boiling water

200 g/7 oz medium-grain polenta

25 g/1 oz butter

2 tbsp finely chopped fresh parsley

2 tsp chopped fresh dill

4 x 175 g/6 oz pieces monkfish fillet

1 tbsp olive oil, plus extra for greasing

salt and pepper

lemon wedges, to serve

1. Lightly grease a rectangular baking dish or tin. Pour the water into a large saucepan, bring to the boil and stir in the polenta. Cook over a medium heat, stirring, for 5 minutes, or until thickened and starting to come away from the sides of the pan.

2. Remove from the heat and stir in the butter, parsley, dill and salt and pepper to taste. Spread evenly in the prepared dish and leave to cool. Chill in the refrigerator until set.

3. Preheat the grill or a griddle pan to high. Brush the monkfish with the oil and sprinkle with salt and pepper. Arrange on the grill rack and cook for 6–8 minutes, turning once, until cooked through.

4. Meanwhile, turn out the polenta and cut into slices. Add to the grill about halfway through the fish cooking time and cook until golden, turning once.

5. Slice the monkfish and arrange on the polenta slices. Serve hot, with lemon wedges for squeezing over.

25 MAY

GARLIC & HERB BREAD SPIRAL

SERVES: 6–8 PREP TIME: 30 MINS PLUS ABOUT 2 HRS RISING TIME COOK TIME: 25 MINS

INGREDIENTS

500 g/1 lb 2 oz strong white flour, plus extra for dusting

1 sachet easy-blend dried yeast

1½ tsp salt

350 ml/12 fl oz lukewarm water

2 tbsp oil, plus extra for greasing

85 g/3 oz butter, melted and cooled

3 garlic cloves, crushed

2 tbsp chopped fresh parsley

2 tbsp snipped fresh chives

beaten egg, for glazing

sea salt flakes, for sprinkling

1. Brush a large baking sheet with oil. Combine the flour, yeast and salt in a mixing bowl. Stir in the water and half the oil, mixing to a soft, sticky dough.

2. Turn out the dough onto a lightly floured work surface and knead until smooth and no longer sticky. Return to the bowl, cover and leave in a warm place for about 1 hour until doubled in size.

3. Meanwhile, preheat the oven to 240°C/475°F/Gas Mark 9. Mix together the butter, garlic, herbs and remaining oil. Roll out the dough to a 33 x 23-cm/13 x 9-inch rectangle and spread the herb mix evenly over the dough to within 1-cm/½-inch of the edge.

4. Roll up the dough from one long side and place on the prepared baking sheet, join underneath. Cut into 12 thick slices and arrange, cut side down, on the baking sheet about 2 cm/¾ inch apart.

5. Cover and leave to rise in a warm place until doubled in size and springy to the touch. Brush with egg and sprinkle with sea salt flakes. Bake in the preheated oven for 20–25 minutes, until golden brown and firm. Leave to cool on a wire rack.

26 MAY

TOASTED MUFFINS WITH BLUEBERRIES & BACON

SERVES: 2 PREP TIME: 10 MINS COOK TIME: 5 MINS

INGREDIENTS

2 muffins

2 lean bacon rashers

100 g/3½ oz fresh blueberries

2 tsp maple syrup (optional)

1. Preheat the grill to medium–high. Slice the muffins horizontally and place them, cut sides down, on the rack in the grill pan.

2. Lay the bacon rashers on the rack and cook until the tops of the muffins are toasted and the bacon is lightly cooked on one side.

3. Turn the muffins and divide the blueberries between the bottom halves. Invert the bacon onto the blueberries, covering them completely. Cook for a further 2 minutes, removing the top halves as soon as they are toasted and the bottom when the bacon is browned and crisp.

4. Place the muffin bases on serving plates, drizzle with maple syrup, if using, and add the muffin tops. Serve.

GARLIC & HERB
BREAD SPIRAL

27 MAY

RUSTIC FISH CASSEROLE

SERVES: 4 | **PREP TIME: 15 MINS** | **COOK TIME: 15 MINS**

INGREDIENTS

300 g/10½ oz live clams, scrubbed

2 tbsp olive oil

1 large onion, chopped

2 garlic cloves, crushed

2 celery sticks, sliced

350 g/12 oz firm white fish fillet

250 g/9 oz prepared squid rings

400 ml/14 fl oz fish stock

6 plum tomatoes, chopped

small bunch of fresh thyme

salt and pepper

crusty bread, to serve

1. Clean the clams under cold running water, scrubbing the shells. Discard any with broken shells and any that refuse to close when tapped.

2. Heat the oil in a large frying pan and fry the onion, garlic and celery for 3–4 minutes, until softened but not browned. Meanwhile, cut the fish into chunks.

3. Stir the fish and squid into the pan, then fry gently for 2 minutes.

4. Stir in the stock, tomatoes and thyme with salt and pepper to taste. Cover and simmer gently for 3–4 minutes.

5. Add the clams, cover and cook over a high heat for a further 2 minutes, or until the shells open. Discard any that remain closed.

6. Serve the casserole with crusty bread.

28 MAY

BAKED CHILLI CHEESE SANDWICHES

MAKES: 4 | **PREP TIME: 10 MINS** | **COOK TIME: 10 MINS**

INGREDIENTS

350 g/12 oz grated cheese, such as Cheddar

115 g/4 oz butter, softened, plus extra to finish

4 fresh green chillies, deseeded and chopped

½ tsp ground cumin

8 thick slices bread

1. Preheat the oven to 190°C/375°F/Gas Mark 5. Mix together the cheese and butter in a bowl until creamy then add the chillies and cumin.

2. Spread this mixture over four slices of bread and top with the remaining slices. Place on a baking sheet.

3. Spread the outside of the sandwiches with extra butter and bake for 8–10 minutes until crisp. Serve.

BEEF, SPRING ONION & PAK CHOI STIR-FRY

SERVES: 4   PREP TIME: 10 MINS   COOK TIME: 8–10 MINS

INGREDIENTS

1 tbsp groundnut oil

2 garlic cloves, crushed

2.5-cm/1-inch piece fresh ginger, chopped

400 g/14 oz lean steak mince

1 bunch spring onions, diagonally sliced

280 g/10 oz pak choi, thickly sliced

200 g/7 oz beansprouts

2 tbsp lime juice

2 tbsp tomato ketchup

2 tbsp soy sauce

cooked egg noodles or rice, to serve

1. Heat the oil in a wok or large frying pan, add the garlic and ginger and stir-fry over a medium heat for a few seconds, without browning.

2. Increase the heat to high, stir in the mince and stir-fry for 4–5 minutes. Add the spring onions and pak choi and stir-fry for 2 minutes.

3. Add the beansprouts and stir-fry for 1–2 minutes until soft.

4. Stir in the lime juice, ketchup and soy sauce, then heat until bubbling. Serve with noodles.

SUMMER FRUIT TARTLETS

MAKES: 12   PREP TIME: 30 MINS PLUS 30 MINS CHILLING TIME   COOK TIME: ABOUT 20 MINS

INGREDIENTS

200 g/7 oz plain flour, plus extra for dusting

85 g/3 oz icing sugar, sifted

55 g/2 oz ground almonds

115 g/4 oz butter

1 egg yolk

1 tbsp milk

FILLING

225 g/8 oz cream cheese

icing sugar, to taste, plus extra, sifted, for dusting

350 g/12 oz fresh summer berries, e.g. strawberries, cut into quarters, raspberries and blueberries

1. Sift the flour and icing sugar into a bowl. Stir in the almonds. Add the butter, rubbing in until the mixture resembles breadcrumbs. Add the egg yolk and milk and work in until the dough binds together. Wrap in clingfilm and chill for 30 minutes. Meanwhile, preheat the oven to 200°C/400°F/Gas Mark 6.

2. Roll out the dough on a lightly floured surface and use it to line 12 deep tartlet tins. Prick the bases and press a piece of foil into each.

3. Bake in the preheated oven for 10–15 minutes, or until light golden brown. Remove the foil and bake for a further 2–3 minutes. Transfer to a wire rack to cool.

4. To make the filling, place the cream cheese and icing sugar in a bowl and mix together. Place a spoonful of filling in each tartlet and arrange the berries on top.

5. Dust with sifted icing sugar and serve.

CHOCOLATE CHIP COOKIES

MAKES: 10–12   PREP TIME: 10 MINS   COOK TIME: ABOUT 15 MINS

INGREDIENTS

unsalted butter, melted, for greasing

175 g/6 oz plain flour, sifted

1 tsp baking powder

125 g/4½ oz margarine, melted

85 g/3 oz light muscovado sugar

55 g/2 oz caster sugar

½ tsp vanilla extract

1 egg

125 g/4½ oz plain chocolate chips

1. Preheat the oven to 190°C/375°F/Gas Mark 5. Line and lightly grease two baking sheets.

2. Place all of the ingredients in a large mixing bowl and beat until well combined.

3. Place tablespoonfuls of the mixture onto the prepared baking sheets, spaced well apart.

4. Bake in the preheated oven for 10–12 minutes, or until golden brown. Transfer to a wire rack and leave to cool.

5. Serve or store in an airtight box.

JUNE

LAMB'S LETTUCE &
CUCUMBER SALAD WITH FIGS

SERVES: 4   PREP TIME: 5 MINS   COOK TIME: NO COOKING

INGREDIENTS

100 g/3½ oz lamb's lettuce

½ cucumber, diced

4 ripe figs

DRESSING

1 small shallot, finely chopped

4 tbsp walnut oil

2 tbsp extra virgin olive oil

2 tbsp cider vinegar

½ tsp clear honey

salt and pepper

1. Place all the dressing ingredients in a screw-top jar, including salt and pepper to taste, and shake well to mix.

2. Put the lettuce and cucumber into a bowl and pour over half the dressing. Toss well to coat evenly, then divide between four serving plates.

3. Cut the figs into quarters and arrange 4 quarters on top of each plate. Drizzle over the remaining dressing and serve immediately.

GRILLED SALMON WITH CITRUS SALSA

SERVES: 4   PREP TIME: 10 MINS   COOK TIME: 10 MINS

INGREDIENTS

4 salmon fillets

1 tbsp olive oil

1 tbsp light soy sauce

CITRUS SALSA

1 large orange

1 lime

2 tomatoes, peeled and diced

2 tbsp extra virgin olive oil

2 tbsp chopped fresh coriander

¼ tsp caster sugar

salt and pepper

1. Preheat the grill to high. To make the salsa, cut all the peel and white pith from the orange and lime and remove the segments, discarding the membranes and reserving the juices.

2. Chop the segments and mix with the reserved juice, the tomatoes, oil and coriander. Add the sugar and season to taste with salt and pepper.

3. Place the salmon fillets on the grill rack. Mix together the oil and soy sauce, brush over the salmon and season to taste with pepper. Place under the preheated grill and cook, turning once, for 8–10 minutes until the fish is firm and flakes easily.

4. Serve the salmon with a spoonful of citrus salsa on the side.

SWORDFISH WITH COCONUT GLAZE

SERVES: 4   PREP TIME: 30 MINS PLUS 1 HR MARINATING TIME   COOK TIME: 25 MINS

INGREDIENTS

4 swordfish steaks, 2 cm/¾ inch thick, about 175 g/6 oz each

sea salt flakes

2 tbsp olive oil, plus extra for oiling

chopped fresh coriander, to garnish

COCONUT GLAZE

425 ml/15 fl oz can cream of coconut

125 ml/4 fl oz rum

4 tbsp soy sauce

1 tbsp black peppercorns, cracked

5-cm/2-inch piece cinnamon stick, broken

1. Put the swordfish steaks in a shallow dish in which they sit snugly in a single layer. Rub with sea salt flakes and olive oil.

2. Put the coconut glaze ingredients in a small saucepan and bring to the boil, stirring. Boil for 12–15 minutes until reduced by half. Strain, pour into a shallow dish and leave until completely cold.

3. Pour the glaze over the swordfish, turning to coat and making sure the steaks are completely covered with the glaze. Cover with clingfilm and leave to marinate in the refrigerator for 30–60 minutes.

4. Preheat the barbecue. Oil a hinged wire grill basket, using a wad of oil-soaked kitchen paper. Drain the steaks, reserving the marinade. Brush the steaks with oil on both sides, and arrange in the basket. Cook over medium–hot coals, covered, for 5–6 minutes until blackened. Turn and cook the other side for 1 minute, or until the flesh is no longer opaque.

5. Meanwhile, pour the marinade into a small saucepan. Bring to the boil and boil for 3 minutes. Pour into a small jug.

6. Carefully remove the steaks from the basket. Arrange in a serving dish, sprinkle with the coriander and serve with the coconut glaze.

ROSEMARY POTATOES

SERVES: 5–6   PREP TIME: 15 MINS   COOK TIME: 45 MINS

INGREDIENTS

675 g/1 lb 8 oz medium-sized potatoes, unpeeled and scrubbed

225 g/8 oz unsalted butter

2 tbsp chopped fresh rosemary leaves

salt and pepper

1. Preheat the barbecue. Slice the potatoes 3 mm/⅛ inch thick. Plunge into a large bowl of water to wash off the starch. Drain and blot dry with kitchen paper.

2. Take a very large sheet of double-thickness foil and smear butter over an area in the middle measuring about 30 x 20 cm/12 x 8 inches. Arrange a single layer of potatoes on the greased area. Sprinkle with some of the rosemary, season to taste with salt and pepper and dot generously with butter. Repeat until all the potato slices are used up – there should be three layers. Fold over the foil to make a flat packet, sealing and crimping the edges well. Wrap the packet in two more large pieces of foil, sealing well.

3. Cook for 45 minutes over hot coals, turning every 10 minutes, or until the potatoes are tender. Serve straight from the packet.

SWORDFISH WITH
COCONUT GLAZE

CRABMEAT & DILL TART

SERVES: 4–6   PREP TIME: 30 MINS PLUS 15 MINS CHILLING TIME   COOK TIME: 45–50 MINS

INGREDIENTS

PASTRY

200 g/7 oz plain flour, plus extra for dusting

1 tbsp chopped fresh dill

100 g/3½ oz butter

2–3 tbsp cold water

FILLING

1 bunch spring onions, chopped

175 g/6 oz crabmeat, light and dark meat

2 tbsp chopped fresh dill

1 large egg, beaten

175 ml/6 fl oz single cream

25 g/1 oz Parmesan cheese, finely grated

salt and pepper

1. Sift the flour into a bowl, add the dill and rub in the butter with your fingertips until the mixture resembles fine breadcrumbs. Stir in just enough water to make a soft dough.

2. Turn out the pastry onto a lightly floured work surface and roll out until it is big enough to line a 23-cm/9-inch flan tin. Press the pastry into the edge of the tin, trim the excess and prick the base with a fork. Chill in the refrigerator for 15 minutes. Preheat the oven to 200°C/400°F/Gas Mark 6.

3. Line the pastry case with a piece of greaseproof paper and fill with baking beans, then blind-bake the base in the preheated oven for 10 minutes. Remove from the oven, take out the greaseproof paper and beans and bake for a further 10 minutes.

4. To make the filling, put the onions, crabmeat and dill into a bowl and mix together. Stir in the egg and cream. Season well with salt and pepper, then spoon into the pastry case and sprinkle with the cheese.

5. Reduce the oven temperature to 190°C/375°F/Gas Mark 5. Bake the tart in the oven for 25–30 minutes, until the filling is just set. Serve warm or cold.

CHOCOLATE TIFFIN CAKE

SERVES: 6–8   PREP TIME: 10 MINS PLUS 1–2 HRS SETTING TIME   COOK TIME: 5 MINS

INGREDIENTS

225 g/8 oz plain chocolate

225 g/8 oz unsalted butter, plus extra for greasing

3 tbsp black coffee

55 g/2 oz soft light brown sugar

few drops of vanilla extract

225 g/8 oz digestive biscuits, crushed

85 g/3 oz raisins

85 g/3 oz walnuts, chopped

1. Grease and line a 450-g/1-lb loaf tin with greaseproof paper.

2. Place the chocolate, butter, coffee, sugar and vanilla extract in a saucepan over a low heat. Stir until the chocolate and butter have melted, the sugar has dissolved and the mixture is well combined.

3. Stir in the crushed biscuits, raisins and walnuts and stir well.

4. Spoon the mixture into the prepared loaf tin. Leave to set for 1–2 hours in the refrigerator, then turn out and cut into thin slices to serve.

ALMOND & RASPBERRY JAM DROPS

MAKES: 25   PREP TIME: 25 MINS   COOK TIME: 15 MINS

INGREDIENTS

225 g/8 oz butter, softened

140 g/5 oz caster sugar

1 egg yolk, lightly beaten

2 tsp almond extract

280 g/10 oz plain flour

55 g/2 oz almonds, toasted and chopped

55 g/2 oz chopped mixed peel

4 tbsp raspberry jam

salt

1. Preheat the oven to 190°C/375°F/Gas Mark 5. Line two baking sheets with greaseproof paper.

2. Put the butter and sugar into a bowl and mix well with a wooden spoon, then beat in the egg yolk and almond extract. Sift together the flour and a pinch of salt into the mixture, add the almonds and mixed peel and stir until thoroughly combined.

3. Scoop out tablespoons of the mixture and shape into balls with your hands, then put them on to the prepared baking sheets, spaced well apart. Use the dampened handle of a wooden spoon to make a hollow in the centre of each cookie and fill the hollows with raspberry jam.

4. Bake for 12–15 minutes, until golden brown. Leave to cool on the baking sheets for 5–10 minutes, then using a palette knife, carefully transfer the cookies to wire racks to cool completely.

BANANA PANCAKES WITH WHIPPED MAPLE BUTTER

SERVES: 4   PREP TIME: 15 MINS   COOK TIME: 10 MINS

INGREDIENTS

150 g/5½ oz plain white flour

1½ tsp baking powder

1 tbsp caster sugar

pinch of salt

250 ml/9 fl oz buttermilk

1 large egg

2 tbsp melted butter

3 ripe bananas

finely grated rind of 1 small orange

sunflower oil, for greasing

MAPLE BUTTER

85 g/3 oz butter

4 tbsp maple syrup

1. Sift the flour, baking powder, sugar and salt into a bowl. Add the buttermilk, egg and butter and whisk to a smooth batter. Mash two bananas and mix thoroughly into the batter with the orange rind. Leave to stand for 5 minutes.

2. Lightly grease a griddle pan or frying pan and heat over a medium heat. Spoon tablespoons of batter into the pan and cook until bubbles appear on the surface.

3. Turn over with a palette knife and cook the other side until golden brown. Repeat this process using the remaining batter, while keeping the cooked pancakes warm.

4. For the maple butter, beat together the butter and maple syrup, whisking until light and fluffy.

5. Slice the remaining banana and serve with the pancakes, with the maple butter spooned over.

TURKEY TERIYAKI

SERVES: 4   **PREP TIME:** 20 MINS PLUS 30 MINS MARINATING TIME   **COOK TIME:** 10 MINS

INGREDIENTS

450 g/1 lb turkey steaks, cut into strips

3 tbsp groundnut oil

1 small yellow pepper, deseeded and sliced into thin strips

8 spring onions, green part included, diagonally sliced into 2.5-cm/1-inch pieces

cooked rice, to serve

TERIYAKI GLAZE

5 tbsp shoyu (Japanese soy sauce)

5 tbsp mirin

2 tbsp clear honey

1 tsp finely chopped fresh ginger

1. Mix the teriyaki glaze ingredients in a small saucepan over a medium–low heat. Stir until the honey has melted, then remove from the heat and leave to cool.

2. Put the turkey in a large shallow dish. Pour over the glaze, turning the strips so they are well coated. Leave to marinate for 30 minutes at room temperature, or overnight in the refrigerator.

3. Using a slotted spoon, remove the turkey from the marinade, shaking off the excess liquid. Reserve the marinade.

4. Heat a wok over a medium–high heat, then add the oil. Add the turkey and stir-fry for 2 minutes. Add the yellow pepper and spring onions, and fry for 1 minute. Pour in the reserved marinade. Bring to the boil, then reduce the heat slightly and cook for 3–4 minutes, until the turkey is cooked through.

5. Transfer the turkey and vegetables to a serving dish. Boil the liquid remaining in the wok until syrupy, then pour over the turkey. Serve with rice.

CAJUN CHICKEN

SERVES: 4 **PREP TIME: 10 MINS** **COOK TIME: 30 MINS**

INGREDIENTS

4 chicken drumsticks

4 chicken thighs

2 fresh corn cobs, husks and silks removed

85 g/3 oz butter, melted

oil, for oiling

SPICE MIX

2 tsp onion powder

2 tsp paprika

1½ tsp salt

1 tsp garlic powder

1 tsp dried thyme

1 tsp cayenne pepper

1 tsp ground black pepper

½ tsp ground white pepper

¼ tsp ground cumin

1. Preheat the barbecue. Using a sharp knife, make two to three diagonal slashes in the chicken drumsticks and thighs, then place them in a large dish. Add the corn cobs. Mix all the ingredients for the spice mix together in a small bowl.

2. Brush the chicken and corn with the melted butter and sprinkle with the spice mix. Toss to coat well.

3. Oil the barbecue rack. Cook the chicken over medium–hot coals, turning occasionally, for 15 minutes, then add the corn cobs and cook, turning occasionally, for a further 10–15 minutes, or until beginning to blacken slightly at the edges. Check the chicken is tender and the juices run clear when a skewer is inserted into the thickest part of the meat. Transfer to a serving plate and serve.

11 JUNE

PASTA WITH ROCKET & MOZZARELLA

SERVES: 4   PREP TIME: 15 MINS   COOK TIME: 15 MINS

INGREDIENTS

400 g/14 oz dried pappardelle

2 tbsp olive oil

1 garlic clove, chopped

350 g/12 oz cherry tomatoes, halved

85 g/3 oz rocket leaves

300 g/10½ oz mozzarella cheese, chopped

salt and pepper

Parmesan cheese shavings, to serve

1. Bring a large, heavy-based saucepan of lightly salted water to the boil. Add the pappardelle, bring back to the boil and cook for 8–10 minutes, or until just tender but still firm to the bite.

2. Meanwhile, heat the oil in a frying pan over a medium heat and fry the garlic, stirring, for 1 minute, without browning.

3. Add the tomatoes, season well with salt and pepper and cook gently for 2–3 minutes, until softened.

4. Drain the pasta and stir into the frying pan. Add the rocket leaves and mozzarella, then stir until the leaves wilt.

5. Serve the pasta with Parmesan cheese.

12 JUNE

TEQUILA-MARINATED BEEF STEAKS

SERVES: 4   PREP TIME: 8 MINS PLUS 2 HRS CHILLING TIME   COOK TIME: ABOUT 10 MINS

INGREDIENTS

2 tbsp olive oil

3 tbsp tequila

3 tbsp freshly squeezed orange juice

1 tbsp freshly squeezed lime juice

3 garlic cloves, crushed

2 tsp chilli powder

2 tsp ground cumin

1 tsp dried oregano

4 sirloin steaks

oil, for oiling

salt and pepper

1. Place the oil, tequila, orange and lime juices, garlic, chilli powder, cumin, oregano and salt and pepper to taste in a large, shallow, non-metallic dish and mix together. Add the steaks and turn to coat in the marinade. Cover and chill in the refrigerator for at least 2 hours or overnight, turning occasionally.

2. Preheat the barbecue. Let the steaks return to room temperature, then remove from the marinade. Oil the barbecue rack. Cook over hot coals for 3–4 minutes on each side for medium, or longer according to taste, basting frequently with the marinade. Serve.

SEAFOOD RISOTTO

SERVES: 4   PREP TIME: 20 MINS   COOK TIME: 25 MINS

INGREDIENTS

150 ml/5 fl oz dry white wine

4 baby squid, cleaned and sliced

250 g/9 oz raw prawns, peeled and deveined

250 g/9 oz live mussels, scrubbed and debearded

2 tbsp olive oil

55 g/2 oz butter

1 onion, finely chopped

2 garlic cloves, finely chopped

2 bay leaves

350 g/12 oz risotto rice

about 1.5 litres/2¾ pints hot fish stock

salt and pepper

chopped fresh flat-leaf parsley, to garnish

1. Heat the wine in a saucepan until boiling. Add the squid and prawns, cover and cook for 2 minutes. Remove the squid and prawns with a slotted spoon and set aside.

2. Discard any mussels with broken shells and any that refuse to close when tapped. Add to the cooking liquid.

3. Heat the oil and butter in a deep saucepan. Add the onion and cook, stirring frequently, for 3–4 minutes, until softened.

4. Add the garlic, bay leaves and rice, and mix to coat in the butter and oil. Cook, stirring constantly, for 2–3 minutes, until the grains are translucent.

5. Stir in the cooking juices from the mussels, then gradually add the hot stock, a ladleful at a time. Cook, stirring, for 15 minutes, until the liquid is absorbed and the rice is creamy.

6. Stir in the cooked seafood, cover and cook for a further 2 minutes to heat through. Season to taste with salt and pepper.

7. Serve garnished with parsley.

TUNA & TOMATO PITTA POCKETS

SERVES: 4 **PREP TIME: 10 MINS** **COOK TIME: NO COOKING**

INGREDIENTS

4 pitta breads

1 Little Gem lettuce, roughly shredded

8 cherry tomatoes, halved

375 g/13 oz canned tuna in oil, drained and flaked

125 ml/4 fl oz mayonnaise

1 tsp finely grated lemon rind

2 tbsp lemon juice

3 tbsp chopped fresh chives

salt and pepper

1. Cut the pitta breads in half and open them out to make a pocket.

2. Divide the lettuce between the pittas, then add the tomatoes and tuna.

3. Put the mayonnaise, lemon rind, lemon juice and chives into a bowl and mix together. Season to taste with salt and pepper and spoon over the pitta filling to serve.

BARBECUED TUNA WITH CHILLI & GINGER SAUCE

SERVES: 4–6 **PREP TIME: 20 MINS PLUS 30–60 MINS MARINATING TIME** **COOK TIME: 15 MINS**

INGREDIENTS

4 tuna steaks, 2 cm/¾ inch thick, about 175 g/6 oz each

2 tbsp olive oil, plus extra for oiling

salt

lime wedges, to serve

CHILLI & GINGER SAUCE

100 g/3½ oz soft brown sugar

125 ml/4 fl oz water

2.5-cm/1-inch piece fresh ginger, finely shredded

1 green chilli, deseeded and finely chopped

1 large garlic clove, crushed

juice of ½ lime

1. Put the tuna steaks in a shallow dish in which they sit snugly in a single layer. Rub with salt and the olive oil.

2. To make the chilli and ginger sauce, put the sugar and water in a small saucepan and bring to the boil. Boil for 7–8 minutes until syrupy. Add the ginger, chilli, garlic and lime, and boil for an additional minute. Pour into a bowl and leave until completely cold.

3. Pour the cold sauce over the tuna steaks, turning to coat. Cover with clingfilm and leave to marinate in the refrigerator for 30–60 minutes, turning occasionally. Meanwhile, preheat the barbecue.

4. Oil a hinged wire grill basket. Place the tuna steaks in the basket, reserving the marinade. Cook over hot coals for 2 minutes. Turn and cook the other side for 1 minute. Remove from the basket and keep warm.

5. Pour the reserved marinade into a small saucepan. Bring to the boil and boil for 2 minutes. Pour into a small jug. Transfer the steaks to serving plates and serve with the hot marinade and lime wedges.

TUNA & TOMATO
PITTA POCKETS

PEPPERED SIRLOIN STEAK WITH BRANDY & CREAM SAUCE

SERVES: 4   PREP TIME: 10 MINS   COOK TIME: ABOUT 20 MINS

INGREDIENTS

2 tbsp black peppercorns, roughly crushed

4 sirloin steaks, about 2 cm/¾ inch thick

cooked jacket potatoes and green salad, to serve

BRANDY & CREAM SAUCE

25 g/1 oz butter

1 tbsp olive oil

1 small onion, finely chopped

3 tbsp brandy

200 ml/7 fl oz double cream

2 tsp Dijon mustard

1. Preheat the barbecue or a griddle pan to high. To make the brandy and cream sauce, melt the butter and oil in a saucepan, add the onion and fry, stirring, for 4–5 minutes until tender and golden.

2. Add the brandy and boil for 30 seconds, then stir in the cream and mustard. Cook over a moderate heat, stirring, for 2 minutes, then remove from the heat and keep warm.

3. Spread the crushed peppercorns on a plate and press the steaks into them, turning to coat on both sides and pressing firmly so the peppercorns stick to the meat.

4. Place the steaks on the barbecue rack and cook, turning once, for 5 minutes for rare, 9–10 minutes for medium and 12–14 minutes for well done. Remove from the heat and leave to rest for 5 minutes before serving with the sauce spooned over, accompanied by jacket potatoes and salad.

SPICED FISH SKEWERS ON TOMATO SALAD

SERVES: 4   PREP TIME: 20 MINS PLUS 1 HR MARINATING TIME   COOK TIME: 10 MINS

INGREDIENTS

450 g/1 lb cod loin or monkfish, cut into 2.5-cm/1-inch cubes

3 tbsp lime juice

4 tbsp sunflower oil

2 tsp mild chilli powder

1 tsp dried oregano

1 lime, cut into 8 wedges

225 g/8 oz cherry tomatoes, halved

225 g/8 oz yellow cherry tomatoes, halved

½ small onion, thinly sliced

2 tbsp roughly chopped fresh coriander

½ tsp sugar

1 tsp mild American mustard

salt and pepper

1. Place the fish cubes in a shallow bowl. Mix together 2 tablespoons of the lime juice and 2 tablespoons of the oil with the chilli powder and oregano. Season to taste with salt and pepper and pour over the fish. Cover and leave to marinate at room temperature for 1 hour.

2. Thread the fish and lime wedges onto presoaked wooden skewers or metal skewers. Preheat the grill to medium and cook the fish skewers for 8–10 minutes, turning occasionally, until just cooked.

3. Meanwhile, mix together the tomatoes, onion and coriander in a bowl. Whisk together the remaining lime juice and oil with the sugar and mustard. Pour the dressing over the tomatoes and toss well to mix. Season to taste with salt and pepper.

4. Divide the tomato salad between four serving dishes and top each with two fish skewers.

CHEESY SWEETCORN FRITTERS

MAKES: 8–10   PREP TIME: 10 MINS   COOK TIME: ABOUT 5 MINS

INGREDIENTS

1 egg

200 ml/7 fl oz milk

100 g/3½ oz plain flour

½ tsp baking powder

85 g/3 oz canned sweetcorn kernels, drained

4 tbsp grated Cheddar cheese

1 tsp snipped fresh chives

2 tsp sunflower oil

1. Put the egg and milk into a small bowl and beat with a fork. Add the flour and baking powder and beat until smooth. Stir in the sweetcorn, cheese and chives. Heat the sunflower oil in a non-stick frying pan. Drop in either teaspoonfuls or tablespoonfuls of the batter. Cook for 1–2 minutes on each side until the fritters are puffed up and golden.

2. Drain on kitchen paper and serve.

GRILLED PEACHES WITH RICOTTA & SPICE

SERVES: 4   **PREP TIME: 10 MINS**   **COOK TIME: ABOUT 5 MINS**

INGREDIENTS

4 peaches or nectarines, halved and stoned

15 g/½ oz unsalted butter, melted, for greasing

150 g/5½ oz ricotta cheese

½ tsp vanilla extract

40 g/1½ oz demerara sugar

1 tsp mixed spice

1. Preheat the grill to high. Place the peach halves cut side up on a flameproof baking dish or baking sheet and brush with the melted butter.

2. Mix the ricotta cheese with the vanilla extract and spoon into the peach cavities.

3. Mix together the sugar and spice, then sprinkle over the peaches.

4. Place under the preheated grill for 3–4 minutes until bubbling and golden brown. Serve warm.

HONEY & LEMON TART

SERVES: 4–6   PREP TIME: 35 MINS PLUS 30 MINS CHILLING TIME   COOK TIME: 50 MINS

INGREDIENTS

375 g/13 oz cottage cheese, cream cheese or ricotta cheese

6 tbsp Greek honey

3 eggs, beaten

½ tsp cinnamon

grated rind and juice of 1 lemon

PASTRY

225 g/8 oz plain flour, plus extra for dusting

pinch of salt

1½ tsp caster sugar

150 g/5½ oz butter, diced

3–4 tbsp cold water

1. To make the pastry, put the flour, salt, sugar and butter into a food processor. Mix in short bursts until the mixture resembles fine breadcrumbs. Sprinkle over the water and mix until a smooth dough forms. Alternatively, make the pastry in a bowl and rub in with your hands. The pastry can be used straight away but is better if allowed to rest in the refrigerator, wrapped in greaseproof paper, for about 30 minutes before use.

2. If using cottage cheese for the filling, push the cheese through a sieve into a bowl. Add the honey to the cheese and beat until smooth. Add the eggs, cinnamon, lemon rind and lemon juice, and mix well together.

3. Preheat the oven to 200°C/400°F/Gas Mark 6. Roll out the pastry on a lightly floured surface and use to line a 23-cm/9-inch tart tin. Prick the base with a fork, cover with a piece of greaseproof paper and fill with baking beans, then blind-bake the base in the preheated oven for 15 minutes. Remove from the oven and take out the greaseproof paper and beans. Bake for a further 5 minutes until the base is firm but not brown.

4. Reduce the oven temperature to 180°C/350°F/Gas Mark 4. Pour the filling into the pastry case and bake in the oven for about 30 minutes until set. Serve cold.

PRAWN NOODLE SOUP

SERVES: 4   PREP TIME: 25 MINS   COOK TIME: 10 MINS

INGREDIENTS

1 bunch spring onions

2 celery sticks

1 red pepper

200 g/7 oz vermicelli rice noodles

2 tbsp groundnut oil

55 g/2 oz unsalted peanuts

1 fresh bird's eye chilli, sliced

1 lemon grass stem, crushed

400 ml/14 fl oz fish stock or chicken stock

200 ml/7 fl oz coconut milk

2 tsp Thai fish sauce

350 g/12 oz cooked peeled tiger prawns

salt and pepper

chopped fresh coriander, to garnish

1. Trim the spring onions and celery and thinly slice diagonally. Deseed and thinly slice the red pepper.

2. Place the noodles in a bowl, cover with boiling water and leave to stand for 4 minutes, or until tender. Drain. Heat the oil in a wok, add the peanuts and stir-fry for 1–2 minutes until golden. Lift out with a slotted spoon. Add the sliced vegetables to the wok and stir-fry over a high heat for 1–2 minutes. Add the chilli, lemon grass, stock, coconut milk and fish sauce and bring to the boil.

3. Stir in the prawns and bring back to the boil, stirring. Season to taste with salt and pepper, then add the noodles. Serve in bowls, sprinkled with fresh coriander.

STRAWBERRIES WITH VANILLA CREAM

SERVES: 4   PREP TIME: 10 MINS   COOK TIME: NO COOKING

INGREDIENTS

400 g/14 oz strawberries

3 tbsp icing sugar

1 tbsp lemon juice

1 vanilla pod

200 ml/7 fl oz double cream

1. Halve the strawberries, place in a bowl and sprinkle with 1 tablespoon of the icing sugar and the lemon juice. Leave to stand for a few minutes.

2. Cut the vanilla pod in half lengthways and scrape out the seeds. Put the cream in a bowl and add the vanilla seeds and the remaining icing sugar.

3. Whisk the cream and vanilla mixture until it just holds its shape.

4. Divide the strawberries between four serving dishes, top with the vanilla cream and serve.

VEGETARIAN CHILLI BURGERS

SERVES: 4–6   PREP TIME: 25 MINS PLUS 1 HR CHILLING TIME   COOK TIME: 20 MINS

INGREDIENTS

85 g/3 oz bulgar wheat

300 g/10½ oz canned red kidney beans, drained and rinsed

300 g/10½ oz canned cannellini beans, drained and rinsed

1–2 fresh red jalapeño chillies, deseeded and roughly chopped

2–3 garlic cloves

6 spring onions, roughly chopped

1 yellow pepper, deseeded, peeled and chopped

1 tbsp chopped fresh coriander

115 g/4 oz mature Cheddar cheese, grated

2 tbsp wholemeal flour

1–2 tbsp sunflower oil

1 large tomato, sliced

salt and pepper

wholemeal buns, to serve

1. Place the bulgar wheat in a sieve and rinse under cold running water. Cook the bulgar wheat in a saucepan of lightly salted water for 12 minutes, or until tender. Drain and reserve.

2. Place the beans in a food processor with the chillies, garlic, spring onions, yellow pepper, coriander and half the cheese. Using the pulse button, chop finely. Add to the cooked bulgar wheat with salt and pepper to taste. Mix well, then shape into four to six equal-sized burgers. Cover and leave to chill for 1 hour. Coat the burgers in the flour.

3. Preheat the grill to medium. Heat a heavy-based frying pan and add the oil. When hot, add the burgers and cook over a medium heat for 5–6 minutes on each side, or until piping hot.

4. Place one to two slices of tomato on top of each burger and sprinkle with the remaining cheese. Cook under the hot grill for 2–3 minutes, or until the cheese begins to melt. Serve in wholemeal buns.

VEGETARIAN HOT DOGS

SERVES: 4 PREP TIME: 25 MINS PLUS 30 MINS CHILLING TIME COOK TIME: 20 MINS

INGREDIENTS

1 tbsp sunflower oil, plus extra for oiling

1 small onion, finely chopped

50 g/1¾ oz mushrooms, finely chopped

½ red pepper, deseeded and finely chopped

400 g/14 oz canned cannellini beans, drained and rinsed

100 g/3½ oz fresh breadcrumbs

100 g/3½ oz Cheddar cheese, grated

1 tsp dried mixed herbs

1 egg yolk

seasoned plain flour

TO SERVE

small bread rolls

fried onion slices

tomato chutney

1. Heat the sunflower oil in a saucepan. Add the onion, mushrooms and pepper and fry until softened.

2. Mash the cannellini beans in a large bowl. Add the onion, mushroom and pepper mixture, the breadcrumbs, cheese, herbs and egg yolk and mix well. Press the mixture together with your fingers and shape into eight sausages. Roll each sausage in the seasoned flour. Leave to chill in the refrigerator for at least 30 minutes.

3. Preheat the barbecue. Brush a sheet of double-thickness foil with oil and cook the sausages over medium–hot coals for 15–20 minutes, turning and basting frequently with oil, until golden. Split bread rolls down the centre and insert a layer of fried onions. Place the sausages in the rolls and serve with tomato chutney.

25 JUNE

SLICED SIRLOIN WITH PARMESAN

SERVES: 4   PREP TIME: 15 MINS PLUS 30 MINS STANDING TIME   COOK TIME: ABOUT 5 MINS

INGREDIENTS

4 sirloin steaks, about 3 cm/
1¼ inches thick, 225 g/8 oz each

olive oil, for oiling

100 g/3½ oz rocket

Parmesan cheese shavings

balsamic vinegar, for drizzling

salt and pepper

1. Snip the fat on the steaks at 1-cm/½-inch intervals to stop it curling and shrinking. Sprinkle both sides with salt and pepper to taste. Cover and leave to stand at room temperature for 30 minutes.

2. Meanwhile, preheat the barbecue. Heap some of the coals on one side leaving a slightly cooler zone with a single layer of coals.

3. Oil the barbecue rack. Cook the steaks on the hottest part of the rack for 2–3 minutes each side until brown. Move to the cooler part and cook the steak to your liking. Transfer to a board and leave to rest for 5 minutes.

4. Carve each steak diagonally into 2-cm/¾-inch slices. Place the rocket on top of the steak, sprinkle with Parmesan cheese shavings and more pepper. Drizzle over a little balsamic vinegar and serve.

26 JUNE

MEXICAN TURKEY BURGERS

SERVES: 4   PREP TIME: 15 MINS PLUS 1 HR CHILLING TIME   COOK TIME: ABOUT 5 MINS

INGREDIENTS

450 g/1 lb fresh turkey mince

200 g/7 oz canned refried beans

2–4 garlic cloves, crushed

1–2 fresh jalapeño chillies, deseeded
and finely chopped

2 tbsp tomato purée

1 tbsp chopped fresh coriander

olive oil, for oiling

salt and pepper

TO SERVE

burger buns

lettuce leaves

tomato slices

tomato salsa

1. Place the turkey mince in a bowl and break up any large lumps. Beat the refried beans until smooth, then add to the turkey in the bowl.

2. Add the garlic, chillies, tomato purée, coriander and salt and pepper to taste and mix together. Shape into four equal-sized burgers, then cover and leave to chill for 1 hour. Meanwhile, preheat the barbecue.

3. Oil the barbecue rack. Cook the burgers over medium–hot coals for 5–6 minutes on each side, or until thoroughly cooked. Transfer to serving plates and serve in the burger buns with the lettuce, tomato slices and salsa.

SLICED SIRLOIN
WITH PARMESAN

27 JUNE

CHICKEN WITH GOAT'S CHEESE

SERVES: 4–6 · PREP TIME: 10 MINS · COOK TIME: 20 MINS

INGREDIENTS

4 skinned chicken breast fillets

100 g/3½ oz soft goat's cheese

small bunch fresh basil

2 tbsp olive oil

salt and pepper

1. Using a sharp knife, slit along one long edge of each chicken breast then carefully open out each breast to make a small pocket. Divide the cheese equally between the pockets and tuck three to four basil leaves in each. Close the openings and season the breasts with salt and pepper to taste.

2. Heat the oil in a frying pan, add the chicken breasts and fry gently for 15–20 minutes, turning several times. Check the chicken is tender and the juices run clear when a skewer is inserted into the thickest part of the meat. Serve warm.

28 JUNE

TURKEY SALAD PITTA

MAKES: 1 · PREP TIME: 20 MINS · COOK TIME: 2 MINS

INGREDIENTS

small handful baby leaf spinach, rinsed, patted dry and shredded

½ red pepper, deseeded and thinly sliced

½ carrot, peeled and coarsely grated

4 tbsp hummus

85 g/3 oz boneless, skinless cooked turkey meat, thinly sliced

½ tbsp toasted sunflower seeds

1 wholemeal pitta bread

salt and pepper

1. Preheat the grill to high.

2. Put the spinach leaves, red pepper, carrot and hummus into a large bowl and stir together, so all the salad ingredients are coated with the hummus. Stir in the turkey and sunflower seeds and season to taste with salt and pepper.

3. Put the pitta bread under the grill for about 1 minute on each side to warm through, but do not brown. Cut it in half to make two 'pockets' of bread.

4. Divide the salad between the bread pockets and serve.

TOFU PARCELS

SERVES: 4   PREP TIME: 10 MINS   COOK TIME: 15 MINS

INGREDIENTS

2 tbsp olive oil, plus extra for brushing

1 garlic clove, crushed

250 g/9 oz firm tofu, cut into chunks

250 g/9 oz cherry tomatoes, halved

1 small red onion, thinly sliced

handful of fresh basil leaves

salt and pepper

crusty bread, to serve

1. Preheat the oven to 220°C/425°F/Gas Mark 7. Brush four 30-cm/ 12-inch squares of double-thickness foil with the oil. Mix the remaining oil with the garlic.

2. Divide the tofu, tomatoes, onion and basil between the foil squares, sprinkle with salt and pepper to taste and spoon over the garlic-flavoured oil.

3. Fold over the foil to enclose the filling and seal firmly. Place on a baking sheet in the preheated oven and cook for 10–15 minutes until heated through.

4. Carefully open the parcels and serve with crusty bread to mop up the juices.

STRAWBERRY PAVLOVA

SERVES: 6–8   PREP TIME: 20 MINS   COOK TIME: 1 HR 20 MINS

INGREDIENTS

3 egg whites

150 g/5½ oz caster sugar

1 tsp cornflour

1 tsp white wine vinegar

1 tsp vanilla extract

150 ml/5 fl oz double cream

150 g/5½ oz Greek-style yogurt

250 g/9 oz strawberries

fresh mint sprigs, to decorate

1. Preheat the oven to 120°C/250°F/Gas Mark ½. Line a baking sheet with greaseproof paper.

2. Put the egg whites into a grease-free bowl and whisk until stiff, then gradually add the sugar, whisking between each addition. Whisk in the cornflour, vinegar and vanilla extract.

3. Spoon the mixture onto the greaseproof paper in a 23-cm/9-inch round, with an indentation in the centre.

4. Bake in the preheated oven for 1 hour–1 hour 20 minutes, until the surface is dry but the centre is still soft. Remove from the oven and leave to cool.

5. Pour the cream into a bowl and whip until it holds stiff peaks, then stir in the yogurt. Chop half the strawberries, stir into the cream and spoon into the pavlova.

6. Decorate with the remaining strawberries, top with mint sprigs and serve chilled.

JULY

BLUEBERRY & CRANBERRY SQUARES

MAKES: 12   PREP TIME: 20 MINS   COOK TIME: 30 MINS

INGREDIENTS

175 g/6 oz unsalted butter, softened, plus extra for greasing

175 g/6 oz caster sugar

1 tsp vanilla extract

3 eggs, beaten

175 g/6 oz self-raising flour

55 g/2 oz dried cranberries

175 g/6 oz blueberries

ICING

200 g/7 oz mascarpone cheese, or full-fat cream cheese

100 g/3½ oz icing sugar

1. Preheat the oven to 180°C/350°F/Gas Mark 4. Grease an 18 x 28-cm/7 x 11-inch shallow rectangular cake tin and line with greaseproof paper.

2. Put the butter, sugar and vanilla extract into a bowl and cream together until pale and fluffy. Add the eggs gradually, beating hard after each addition.

3. Fold in the flour with a metal spoon, then stir in the cranberries and 100 g/3½ oz of the blueberries.

4. Spoon the mixture into the prepared tin and spread evenly over the base. Bake in the preheated oven for 25–30 minutes or until risen, firm and golden brown. Leave to cool in the tin for 15 minutes, then turn out and transfer to a wire rack to cool completely.

5. To make the icing, beat together the mascarpone cheese and sugar until smooth, then spread over the cake with a palette knife.

6. Scatter the remaining blueberries over the cake and cut into 12 squares to serve.

SUMMER BERRY PANCAKE STACK

SERVES: 4   PREP TIME: 10 MINS   COOK TIME: 10 MINS

INGREDIENTS

150 g/5½ oz plain white flour

1½ tsp baking powder

pinch of salt

1 tbsp caster sugar

250 ml/9 fl oz milk

1 large egg

2 tbsp melted butter

2 tbsp finely chopped fresh mint

sunflower oil, for greasing

fresh mint sprigs, to decorate

TO SERVE

200 g/7 oz Greek-style natural yogurt

350 g/12 oz mixed berries, such as blackberries, raspberries, redcurrants and blueberries

icing sugar, for dusting

1. Sift the flour, baking powder, salt and sugar into a bowl. Add the milk, egg, butter and mint and whisk to a smooth batter. Leave to stand for 5 minutes.

2. Lightly grease a griddle pan or frying pan and heat over a medium heat. Spoon tablespoons of batter into the pan and cook until bubbles appear on the surface.

3. Turn over with a palette knife and cook the other side until golden brown. Repeat this process using the remaining batter, while keeping the cooked pancakes warm.

4. To serve, stack the pancakes with the yogurt and berries, dust with icing sugar and decorate with mint sprigs.

CAESAR SALAD

SERVES: 4   **PREP TIME: 20 MINS**   **COOK TIME: ABOUT 5 MINS**

INGREDIENTS

1 large egg

2 cos lettuces or 3 Little Gem lettuces

6 tbsp olive oil

2 tbsp lemon juice

8 canned anchovy fillets, drained and roughly chopped

salt and pepper

Parmesan cheese shavings, to garnish

GARLIC CROÛTONS

4 tbsp olive oil

2 garlic cloves

5 slices white bread, crusts removed, cut into 1-cm/½-inch cubes

1. Bring a small, heavy-based saucepan of water to the boil.

2. Meanwhile, make the garlic croûtons. Heat the oil in a heavy-based frying pan. Add the garlic and diced bread and cook, stirring and tossing frequently, for 4–5 minutes, or until the bread is crispy and golden all over. Remove from the pan with a slotted spoon and drain on kitchen paper.

3. While the bread is frying, add the egg to the boiling water and cook for 1 minute, then remove from the pan and reserve.

4. Arrange the lettuce leaves in a salad bowl. Mix together the oil and lemon juice, then season to taste with salt and pepper. Crack the egg into the dressing and whisk to blend. Pour the dressing over the lettuce leaves, toss well, then add the croûtons and anchovies and toss the salad again. Sprinkle with Parmesan cheese shavings and serve.

CHEESE & BACON BURGERS

SERVES: 4   PREP TIME: 10 MINS   COOK TIME: 15 MINS

INGREDIENTS

675 g/1 lb 8 oz freshly minced sirloin or rump steak

2 tbsp grated onion

1 tsp Worcestershire sauce

olive oil, for brushing and oiling

4 rashers streaky bacon

4 thin squares Cheddar cheese

salt and pepper

burger buns and toppings of your choice, to serve

1. Preheat the barbecue. Using a fork, lightly mix the beef with the onion, Worcestershire sauce, and salt and pepper to taste. Divide the mixture into balls and flatten into patties about 2.5 cm/1 inch thick. Season the outside with salt and pepper, and lightly brush with oil.

2. Oil the barbecue rack. Cook the bacon for 3–4 minutes, turning once. Set aside and keep warm. Cook the burgers for 5 minutes, then turn and place the cheese squares on top. Cook for a further 3–4 minutes. Brush the inside of the buns with oil and toast over the barbecue, cut-side down, for 1–2 minutes. Serve in burger buns with toppings of your choice.

WINE-STEAMED MUSSELS

SERVES: 4   PREP TIME: 15 MINS   COOK TIME: 10 MINS

INGREDIENTS

115 g/4 oz butter

1 shallot, chopped

3 garlic cloves, finely chopped

2 kg/4 lb 8 oz live mussels, scrubbed and debearded

225 ml/8 fl oz dry white wine

4 tbsp chopped fresh parsley

salt and pepper

crusty bread, to serve

1. Place half the butter in a large saucepan and melt over a low heat. Add the shallot and garlic and cook for 2 minutes.

2. Discard any mussels with broken shells and any that refuse to close when tapped. Add the mussels and wine to the pan with salt and pepper to taste. Cover and bring to the boil, then cook for 3 minutes, shaking the pan from time to time.

3. Remove the mussels from the pan with a slotted spoon and place in serving bowls. Discard any mussels that remain closed.

4. Stir the remaining butter and the parsley into the cooking juices in the pan. Bring to the boil, then pour over the mussels.

5. Serve with crusty bread for mopping up the juices.

CHEESE &
BACON BURGERS

GRILLED FILLET STEAK

SERVES: 4–6   PREP TIME: 10 MINS PLUS 30 MINS MARINATING TIME   COOK TIME: 15 MINS

INGREDIENTS

2 tbsp olive oil

3 tbsp raspberry vinegar

1 tbsp caster sugar

1 tbsp finely chopped fresh rosemary

4 beef fillet steaks

1 small red onion, finely chopped

100 ml/3½ fl oz red wine

200 g/7 oz raspberries

salt and pepper

1. Put the oil, vinegar, sugar and rosemary into a small bowl and mix together. Place the steak in a non-metallic dish and pour over the vinegar mixture. Cover and leave to marinate for 30 minutes.

2. Preheat the grill to high. Drain the meat well, season to taste with salt and pepper, place on the grill rack and cook under the preheated grill, turning once, for 2 minutes on each side for medium–rare, and for 2½ minutes on each side for medium. Remove from the rack and leave to stand for 5 minutes.

3. Meanwhile, put the marinade into a saucepan with the onion and bring to the boil, then cook over a moderate heat, stirring, for 3–4 minutes until the onion is soft. Add the wine, bring to the boil and boil for 2–3 minutes until the liquid is reduced by half. Add the raspberries and cook, stirring, for 1 minute.

4. Season the raspberry sauce with salt and pepper to taste, spoon over the steaks and serve immediately.

ROAST SUMMER VEGETABLES

SERVES: 4   PREP TIME: 25 MINS   COOK TIME: 25 MINS

INGREDIENTS

150 ml/5 fl oz olive oil, plus extra for brushing

1 fennel bulb, cut into wedges

2 red onions, cut into wedges

2 beef tomatoes, cut into wedges

1 aubergine, thickly sliced

2 courgettes, thickly sliced

1 yellow pepper, deseeded and cut into chunks

1 red pepper, deseeded and cut into chunks

1 orange pepper, deseeded and cut into chunks

4 garlic cloves

4 fresh rosemary sprigs

pepper

crusty bread, to serve

1. Preheat the oven to 200°C/400°F/Gas Mark 6. Brush a large ovenproof dish with a little of the oil. Arrange the prepared vegetables in the dish and tuck the garlic cloves and rosemary sprigs among them. Drizzle with the remaining oil and season to taste with plenty of pepper.

2. Roast the vegetables in the preheated oven for 20–25 minutes, turning once, until they are tender and beginning to turn golden brown.

3. Serve the vegetables with crusty bread.

GRILLED FILLET
STEAK

CHILLI-PRAWN TACOS

SERVES: 4–6   PREP TIME: 15 MINS   COOK TIME: 40 MINS

INGREDIENTS

600 g/1 lb 5 oz raw prawns, shelled and deveined

2 tbsp chopped fresh flat-leaf parsley

12 tortilla shells

spring onions, chopped, to garnish

soured cream and lemon wedges, to serve

TACO SAUCE

1 tbsp olive oil

1 onion, finely chopped

1 green pepper, deseeded and diced

1–2 fresh hot green chillies, such as jalapeño, deseeded and finely chopped

3 garlic cloves, crushed

1 tsp ground cumin

1 tsp ground coriander

1 tsp brown sugar

450 g/1 lb ripe tomatoes, peeled and coarsely chopped

juice of ½ lemon

salt and pepper

1. To make the taco sauce, heat the oil in a deep frying pan over a medium heat. Add the onion and cook for 5 minutes, or until softened. Add the pepper and chillies and cook for 5 minutes. Add the garlic, cumin, coriander and sugar and cook the sauce for a further 2 minutes, stirring.

2. Preheat the oven to 180°C/350°F/Gas Mark 4. Add the tomatoes, lemon juice and salt and pepper to taste. Bring to the boil, then reduce the heat and simmer for 10 minutes. Stir in the prawns and parsley, cover and cook gently for 5–8 minutes, or until the prawns are pink and tender.

3. Meanwhile, place the tortilla shells, open-side down, on a baking sheet. Warm in the preheated oven for 2–3 minutes. To serve, spoon the prawn mixture into the tortilla shells, garnish with spring onions and serve with soured cream and lemon wedges.

SEARED SESAME SALMON WITH PAK CHOI

SERVES: 4   PREP TIME: 25 MINS   COOK TIME: 10 MINS

INGREDIENTS

2.5-cm/1-inch piece fresh ginger

1 tbsp soy sauce

1 tsp sesame oil

4 skinless salmon fillets

2 tbsp sesame seeds

lime wedges, to serve

STIR-FRY

1 tbsp sunflower oil

1 tsp sesame oil

2 small pak choi, cut lengthways into quarters

1 bunch spring onions, cut diagonally into thick slices

salt and pepper

1. Peel and finely grate the ginger and mix with the soy sauce and sesame oil in a shallow dish. Add the salmon fillets, turning to coat evenly on both sides.

2. Sprinkle the salmon on one side with half the sesame seeds, then turn and sprinkle the other side with the remaining sesame seeds.

3. Preheat a heavy-based frying pan. Add the salmon and cook for 3–4 minutes. Turn and cook for a further 3–4 minutes.

4. Meanwhile, heat the sunflower and sesame oils in a wok, add the pak choi and spring onions and stir-fry for 2–3 minutes. Season to taste with salt and pepper.

5. Divide the vegetables between serving plates and place the salmon on top.

6. Serve with lime wedges for squeezing over.

SCRAMBLED EGGS WITH SMOKED SALMON

SERVES: 4 | PREP TIME: 10 MINS | COOK TIME: 10 MINS

INGREDIENTS

8 eggs

90 ml/3 fl oz single cream

2 tbsp chopped fresh dill, plus extra to garnish

100 g/3½ oz smoked salmon, cut into small pieces

25 g/1 oz butter

8 slices rustic bread, toasted

salt and pepper

1. Break the eggs into a large bowl and whisk together with the cream and dill. Season to taste with salt and pepper. Add the smoked salmon and mix to combine.

2. Melt the butter in a large non-stick frying pan and pour in the egg and smoked salmon mixture. Gently scrape the egg away from the sides of the pan as it begins to set and swirl the pan slightly to allow the uncooked egg to fill the surface. When the eggs are almost cooked but still creamy, remove from the heat and spoon onto the prepared toast. Garnish with dill and serve.

FRUIT & NUT GRANOLA

MAKES: ABOUT 20 SERVINGS | PREP TIME: 5 MINS PLUS 12 HRS SOAKING TIME | COOK TIME: NO COOKING

INGREDIENTS

150 g/5½ oz jumbo rolled oats

150 g/5½ oz rolled wheat flakes

70 g/2½ oz rice flakes

70 g/2½ oz rye flakes

100 g/3½ oz raisins or sultanas

100 g/3½ oz dried banana flakes

55 g/2 oz toasted hazelnuts

55 g/2 oz sunflower seeds or linseeds

55 g/2 oz wheatgerm

milk, for soaking

1. Put all the dried ingredients into a large jar with an airtight seal. Seal the jar and shake to mix together.

2. Make sure that the ingredients are well distributed, then pour over enough milk to cover the servings for the next day and leave to soak overnight. The dry muesli will keep for at least a month in a well-sealed jar.

BARBECUED CHICKEN WITH TARRAGON BUTTER

SERVES: 4   PREP TIME: 10 MINS PLUS 30 MINS MARINATING TIME   COOK TIME: 10 MINS

INGREDIENTS

4 skinless, boneless chicken breasts, about 225 g/8 oz each

oil, for brushing and oiling

TARRAGON BUTTER

100 g/3½ oz unsalted butter, at room temperature

5 tbsp chopped fresh tarragon

1 shallot, finely chopped

salt and pepper

MARINADE

1½ tbsp lemon juice

2 tbsp water

1 tsp sugar

1 tsp salt

½ tsp pepper

3 tbsp olive oil

1. To make the tarragon butter, mash the butter with a fork until soft, then add the remaining ingredients, mixing well. Scrape the mixture onto a piece of clingfilm and form into a log. Wrap tightly and chill in the refrigerator.

2. Slice the chicken breasts lengthways to make eight portions. Trim any excess fat. Place in a single layer in a shallow dish. Whisk together the marinade ingredients and pour over the chicken. Cover with clingfilm and marinate for 30 minutes, turning halfway through. Meanwhile, preheat the barbecue.

3. Drain the chicken and discard the marinade. Pat dry and lightly brush with oil. Oil the barbecue rack. Place the chicken on the rack, and cover with a disposable foil tray. Grill over medium–hot coals for 5–6 minutes until the underside is striped with grill marks and is no longer translucent. Using tongs, turn and cook the other side for 4–5 minutes. Check the chicken is tender and the juices run clear when a skewer is inserted into the thickest part of the meat.

4. Place in a warmed dish, cover with foil and leave to rest in a warm place for 5 minutes. Serve with slices of tarragon butter.

STRAWBERRY SHORTCAKE

SERVES: 6–8   PREP TIME: 25 MINS   COOK TIME: 20 MINS

INGREDIENTS

BASE

250 g/9 oz self-raising flour

50 g/1¾ oz butter, diced, plus extra for greasing

50 g/1¾ oz caster sugar

125–150 ml/4–5 fl oz milk

fresh mint leaves, to garnish

TOPPING

4 tbsp milk

500 g/1 lb 2 oz mascarpone cheese

5 tbsp caster sugar

500 g/1 lb 2 oz strawberries, hulled and quartered

finely grated rind of 1 orange

1. Preheat the oven to 200°C/400°F/Gas Mark 6. Lightly grease a 20-cm/8-inch loose-based cake tin.

2. To make the base, sift the flour into a large bowl, add the butter and rub in with your fingertips until the mixture resembles fine breadcrumbs. Add the caster sugar. Stir in enough of the milk to form a soft but smooth dough. Gently press the dough evenly into the prepared cake tin. Bake in the preheated oven for 15–20 minutes until risen, firm to the touch and golden brown. Leave to cool for 5 minutes in the tin, then turn out onto a wire rack and leave to cool completely.

3. To make the topping, beat together the milk and mascarpone cheese with 3 tablespoons of the caster sugar in a bowl until smooth and fluffy. Put the strawberries in a separate bowl and sprinkle with the remaining caster sugar and the orange rind.

4. Spread the mascarpone mixture over the scone base and pile the strawberries on top. Spoon over any juices left over from the strawberries in the bowl, scatter with mint leaves and serve.

BLUEBERRY FROZEN YOGURT

SERVES: 6–8   PREP TIME: 10 MINS PLUS 6 HRS FREEZING TIME   COOK TIME: NO COOKING

INGREDIENTS

175 g/6 oz fresh blueberries

finely grated rind and juice of 1 orange

3 tbsp maple syrup

500 g/1 lb 2 oz natural low-fat yogurt

1. Put the blueberries and orange juice into a food processor and process to a purée. Strain through a nylon sieve into a bowl or jug.

2. Stir together the maple syrup and yogurt in a large mixing bowl, then fold in the fruit purée.

3. Churn the mixture in an ice-cream machine, following the manufacturer's instructions, then freeze for 5–6 hours. If you don't have an ice-cream machine, transfer the mixture to a freezerproof container and freeze for 2 hours. Remove from the freezer, turn out into a bowl and beat until smooth. Return to the freezer and freeze until firm. When ready to serve, decorate with the orange rind.

STRAWBERRY
SHORTCAKE

AVOCADO, FETA & ROCKET SALAD

SERVES: 4   PREP TIME: 10 MINS   COOK TIME: 5 MINS

INGREDIENTS

2 ripe avocados

100 g/3½ oz rocket leaves

250 g/9 oz feta cheese, crumbled

DRESSING

6 tbsp olive oil

2 tbsp white wine vinegar

1 shallot, finely chopped

2 large ripe tomatoes, deseeded and diced

1 tbsp lemon juice

1 tsp caster sugar

salt and pepper

1. Halve, stone, peel and slice the avocados and arrange on a serving dish with the rocket leaves. Top with the cheese.

2. To make the dressing, put the oil and vinegar into a saucepan and gently heat, then add the shallot and cook, stirring, for 2–3 minutes until soft. Add the tomatoes, lemon juice and sugar and gently heat, stirring, for 30 seconds.

3. Season the dressing to taste with salt and pepper, then spoon it over the salad and serve immediately.

GAZPACHO

SERVES: 4   PREP TIME: 25 MINS PLUS 2 HRS COOLING TIME   COOK TIME: NO COOKING

INGREDIENTS

1 red pepper, deseeded
and chopped

1 kg/2 lb 4 oz ripe tomatoes, peeled,
deseeded and chopped

2 tbsp very finely chopped onion

3 garlic cloves, crushed

1 cucumber, peeled and chopped

100 g/3½ oz stale bread, crumbled

3 tbsp red wine vinegar or
sherry vinegar

3½ tbsp olive oil, plus
extra for drizzling

200 g/7 oz ice cubes (optional)

salt and pepper

1. Set aside a handful of the red pepper, a handful of the tomatoes and half the chopped onion in the refrigerator. Put the rest in a food processor with the garlic and cucumber and purée until smooth. Add the bread, vinegar and oil and whizz again. Season to taste with salt and pepper. If the soup is too thick, add the ice, then place in the refrigerator for 2 hours.

2. When ready to serve, check the vinegar and seasoning and ladle into bowls. Scatter over the reserved red pepper, tomatoes and onions, then drizzle over a swirl of olive oil. Serve.

CRAB CAKES WITH TARTARE SAUCE

MAKES: 6   **PREP TIME: 25 MINS PLUS 2 HRS CHILLING TIME**   **COOK TIME: ABOUT 10 MINS**

INGREDIENTS

1 large egg, beaten

2 tbsp mayonnaise

½ tsp Dijon mustard

¼ tsp Worcestershire sauce

½ tsp celery salt

¼ tsp salt

40 g/1½ oz cream crackers, finely crushed

450 g/1 lb fresh crabmeat

85–140 g/3–5 oz fresh breadcrumbs

25 g/1 oz unsalted butter

1 tbsp vegetable oil

salad leaves and lemon wedges, to serve

TARTARE SAUCE

225 ml/8 fl oz mayonnaise

4 tbsp sweet pickle relish

1 tbsp very finely chopped onion

1 tbsp chopped capers

1½ tbsp freshly squeezed lemon juice

dash of Worcestershire sauce

salt and pepper

1. To make the crab cakes, whisk together the egg, mayonnaise, mustard, Worcestershire sauce, celery salt and salt in a large bowl until combined. Stir in the cracker crumbs with a spatula, then leave to stand for 5 minutes.

2. Pick over the crabmeat to remove any pieces of shell or cartilage, then gently fold into the mixture, trying to avoid breaking it up too much. Cover the bowl with clingfilm and chill in the refrigerator for at least 1 hour.

3. Meanwhile, make the tartare sauce. Mix together all the ingredients in a bowl and season to taste with salt and pepper. Cover and chill in the refrigerator for at least 1 hour before serving.

4. Sprinkle the breadcrumbs over a large plate until lightly covered. Shape the crab mixture into six even-sized cakes, about 2.5 cm/1 inch thick, placing them on the plate as they are formed. Dust the tops of each crab cake lightly with more breadcrumbs.

5. Melt the butter with the oil in a large frying pan over a medium–high heat. Carefully transfer each crab cake from the plate to the pan using a metal spatula.

6. Cook the crab cakes for 4 minutes on each side, until golden brown. Remove from the pan and drain on kitchen paper. Serve with the tartare sauce, salad leaves and lemon wedges.

LAMB KOFTAS WITH YOGURT, THYME & LEMON DIP

SERVES: 4   **PREP TIME: 20 MINS**   **COOK TIME: ABOUT 10 MINS**

INGREDIENTS

500 g/1 lb 2 oz lean lamb mince

25 g/1 oz fresh white breadcrumbs

1 onion, grated

1 garlic clove, crushed

1 tsp ground coriander

1 tsp ground cumin

2 tbsp chopped fresh mint

olive oil, for brushing

salt and pepper

lemon wedges, to serve

YOGURT, THYME & LEMON DIP

150 ml/5 fl oz natural yogurt

finely grated rind and juice of ½ lemon

1 tbsp chopped fresh thyme

salt and pepper

1. Preheat the barbecue. Put the mince, breadcrumbs, onion, garlic, coriander, cumin and mint into a bowl and mix together. Season well with salt and pepper.

2. Divide the mixture into eight equal portions and press evenly onto eight presoaked wooden skewers or metal skewers.

3. To make the yogurt, thyme and lemon dip, put the yogurt and lemon rind and juice into a bowl and mix together. Stir in the thyme and season to taste with salt and pepper.

4. Brush the koftas with oil, place on the barbecue rack and cook, turning occasionally, for 10–12 minutes until golden brown and cooked through. Serve with the yogurt, thyme and lemon dip and with lemon wedges.

MEXICAN TURKEY STEAK

SERVES: 4–6   PREP TIME: 20 MINS PLUS AT LEAST 4 HRS MARINATING TIME   COOK TIME: 5 MINS

INGREDIENTS

4 turkey steaks, 500 g/
1 lb 2 oz in total

olive oil, for brushing and oiling

avocado salsa and warm tortillas,
to serve

MARINADE

juice of 1 orange

juice of 2 limes

2 garlic cloves, crushed

1 tsp paprika

½ tsp salt

½ tsp chilli powder

½ tsp cumin seeds, crushed

¼ tsp pepper

4 tbsp olive oil

1. Halve the turkey steaks horizontally to make eight thinner pieces. Place between two sheets of polythene and pound with a meat mallet until flattened to 1 cm/½ inch thick. Slice into strips about 4 cm/1½ inches wide and 6 cm/2½ inches long. Place in a single layer in a shallow dish.

2. Whisk together the marinade ingredients and pour over the turkey. Cover with clingfilm and leave in the refrigerator to marinate for at least 4 hours or overnight. Allow to come to room temperature before cooking. When ready to cook, preheat the barbecue.

3. Drain the turkey, discarding the marinade. Lightly brush with oil and thread concertina-style onto presoaked wooden skewers or metal skewers. Oil the barbecue rack. Grill for 2–2½ minutes on each side over hot coals until no longer pink when cut into with a small vegetable knife. Remove from the skewers and serve with the avocado salsa and warm tortillas.

SPICY TURKEY & SAUSAGE KEBABS

SERVES: 8   PREP TIME: 15 MINS PLUS 1 HR STANDING TIME   COOK TIME: 15 MINS

INGREDIENTS

6 tbsp olive oil, plus extra for oiling

2 garlic cloves, crushed

1 fresh red chilli, deseeded and
chopped

350 g/12 oz turkey breast fillet

300 g/10½ oz chorizo sausage

1 dessert apple

1 tbsp lemon juice

8 bay leaves

salt and pepper

1. Place the olive oil, garlic, chilli and salt and pepper to taste in a small screw-top jar and shake well to combine. Leave to stand for 1 hour for the garlic and chilli to flavour the oil.

2. Preheat the barbecue. Using a sharp knife, cut the turkey into 2.5-cm/1-inch pieces. Cut the sausage into 2.5-cm/1-inch lengths. Cut the apple into chunks and remove the core. Toss the apple in the lemon juice to prevent discoloration.

3. Thread the turkey and sausage pieces onto presoaked wooden skewers or metal skewers, alternating with the apple chunks and bay leaves.

4. Oil the barbecue rack. Cook the kebabs over hot coals for 15 minutes, or until the turkey is cooked through. Turn and baste the kebabs frequently with the flavoured oil.

5. Transfer the kebabs to warmed serving plates and serve immediately. Do not eat the bay leaves.

MEXICAN TURKEY
STEAK

21 JULY

MIXED VEGETABLE BRUSCHETTA

SERVES: 4 | **PREP TIME: 15 MINS** | **COOK TIME: 10 MINS**

INGREDIENTS

olive oil, for greasing and drizzling

1 large red pepper, halved and deseeded

1 large orange pepper, halved and deseeded

4 thick slices baguette or ciabatta

1 fennel bulb, sliced

1 red onion, sliced

2 courgettes, sliced diagonally

2 garlic cloves, halved

1 tomato, halved

salt and pepper

1. Preheat the barbecue. Oil the grill rack. Cut each pepper half lengthways into four strips. Toast the bread on both sides in a toaster or under a grill.

2. Cook the pepper strips and fennel over medium–hot coals for 4 minutes, then add the onion and courgettes and cook for a further 5 minutes, until all the vegetables are tender but still firm to the bite.

3. Meanwhile, rub the garlic halves over the toasted bread, then rub with the tomato halves. Place on serving plates. Pile the chargrilled vegetables on top, drizzle with oil and season to taste with salt and pepper. Serve.

22 JULY

ROMAINE, BACON & BLUE CHEESE SALAD

SERVES: 4 | **PREP TIME: 10 MINS** | **COOK TIME: 5 MINS**

INGREDIENTS

4 thin streaky bacon rashers

1 small romaine lettuce

100 g/3½ oz blue cheese, such as Roquefort or Gorgonzola cheese

DRESSING

finely grated rind and juice of ½ lemon

3 tbsp olive oil

2 tsp poppy seeds

½ tsp caster sugar

salt and pepper

1. Preheat the grill to high. Place the bacon on the grill rack and cook under the preheated grill, turning once, for 4–5 minutes until golden brown and crisp. Place on absorbent kitchen paper and leave to cool.

2. Tear or cut the lettuce into bite-sized pieces and place in a large bowl. Crumble the cheese over the leaves. Chop the bacon and scatter over the salad.

3. To make the dressing, put the lemon rind and juice, the oil, poppy seeds and sugar into a screw-top jar and shake well to mix. Season to taste with salt and pepper, then pour over the salad, lightly toss and serve.

POTATO KEBABS WITH FETA

SERVES: 4–6   PREP TIME: 25 MINS   COOK TIME: ABOUT 20 MINS

INGREDIENTS

4 large garlic cloves, peeled

1 tsp sea salt flakes

1 tbsp finely chopped fresh rosemary

½ tsp pepper

4 tbsp olive oil, plus extra for oiling

850 g/1 lb 14 oz oval red-skinned salad potatoes, about 5 cm/ 2 inches long

40 g/1½ oz crumbled feta cheese

1 tbsp chopped fresh flat-leaf parsley

1. Preheat the barbecue. Using a pestle and mortar, crush the garlic cloves with the sea salt until smooth and creamy. If necessary, push through a sieve to remove any fibrous shreds which could burn. Add the rosemary and pepper, and pound to a paste. Whisk in the olive oil, then pour the mixture into a large bowl and leave to stand.

2. Scrub the potatoes and slice in half crossways. Steam over boiling water for 7 minutes until only just tender. Spread out on a clean tea towel to dry. Add to the garlic mixture in the bowl and toss to coat.

3. Arrange the potatoes cut-side down on a board, reserving the remaining garlic mixture in the bowl. Thread onto six presoaked wooden skewers or metal skewers, piercing the potato halves through the middle so that the cut sides remain facing downwards.

4. Heap some of the coals to one side, leaving a slightly cooler zone with a single layer of coals. Oil the barbecue rack. Cook the kebabs over hot coals, cut-side down, for 3–4 minutes, turning when each side is striped from the grill. Brush the upper surface with the garlic oil as you turn. Move to the cooler zone and cook for about 5–7 minutes more, turning and brushing, until tender when pierced with the tip of a knife.

5. Arrange the kebabs on a serving platter, and sprinkle with the feta cheese and parsley. Serve while still hot.

GRILLED ITALIAN SAUSAGES WITH DOUBLE CHILLI SALSA

SERVES: 4   PREP TIME: 10 MINS PLUS AT LEAST 1 HR CHILLING TIME   COOK TIME: 15 MINS

INGREDIENTS

8 Italian-style sausages

oil, for brushing

crusty bread rolls, to serve

SALSA

1 red pepper, deseeded and finely diced

2 tomatoes, finely diced

1 red finger chilli, finely chopped

2 jalapeño chillies, finely chopped

2 tbsp extra virgin olive oil

1 tbsp balsamic vinegar

salt and pepper

1. To make the salsa, put the red pepper, tomatoes and chillies into a bowl and mix together. Stir in the oil and vinegar, then season to taste with salt and pepper. Cover and chill in the refrigerator for at least 1 hour, or until required.

2. Preheat the grill to medium. Arrange the sausages on the grill rack and brush lightly with oil. Cook under the preheated grill, turning occasionally, for 12–15 minutes until golden and thoroughly cooked.

3. Serve the sausages hot, with a large spoonful of salsa on the side, accompanied by bread rolls.

PEA & MINT RISOTTO

SERVES: 4   PREP TIME: 10 MINS   COOK TIME: 20 MINS

INGREDIENTS

2 tbsp olive oil

40 g/1½ oz butter

1 onion, finely chopped

1 garlic clove, crushed

400 g/14 oz arborio rice

150 ml/5 fl oz dry white wine

1.5 litres/2¾ pints boiling chicken stock or vegetable stock

400 g/14 oz fresh or frozen peas

2 tbsp chopped fresh mint

salt and pepper

1. Heat the oil with 15 g/½ oz of the butter in a large, heavy-based saucepan. Add the onion and fry gently over a medium heat, stirring, for 4–5 minutes until soft but not brown.

2. Add the garlic and rice and cook, stirring, for 1–2 minutes. Stir in the wine, bring to the boil and cook, stirring, for about 1 minute.

3. Gradually add the stock, stirring until each addition is absorbed before adding the next. Stir in the peas and half the mint with the final addition of stock.

4. Continue stirring until most of the liquid has been absorbed and the rice is almost tender, with a slight firmness in the centre. Stir in the remaining butter.

5. Season to taste with salt and pepper, stir in the remaining mint and serve.

SPAGHETTI WITH TOMATOES & BLACK OLIVES

SERVES: 4   PREP TIME: 10 MINS   COOK TIME: 40 MINS

INGREDIENTS

1 tbsp olive oil

1 garlic clove, finely chopped

2 tsp bottled capers, drained, rinsed and chopped

12 black olives, stoned and chopped

½ dried red chilli, crushed

1.25 kg/2 lb 12 oz canned chopped tomatoes

1 tbsp chopped fresh parsley, plus extra to garnish

350 g/12 oz dried spaghetti

2 tbsp freshly grated Parmesan cheese

salt

1. Heat the olive oil in a large, heavy-based frying pan. Add the garlic and cook over a low heat for 30 seconds. Add the capers, olives, dried chilli and tomatoes and season to taste with salt. Partially cover the pan and simmer gently for 20 minutes.

2. Stir in the parsley, partially cover the frying pan again and simmer for a further 10 minutes.

3. Meanwhile, bring a large, heavy-based saucepan of lightly salted water to the boil. Add the spaghetti, bring back to the boil and cook for 8–10 minutes, or until just tender but still firm to the bite. Drain and transfer to a serving dish. Add the tomato and olive sauce and toss well. Sprinkle the Parmesan cheese over the pasta and garnish with chopped parsley. Serve.

PRAWN & MUSSEL PAELLA

SERVES: 6–8   **PREP TIME: 25 MINS PLUS 10 MINS SOAKING TIME**   **COOK TIME: 35–40 MINS**

INGREDIENTS

16 live mussels

½ tsp saffron threads

2 tbsp hot water

350 g/12 oz paella rice

6 tbsp olive oil

6–8 boned chicken thighs

140 g/5 oz Spanish chorizo
sausage, sliced

2 large onions, chopped

4 large garlic cloves, crushed

1 tsp mild or hot Spanish paprika

100 g/3½ oz green beans, chopped

125 g/4½ oz frozen peas

1.3 litres/2¼ pints fish stock

16 raw prawns, peeled and deveined

2 red peppers, halved and deseeded,
then grilled, peeled and sliced

salt and pepper

chopped fresh flat-leaf parsley,
to garnish

1. Soak the mussels in lightly salted water for 10 minutes. Put the saffron threads and hot water in a small bowl or cup and leave to infuse for a few minutes. Meanwhile, put the rice in a sieve and rinse in cold water until the water runs clear. Set aside.

2. Heat 3 tablespoons of the oil in a 30-cm/12-inch paella pan or flameproof casserole. Cook the chicken thighs over a medium–high heat, turning frequently, for 5 minutes, or until golden and crispy. Using a slotted spoon, transfer to a bowl. Add the chorizo to the pan and cook, stirring, for 1 minute, or until beginning to crisp. Add to the chicken.

3. Heat the remaining oil in the pan and cook the onions, stirring frequently, for 2 minutes. Add the garlic and paprika and cook for a further 3 minutes, or until the onions are soft but not browned.

4. Add the drained rice, beans and peas and stir until coated in oil. Return the chicken and chorizo and any accumulated juices to the pan. Stir in the stock, saffron and its soaking liquid, and salt and pepper to taste and bring to the boil, stirring constantly. Reduce the heat to low and simmer, uncovered and without stirring, for 15 minutes, or until the rice is almost tender.

5. Arrange the mussels, prawns and red peppers on top, then cover and simmer, without stirring, for a further 5 minutes, or until the prawns turn pink and the mussels open. Discard any mussels that remain closed. Check the chicken is tender and the juices run clear when a skewer is inserted into the thickest part of the meat. Taste and adjust the seasoning if necessary. Sprinkle with the parsley and serve.

RASPBERRY RIPPLE ICE CREAM

SERVES: 6–8   PREP TIME: 20 MINS PLUS 30 MINS INFUSING TIME, PLUS 2–3 HRS FREEZING TIME   COOK TIME: 25 MINS

INGREDIENTS

300 ml/10 fl oz milk

1 vanilla pod

210 g/7½ oz caster sugar

3 egg yolks

350 g/12 oz fresh raspberries

6 tbsp water

300 ml/10 fl oz whipping cream

1. Pour the milk into a heavy-based saucepan, add the vanilla pod and bring almost to the boil. Remove from the heat and leave to infuse for 30 minutes. Put 85 g/3 oz of the sugar and the egg yolks in a large bowl and whisk together until pale and the mixture leaves a trail when the whisk is lifted. Remove the vanilla pod from the milk, then slowly add the milk to the sugar mixture, stirring all the time with a wooden spoon.

2. Strain the mixture into the rinsed-out saucepan or a double boiler and cook over a low heat for 10–15 minutes, stirring all the time, until the mixture thickens enough to coat the back of the wooden spoon. Do not allow the mixture to boil or it will curdle. Remove the custard from the heat and leave to cool for at least 1 hour, stirring from time to time to prevent a skin from forming.

3. Meanwhile, put the raspberries in a heavy-based saucepan with the remaining 125 g/4½ oz of sugar and the water. Heat gently, stirring, until the sugar has dissolved, then simmer gently for 5 minutes, or until the raspberries are very soft. Pass the raspberries through a nylon sieve into a bowl to remove the seeds, then leave the purée to cool. Meanwhile, whip the cream until it holds its shape. Keep in the refrigerator until ready to use.

4. If using an ice cream machine, fold the whipped cream into the cold custard, then churn the mixture in the machine following the manufacturer's instructions. Just before the ice cream freezes, spread half into a freezer-proof container. Pour over half the raspberry purée then repeat the layers. Freeze for 1–2 hours or until firm or required. Alternatively, fold the whipped cream into the mixture and freeze in a freezer-proof container, uncovered, for 1–2 hours, or until it begins to set around the edges. Turn the mixture into a bowl and stir with a fork until smooth. Spread half the mixture into another container. Pour over half the raspberry purée then repeat the layers. Return to the container and freeze until completely frozen.

CHILLED PEA SOUP

SERVES: 3–4   PREP TIME: 15 MINS PLUS 2 HRS CHILLING TIME   COOK TIME: 10 MINS

INGREDIENTS

425 ml/15 fl oz vegetable stock or water

450 g/1 lb frozen peas

55 g/2 oz spring onions, coarsely chopped

300 ml/10 fl oz natural yogurt

salt and pepper

TO GARNISH

2 tbsp chopped fresh mint

2 tbsp chopped spring onions or chives

grated lemon rind

olive oil

1. Bring the stock to the boil in a large saucepan over a medium heat. Reduce the heat, add the peas and spring onions and simmer for 5 minutes.

2. Leave to cool slightly, then strain twice, making sure that you remove any bits of skin. Pour into a large bowl, season to taste with salt and pepper and stir in the yogurt. Cover the bowl with clingfilm and chill in the refrigerator for several hours, or until well chilled.

3. To serve, remove from the refrigerator, mix well and ladle into serving bowls. Garnish with the chopped mint, spring onions, grated lemon rind and olive oil.

PEACH MELBA MERINGUE

SERVES: 8   PREP TIME: 25 MINS PLUS 15 MINS COOLING TIME   COOK TIME: 50 MINS

INGREDIENTS

sunflower oil, for brushing

RASPBERRY COULIS

350 g/12 oz fresh raspberries

115 g/4 oz icing sugar

MERINGUE

2 tsp cornflour

300 g/10½ oz caster sugar

5 large egg whites

1 tsp cider vinegar

FILLING

3 peaches, peeled, stoned and chopped

250 g/9 oz fresh raspberries

200 ml/7 fl oz crème fraîche

150 ml/5 fl oz double cream

1. Preheat the oven to 150°C/300°F/Gas Mark 2. Brush a 35 x 25-cm/ 14 x 10-inch Swiss roll tin with oil and line with greaseproof paper.

2. To make the raspberry coulis, process the raspberries and icing sugar to a purée. Press through a sieve into a bowl and reserve.

3. To make the meringue, sift the cornflour into a bowl and stir in the sugar. In a separate, grease-free bowl, whisk the egg whites into stiff peaks, then whisk in the vinegar. Gradually whisk in the cornflour and sugar mixture until stiff and glossy.

4. Spread the mixture evenly in the prepared tin, leaving a 1-cm/½-inch border. Bake in the centre of the preheated oven for 20 minutes, then reduce the heat to 110°C/225°F/Gas Mark ¼ and cook for a further 25–30 minutes, or until puffed up. Remove from the oven. Leave to cool for 15 minutes. Turn out onto another piece of greaseproof paper and carefully remove the greaseproof paper.

5. To make the filling, place the peaches in a bowl with the raspberries. Add 2 tablespoons of the coulis and mix. In a separate bowl, whisk together the crème fraîche and cream until thick. Spread over the meringue. Scatter the fruit over the cream, leaving a 3-cm/1¼-inch border at one short edge. Using the greaseproof paper, lift and roll the meringue, starting at the short edge without the border, ending up seam-side down. Lift onto a plate and serve with the coulis.

CHOCOLATE BANANA SPLITS

SERVES: 4   PREP TIME: 15 MINS PLUS COOLING AND CHILLING TIME, PLUS 2 HRS FREEZING TIME   COOK TIME: 5 MINS

INGREDIENTS

4 bananas

6 tbsp chopped, mixed nuts and chocolate rum sauce, to serve

VANILLA ICE CREAM

300 ml/10 fl oz milk

1 tsp vanilla extract

3 egg yolks

100 g/3½ oz caster sugar

300 ml/10 fl oz double cream, whipped

1. To make the vanilla ice cream, heat the milk and vanilla extract in a saucepan over a medium heat until almost boiling. Beat together the egg yolks and sugar in a bowl. Remove the milk from the heat and stir a little into the egg mixture. Transfer the mixture to the pan and stir over a low heat until thickened. Do not allow to boil. Remove from the heat.

2. Leave to cool for about 30 minutes, fold in the cream, cover with clingfilm and chill in the refrigerator for 1 hour. If using an ice cream machine, transfer the mixture and churn in the machine following the manufacturer's instructions. Alternatively, freeze in a freezer-proof container, uncovered, for 1–2 hours, or until it begins to set around the edges. Turn the mixture into a bowl and stir with a fork until smooth. Return to the container and freeze for 30 minutes. Repeat twice more or until completely frozen.

3. Peel the bananas, slice lengthways and arrange on four serving dishes. Top with ice cream and nuts and serve with the chocolate rum sauce.

PEACH MELBA
MERINGUE

TURBOT GOUJONS WITH CAPER MAYONNAISE

SERVES: 4 **PREP TIME: 20 MINS** **COOK TIME: 5 MINS**

INGREDIENTS

70 g/2½ oz stale white breadcrumbs

finely grated rind of 1 lemon

2 tbsp finely chopped fresh parsley

500 g/1 lb 2 oz skinless turbot fillet

3 tbsp plain flour

1 egg, beaten

sunflower oil, for frying

salt and pepper

CAPER MAYONNAISE

4 tbsp mayonnaise

1 tbsp capers, chopped

1 tbsp lemon juice

1. Put the breadcrumbs, lemon rind and parsley into a food processor and process to fine crumbs. Place in a wide dish.

2. Cut the turbot into 2 x 7.5-cm/¾ x 3-inch strips. Season the flour with salt and pepper to taste and place in a wide dish. Put the egg into a separate wide dish.

3. Toss the fish in the seasoned flour to coat evenly, then dip in the beaten egg and, finally, in the breadcrumb mixture, turning to coat completely.

4. To make the dip, mix together the mayonnaise, capers and lemon juice.

5. Heat enough oil for deep-frying in a large saucepan or deep-fryer to 190°C/375°F, checking the temperature with a thermometer. Add the fish strips in batches and fry, turning once, for 2–3 minutes until golden. Drain on absorbent kitchen paper.

6. Serve the goujons hot, with the caper mayonnaise on the side.

EGGS BAKED IN TOMATOES

SERVES: 4 | **PREP TIME: 10 MINS** | **COOK TIME: 25 MINS**

INGREDIENTS

4 large beef tomatoes

4 eggs

2 tbsp chopped fresh oregano

4 tbsp freshly grated Parmesan cheese

1 garlic clove, halved

4 slices country bread

2 tbsp olive oil

salt and pepper

1. Preheat the oven to 220°C/425°F/Gas Mark 7. Cut a slice from the top of each tomato and scoop out the seeds and pulp. Place the tomatoes in a baking dish or tin.

2. Break an egg into each tomato, then sprinkle with oregano and salt and pepper. Sprinkle with the cheese and bake in the preheated oven for about 20 minutes, or until the eggs are just set, with runny yolks.

3. Meanwhile, rub the garlic over the bread, place on a baking sheet and drizzle with oil. Bake in the oven for 5–6 minutes, or until golden.

4. Put each egg on a slice of toast and serve immediately.

COLESLAW

SERVES: 10–12 **PREP TIME: 15 MINS** **COOK TIME: NO COOKING**

INGREDIENTS

150 ml/5 fl oz mayonnaise

150 ml/5 fl oz natural yogurt

dash of Tabasco sauce

1 head of white cabbage

4 carrots

1 green pepper, deseeded

salt and pepper

1. Mix together the mayonnaise, yogurt, Tabasco sauce, and salt and pepper to taste in a small bowl. Chill the dressing in the refrigerator until required.

2. Cut the cabbage in half and then into quarters. Remove and discard the tough centre stalk. Finely shred the cabbage leaves. Wash the leaves under cold running water and dry thoroughly on kitchen paper. Roughly grate the carrots and pepper or shred in a food processor or on a mandoline.

3. Mix the vegetables together in a large serving bowl and toss to mix. Pour over the dressing and toss until the vegetables are well coated. Cover and chill in the refrigerator until required.

SIMPLE SAVOURY BEEF

SERVES: 4 **PREP TIME: 15 MINS** **COOK TIME: 1 HR 15 MINS**

INGREDIENTS

55 g/2 oz butter

1 onion, finely chopped

2 carrots, finely chopped

4 tomatoes, peeled and chopped

25 g/1 oz plain flour

1 tsp mustard powder

600 ml/1 pint beef stock

500 g/1 lb 2 oz fresh beef mince

175 g/6 oz frozen peas

salt and pepper

chopped fresh parsley, to garnish

1. Melt the butter in a saucepan. Add the onion and carrots and cook over a low heat, stirring occasionally, for 5 minutes, until softened. Add the tomatoes and cook, stirring occasionally, for a further 3 minutes.

2. Remove the pan from the heat and stir in the flour and mustard powder, then return to the heat and cook, stirring constantly, for 2 minutes. Gradually stir in the stock, a little at a time, then bring to the boil, stirring constantly. Cook, stirring constantly, for a further few minutes, until thickened.

3. Add the beef and stir to break it up. Season to taste with salt and pepper, then cover and simmer, stirring occasionally, for 45 minutes.

4. Gently stir in the peas, re-cover the pan and simmer, stirring occasionally, for a further 15 minutes. Taste and adjust the seasoning, adding salt and pepper if needed. Garnish with parsley and serve.

TUNA MELT BAGELS

SERVES: 8   PREP TIME: 35 MINS PLUS 1 HR 20 MINS RISING TIME   COOK TIME: 30 MINS

INGREDIENTS

500 g/1 lb 2 oz strong white flour, plus extra for dusting

1 sachet easy-blend dried yeast

1 tbsp caster sugar

1½ tsp salt

325 ml/11 fl oz lukewarm water

olive oil, for greasing

55 g/2 oz poppy seeds

375 g/13 oz canned tuna in brine, drained and flaked

3 tbsp mayonnaise

2 tbsp snipped chives, plus extra to garnish

200 g/7 oz Cheddar cheese, grated

1. Mix the flour, yeast, sugar and salt in a large bowl. Make a well in the centre and stir in just enough of the water to mix to a soft dough.

2. Turn out the dough onto a lightly floured work surface and knead for about 10 minutes until smooth. Cover and leave in a warm place for about 1 hour until doubled in size.

3. Turn out the dough onto a lightly floured work surface and lightly knead until smooth. Divide into eight pieces and roll each piece into a smooth ball. Make a hole in the centre of each ball with a floured finger, then swirl your finger around to stretch and open out the ball to a ring. Cover and leave to stand for 20 minutes.

4. Preheat the oven to 220°C/425°F/Gas Mark 7 and grease a baking sheet. Bring a large saucepan of water to the boil, then lower the bagels into the water in batches and cook, turning once, for about 2 minutes until they puff up.

5. Put the poppy seeds into a shallow bowl. Lift out the bagels with a slotted spoon and press them into the poppy seeds. Place the bagels on the prepared baking sheet and bake in the preheated oven for 20–25 minutes until golden brown and firm. Transfer to a wire rack and leave to cool.

6. Preheat the grill to high. Mix the tuna with the mayonnaise and chives. Split the bagels in half and top with the tuna mixture. Sprinkle with the cheese, place on the grill rack and cook under the preheated grill until the cheese is melted. Replace the bagel lids and serve sprinkled with chives.

BARBECUED CHICKEN

SERVES: 4–6   PREP TIME: 15 MINS PLUS 2 HRS MARINATING TIME   COOK TIME: 25 MINS

INGREDIENTS

4 chicken drumsticks, about 100 g/3½ oz each, skinned

chopped fresh parsley, to garnish

salad, to serve

SAUCE

1 shallot, finely chopped

1 garlic clove, crushed

1 tbsp tomato purée blended with 150 ml/5 fl oz water

2 tbsp red wine vinegar

1 tbsp mustard

1 tbsp Worcestershire sauce

1. To make the sauce, place all the sauce ingredients into a screw-top jar and shake vigorously until well blended.

2. Rinse the chicken drumsticks and pat dry with kitchen paper. Place the drumsticks in a large ovenproof dish, pour over the sauce and leave to marinate for at least 2 hours, occasionally spooning the sauce over the chicken. When ready to cook, preheat the oven to 190°C/375°F/ Gas Mark 5.

3. Cook the chicken drumsticks in the preheated oven for 20–25 minutes. Spoon the sauce over the chicken or turn the chicken over during cooking. Check the chicken is tender and the juices run clear when a skewer is inserted into the thickest part of the meat.

4. Transfer to a serving plate, sprinkle with chopped parsley, and serve with salad.

SPARE RIBS IN BARBECUE SAUCE

SERVES: 4–6   PREP TIME: 15 MINS   COOK TIME: 1 HR 40 MINS

INGREDIENTS

25 g/1 oz butter

2 tbsp olive oil

1 onion, finely chopped

2 garlic cloves, finely chopped

1 celery stick, finely chopped

400 g/14 oz canned chopped tomatoes

2 tbsp tomato purée

2–3 tbsp brown sugar

2 tbsp orange juice

1 tbsp clear honey

1 tsp wholegrain mustard

2 tbsp red wine vinegar

1 tbsp Worcestershire sauce

1.5 kg/3 lb 5 oz pork spare ribs

salt and pepper

1. Preheat the oven to 200°C/400°F/Gas Mark 6. Melt the butter with the oil in a saucepan. Add the onion, garlic and celery and cook over a low heat, stirring occasionally, for 5 minutes, until softened. Stir in the tomatoes, tomato purée, sugar, orange juice, honey, mustard, vinegar and Worcestershire sauce and season to taste with salt and pepper. Increase the heat to medium and bring to the boil, then reduce the heat and simmer, stirring occasionally, for 15–20 minutes, until thickened. Remove the pan from the heat.

2. Spread out the spare ribs in a shallow roasting tin and bake in the preheated oven for 25 minutes. Remove from the oven and spoon half the sauce over them. Reduce the oven temperature to 180°C/350°F/ Gas Mark 4, return the tin to the oven and cook for a further 20 minutes.

3. Remove the tin from the oven and turn the ribs over. Spoon the remaining sauce over them and return the tin to the oven. Cook for a further 25–30 minutes, until the meat is tender. Serve.

PEPPERONI & ONION PIZZA

SERVES: 2–4 | **PREP TIME: 20 MINS** | **COOK TIME: 30 MINS**

INGREDIENTS

olive oil, for brushing and drizzling

1 x 25-cm/10-inch ready-made pizza base

4 tbsp sun-dried tomato paste

4 tomatoes, skinned and thinly sliced

2 red onions, finely chopped

4 slices prosciutto or other cooked ham, coarsely shredded

12 slices pepperoni sausage

12 black olives

½ tsp dried oregano

55 g/2 oz mozzarella cheese, roughly torn

salt

1. Preheat the oven to 220°C/425°F/Gas Mark 7. Brush a baking sheet with oil and place the pizza base on it.

2. Spread the sun-dried tomato paste evenly over the base. Arrange the tomato slices on the base and season to taste with salt. Sprinkle over the chopped onion and prosciutto and arrange the pepperoni on top. Add the olives and sprinkle with oregano. Add the cheese and drizzle with oil.

3. Bake in the preheated oven for 20–30 minutes, until golden and sizzling. Cut into slices and serve.

SPICY SALMON FISH CAKES

SERVES: 4   PREP TIME: 25 MINS   COOK TIME: 35 MINS

INGREDIENTS

400 g/14 oz potatoes, cut into medium-sized chunks

400 g/14 oz skinless salmon fillet

2 tbsp mayonnaise

1 egg, beaten

dash of milk, if needed

2 fresh jalapeño chillies, deseeded and finely chopped

1 small bunch fresh coriander leaves

plain flour, for dusting

1 tbsp olive oil

salt and pepper

1. Cook the potatoes in a large saucepan of lightly salted boiling water for 15 minutes, or until tender.

2. Meanwhile, lightly poach the salmon fillet in a saucepan of gently simmering water for 5–6 minutes (if in one piece), or until just cooked but still moist. Alternatively, cut into four equal-sized pieces and cook in a microwave oven on medium for 3 minutes, then turn the pieces around so that the cooked parts are in the centre, and cook for a further 1–2 minutes – check after 1 minute; the fish should be barely cooked. Using a fork, flake the flesh into a bowl.

3. Drain the potatoes, return to the saucepan and, while still warm, roughly mash with a fork, adding the mayonnaise, egg and milk, if needed – the mixture must remain firm, so only add the milk if necessary. Stir in the chillies, coriander leaves and salt and pepper to taste, then lightly mix in the salmon flakes.

4. With floured hands, form the mixture into 8 small patties. Heat the oil in a large non-stick frying pan over a medium–high heat, add the patties and cook for 5 minutes on each side, or until golden brown. Carefully remove with a fish slice and serve.

PAN-FRIED HALIBUT STEAKS WITH TOMATO SALSA

SERVES: 4   PREP TIME: 20 MINS   COOK TIME: ABOUT 10 MINS

INGREDIENTS

1 tbsp vegetable oil

50 g/1¾ oz butter

4 halibut steaks, about 2.5 cm/1 inch thick

plain flour, for dusting

juice of ½ lemon

salt and pepper

TOMATO SALSA

3 firm tomatoes, halved, deseeded and finely diced

1 small red onion, finely diced

1 green chilli, deseeded and finely chopped

3 tbsp chopped fresh coriander

juice of 1 lime

½ tsp sea salt

1. Combine all the tomato salsa ingredients in a serving bowl and leave to stand at room temperature.

2. Heat the oil and 40 g/1½ oz of the butter in a large frying pan over a medium–high heat. Dust the halibut steaks with flour and season to taste with salt and pepper. Place in the pan and cook for 5 minutes on one side and 3–4 minutes on the other, until golden and cooked through. Transfer to a warmed serving dish.

3. Add the lemon juice to the pan and simmer over a medium heat for a few seconds, scraping up any sediment from the base of the pan. Stir in the remaining butter and cook for a few seconds. Pour over the fish and serve with the tomato salsa.

SPICY SALMON
FISH CAKES

BEEF WRAPS WITH LIME & HONEY

SERVES: 4   PREP TIME: 10 MINS PLUS 20 MINS MARINATING TIME   COOK TIME: ABOUT 5 MINS

INGREDIENTS

finely grated rind and juice of 1 lime

1 tbsp clear honey

1 garlic clove, crushed

450 g/1 lb sirloin steak

oil, for brushing

4 tbsp mayonnaise

4 large wheat tortillas

1 red onion, thinly sliced

7.5-cm/3-inch piece cucumber, sliced into ribbons

salt and pepper

1. Mix together the lime juice, honey and garlic in a bowl and add the steak. Cover and leave to marinate in the refrigerator for 20 minutes.

2. Remove the steak from the marinade and season to taste with salt and pepper. Heat a heavy-based frying pan or griddle pan and brush with oil. Add the steak to the pan and cook, turning once, for 5–6 minutes until golden brown.

3. Remove the steak from the heat, leave to stand for 2 minutes, then cut into thin strips.

4. Mix together the mayonnaise and grated lime rind and spread over the tortillas. Scatter the onion over and add the steak strips and cucumber. Wrap the sides over and turn over one end. Serve.

12 AUGUST

TRADITIONAL SCONES

MAKES: 10–12   PREP TIME: 20 MINS   COOK TIME: ABOUT 10 MINS

INGREDIENTS

450 g/1 lb plain flour, plus extra for dusting

½ tsp salt

2 tsp baking powder

55 g/2 oz butter

2 tbsp caster sugar

250 ml/9 fl oz milk, plus 3 tbsp for glazing

strawberry jam and cream, to serve

1. Preheat the oven to 220°C/425°F/Gas Mark 7. Lightly dust a baking sheet with flour.

2. Sift the flour, salt and baking powder into a bowl. Rub in the butter until the mixture resembles breadcrumbs. Stir in the sugar.

3. Make a well in the centre and pour in the milk. Stir in using a round-bladed knife and make a soft dough.

4. Turn the mixture onto a floured work surface and lightly flatten the dough until it is an even thickness, about 1 cm/½ inch. Don't be too heavy-handed – scones need a light touch.

5. Use a 6-cm/2½-inch pastry cutter to cut out the scones, then place them on the prepared baking sheet.

6. Glaze with a little milk and bake in the preheated oven for 10–12 minutes, until golden and well risen.

7. Leave to cool on a wire rack and serve freshly baked with strawberry jam and cream.

13 AUGUST

CHOCOLATE & ORANGE SLICES

SERVES: 8   PREP TIME: 15 MINS PLUS 4 HRS CHILLING TIME   COOK TIME: 5 MINS

INGREDIENTS

butter, for greasing

450 g/1 lb plain chocolate, broken into pieces

3 small, loose-skinned oranges, such as tangerines, mandarins or satsumas

4 egg yolks

200 ml/7 fl oz crème fraîche

2 tbsp raisins

whipped cream, to serve

1. Lightly grease a 450-g/1-lb loaf tin and line it with clingfilm. Put the chocolate in a heatproof bowl set over a saucepan of gently simmering water. Stir over a low heat until melted. Remove from the heat and leave to cool slightly.

2. Meanwhile, peel the oranges, removing all traces of pith. Cut the zest into very thin strips. Beat the egg yolks into the chocolate, one at a time, then add most of the orange zest (reserving the rest for decoration), and all the crème fraîche and raisins, and beat until thoroughly combined. Spoon the mixture into the prepared tin, cover with clingfilm and chill for 3–4 hours, until set.

3. To serve, remove the tin from the refrigerator and turn out the chocolate mould. Remove the clingfilm and cut the mould into slices. Place a slice on serving plates and add whipped cream to serve. Decorate with the remaining orange zest.

TOMATO & HERB RICOTTA TART

SERVES: 6 **PREP TIME: 20 MINS** **COOK TIME: 35 MINS**

INGREDIENTS

500 g/1 lb 2 oz ready-rolled puff pastry

plain flour, for dusting

1 tbsp olive oil

4 spring onions, finely chopped

250 g/9 oz ricotta cheese

2 eggs, beaten

3 tbsp chopped fresh parsley

2 tbsp chopped fresh mint

450 g/1 lb plum or salad tomatoes, sliced

salt and pepper

chopped fresh herbs, to garnish

1. Preheat the oven to 200°C/400°C/Gas Mark 6. Roll out the pastry on a lightly floured work surface to a rectangle about 2.5 cm/1 inch larger than a 33 x 23-cm/13 x 9-inch Swiss roll tin. Carefully lift the pastry into the tin, tucking the edges evenly up the sides.

2. Heat the oil in a frying pan, add the spring onions and stir-fry for 1 minute. Put the ricotta cheese and the eggs into a bowl, add the spring onions and stir to combine. Add the parsley and mint, then season well with salt and pepper.

3. Spread the filling over the pastry case and arrange the tomato slices over the filling in an overlapping pattern.

4. Bake the tart in the preheated oven for 30–35 minutes, until the pastry is golden brown. Sprinkle with fresh herbs and serve warm.

GRILLED HALIBUT WITH BLUE CHEESE & BASIL BUTTER

SERVES: 4   PREP TIME: 10 MINS   COOK TIME: 10 MINS

INGREDIENTS

140 g/5 oz unsalted butter, at room temperature

140 g/5 oz Roquefort cheese or other blue cheese, crumbled

2 tbsp chopped fresh basil

4 halibut steaks, about 200 g/7 oz each

olive oil, for brushing

salt and pepper

1. Put the butter into a bowl and beat until soft, then stir in the cheese and basil, mixing evenly. Season to taste with salt and pepper.

2. Spoon the mixture onto a sheet of clingfilm, shape into a long roll and roll up in the clingfilm. Leave to chill in the refrigerator until firm.

3. Preheat the grill to high. Brush the halibut steaks with a little oil and season to taste with salt and pepper. Grill the steaks for 8–10 minutes, turning once, until it flakes easily.

4. Serve the fish with a slice of chilled butter on each piece.

COURGETTES WITH BUTTER & LEMON

SERVES: 4   PREP TIME: 5 MINS PLUS 30 MINS MARINATING TIME   COOK TIME: 5 MINS

INGREDIENTS

4 courgettes, sliced lengthways into 5-mm/¼-inch slices

1 tbsp olive oil

25 g/1 oz butter, melted

1 garlic clove, crushed

finely grated rind of 1 lemon

1 tbsp lemon juice

salt and pepper

1. Place the courgette slices in a bowl and add the oil, butter, garlic, lemon rind and lemon juice. Turn to coat evenly, then cover and leave to stand for 30 minutes.

2. Preheat a griddle pan or large frying pan. Season the courgettes with salt and pepper to taste.

3. Place the courgettes in the saucepan and cook, turning occasionally and basting with any extra lemon butter, for 4–5 minutes until golden and tender. Serve.

17 AUGUST

SUMMER COUSCOUS SALAD

SERVES: 4–6   PREP TIME: 20 MINS PLUS 10 MINS TO ABSORB THE WATER   COOK TIME: 15 MINS

INGREDIENTS

350 g/12 oz couscous

½ tsp salt

400 ml/14 fl oz warm water

1–2 tbsp olive oil

4 spring onions, finely chopped or sliced

1 bunch fresh mint, finely chopped

1 bunch fresh flat-leaf parsley, finely chopped

1 bunch fresh coriander, finely chopped

15 g/½ oz butter

½ preserved lemon, finely chopped

1. Preheat the oven to 180°C/350°F/Gas Mark 4. Tip the couscous into an ovenproof dish. Stir the salt into the water and then pour over the couscous. Cover and leave the couscous to absorb the water for 10 minutes.

2. Drizzle the oil over the couscous. Using your fingers, rub the oil into the grains to break up the lumps and aerate them. Toss in the spring onions and half the herbs. Dot the surface with the butter and cover with a piece of foil or wet greaseproof paper. Bake in the preheated oven for about 15 minutes to heat through.

3. Fluff up the grains with a fork and tip the couscous into a serving dish. Toss the remaining herbs into the couscous and scatter the preserved lemon over the top. Serve.

18 AUGUST

BACON-WRAPPED CHICKEN BURGERS

SERVES: 4   PREP TIME: 15 MINS PLUS 1 HR CHILLING TIME   COOK TIME: 10 MINS

INGREDIENTS

450 g/1 lb fresh chicken mince

1 onion, grated

2 garlic cloves, crushed

55 g/2 oz pine kernels, toasted

55 g/2 oz Gruyère cheese, grated

2 tbsp fresh, snipped chives

2 tbsp wholemeal flour

8 slices lean back bacon

oil, for brushing and oiling

salt and pepper

crusty rolls and toppings of your choice, to serve

1. Place the chicken mince, onion, garlic, pine kernels, Gruyère cheese, chives and salt and pepper to taste in a food processor. Using the pulse button, process the mixture together using short sharp bursts. Scrape out onto a board and shape into four even-sized burgers. Coat in the flour, then cover and chill for 1 hour. Meanwhile, preheat the barbecue.

2. Wrap each burger with two bacon slices, securing in place with a presoaked wooden cocktail stick.

3. Oil the barbecue rack. Lightly brush each burger with a little oil and cook the burgers for 5 minutes on each side, or until cooked through. Transfer to serving plates and serve in crusty rolls with toppings of your choice.

19 AUGUST

TARRAGON TURKEY

SERVES: 4   PREP TIME: 10 MINS   COOK TIME: ABOUT 15 MINS

INGREDIENTS

4 turkey breasts, about 175 g/6 oz each

4 tsp wholegrain mustard

8 fresh tarragon sprigs, plus extra to garnish

4 smoked back bacon rashers

oil, for oiling

salt and pepper

salad leaves, to serve

1. Preheat the barbecue. Season the turkey to taste with salt and pepper, and using a round-bladed knife, spread the mustard evenly over the turkey.

2. Place two tarragon sprigs on top of each turkey breast and wrap a bacon rasher around it to hold the herbs in place. Secure with a presoaked wooden cocktail stick.

3. Oil the barbecue rack. Cook the turkey over medium–hot coals for 5–8 minutes on each side. Transfer to serving plates and garnish with tarragon sprigs. Serve with salad leaves.

BACON-WRAPPED
CHICKEN BURGERS

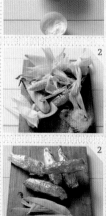

CORN ON THE COB WITH BLUE CHEESE DRESSING

SERVES: 6   PREP TIME: 15 MINS PLUS CHILLING TIME   COOK TIME: 20 MINS

INGREDIENTS

140 g/5 oz Danish Blue cheese

140 g/5 oz curd cheese

125 ml/4 fl oz natural Greek yogurt

6 corn cobs in their husks

salt and pepper

1. Crumble the Danish Blue cheese, then place in a bowl. Beat with a wooden spoon until creamy. Beat in the curd cheese until thoroughly blended. Gradually beat in the yogurt and season to taste with salt and pepper. Cover with clingfilm and leave to chill somewhere cool until required. Meanwhile, preheat the barbecue.

2. Fold back the husks on each corn cob and remove the silks. Smooth the husks back into place. Cut out six rectangles of foil, each large enough to enclose a corn cob. Wrap the corn cobs in the foil.

3. Cook the corn cobs on the barbecue for 15–20 minutes, turning frequently. Unwrap the corn cobs and discard the foil. Peel back the husk on one side of each and trim off with a sharp knife. Serve with the blue cheese dressing.

PROSECCO & LEMON SORBET

SERVES: 4 | PREP TIME: 10 MINS PLUS FREEZING TIME | COOK TIME: 5 MINS

INGREDIENTS

140 g/5 oz caster sugar

100 ml/3½ fl oz water

finely grated rind and juice of 1 lemon

350 ml/12 fl oz prosecco

fresh mint sprigs, to decorate

1. Put the sugar and water into a saucepan with the grated lemon rind and stir over a low heat until the sugar dissolves.

2. Bring to the boil, then boil for 1 minute until slightly reduced. Leave to cool, then strain through a sieve.

3. Add the lemon juice and prosecco to the lemon syrup and stir to combine, then pour into an ice cream machine and churn in the machine following the manufacturer's instructions. Alternatively, pour into a container to freeze and whisk once an hour until completely frozen.

4. Remove the sorbet from the freezer about 15 minutes before serving, then scoop into serving dishes. Decorate with mint sprigs and serve.

PEANUT BUTTER S'MORES

SERVES: 4   PREP TIME: 5 MINS   COOK TIME: 5 MINS

INGREDIENTS

115 g/4 oz smooth peanut butter

8 graham crackers or digestive biscuits

85 g/3 oz plain chocolate, broken into squares

1. Preheat the barbecue. Spread the peanut butter on one side of each cracker.

2. Place the chocolate pieces on four of the crackers and invert the remaining crackers on top.

3. Toast the s'mores on the preheated barbecue for about 1 minute until the filling starts to melt. Turn carefully using tongs. Serve.

CARROT CAKE

SERVES: 8   PREP TIME: 25 MINS   COOK TIME: 40 MINS

INGREDIENTS

butter, for greasing

115 g/4 oz self-raising flour

pinch of salt

1 tsp mixed spice

½ tsp ground nutmeg

125 g/4½ oz soft light brown sugar

2 eggs, beaten

5 tbsp sunflower oil

125 g/4½ oz carrots, peeled and grated

1 banana, peeled and chopped (100 g/3½ oz peeled weight)

25 g/1 oz walnut halves, chopped

ready-made frosting, to decorate

1. Preheat the oven to 180°C/350°F/Gas Mark 4. Grease an 18-cm (7-inch) square cake tin and line the base and two sides with greaseproof paper.

2. Sift the flour, salt, mixed spice and nutmeg into a large bowl. Stir in the brown sugar then add the eggs and sunflower oil and beat well. Stir in the carrots, banana and chopped nuts.

3. Spoon the mixture into the prepared tin and level the surface. Bake in the preheated oven for 35–40 minutes or until risen, golden and just firm to the touch. Cool in the tin for 5 minutes then transfer to a wire rack to cool completely.

4. Spread the frosting over the top of the cake and serve.

PEANUT BUTTER
S'MORES

STICKY LIME CHICKEN

SERVES: 4   PREP TIME: 25 MINS   COOK TIME: 40 MINS

INGREDIENTS

4 part-boned, skinless chicken breasts, about 140 g/5 oz each

juice and grated rind of 1 lime

1 tbsp clear honey

1 tbsp olive oil

1 garlic clove, chopped (optional)

1 tbsp chopped fresh thyme

pepper

grated lemon rind, to garnish

roasted cherry tomatoes and chargrilled courgettes, to serve

1. Preheat the oven to 190°C/375°F/Gas Mark 5. Arrange the chicken breasts in a shallow roasting tin.

2. Put the lime juice and rind, honey, oil, garlic (if using) and thyme in a small bowl and combine thoroughly. Spoon the mixture evenly over the chicken breasts and season to taste with pepper.

3. Roast the chicken in the preheated oven, basting occasionally, for 35–40 minutes, or until tender and the juices run clear when a skewer is inserted into the thickest part of the meat. As the chicken cooks, the liquid in the pan will thicken to give a sticky coating.

4. Remove from the oven and transfer to plates. Garnish with lemon rind and serve with roasted cherry tomatoes and chargrilled courgettes.

25 AUGUST

ROASTED VEGETABLE & FETA CHEESE WRAPS

MAKES: 4   PREP TIME: 20 MINS   COOK TIME: 20 MINS

INGREDIENTS

1 red onion, cut into eighths

1 red pepper, cored and cut into eighths

1 small aubergine, cut into eighths

1 courgette, cut into eighths

4 tbsp extra virgin olive oil

1 garlic clove, crushed

100 g/3½ oz feta cheese, crumbled

small bunch fresh mint, shredded

4 x 25-cm/10-inch sun-dried tomato wraps

salt and pepper

1. Preheat the oven to 220°C/425°F/Gas Mark 7. Mix together all of the vegetables, olive oil, garlic and salt and pepper to taste and place in the oven in a non-stick oven tray. Roast for 15–20 minutes or until golden and cooked through.

2. Remove from the oven and leave to cool. Once cool, mix in the feta and mint.

3. Preheat a non-stick saucepan or grill pan until almost smoking, then cook the wraps one at a time on both sides for 10 seconds.

4. Divide the vegetable and feta mixture between the wraps, placing it along the middle of each wrap. Roll up the wrap, cut them in half and serve.

PRAWN & SCALLOP KEBABS

SERVES: 4–6 | **PREP TIME: 25 MINS PLUS 15 MINS MARINATING TIME** | **COOK TIME: 5 MINS**

INGREDIENTS

24 raw tiger prawns, heads removed

12 large scallops, corals attached

4–5 tbsp olive oil, plus extra for oiling

juice of 1 lime

1 tbsp chopped fresh coriander

salt and pepper

lime wedges, to serve

1. Preheat the barbecue. Peel the prawns but leave the tails attached. Slit down the back and remove the dark intestinal vein. Remove the tough muscle from the side of the scallops. Slice in half lengthways through the coral.

2. Combine the olive oil and lime juice in a shallow dish. Add a pinch of salt and pepper to taste. Add the scallops and prawns and leave to marinate for 15 minutes.

3. Oil the barbecue rack. Reserving the marinade, thread the scallops and prawns alternately onto eight presoaked wooden skewers or metal skewers. Cook over hot coals for 4–6 minutes, turning and brushing with the marinade, until the prawns are pink and cooked through. Transfer to serving plates and sprinkle with coriander. Serve with lime wedges.

VEGETABLE KEBABS WITH BLUE CHEESE

SERVES: 4–6 | **PREP TIME: 15 MINS** | **COOK TIME: 10 MINS**

INGREDIENTS

5 thin leeks

18 small vine-ripened tomatoes, halved lengthways

250 g/9 oz chestnut mushrooms, stalks removed

100 g/3½ oz butter, melted

oil, for oiling

125 g/4½ oz blue cheese, crumbled

salt and pepper

1. Preheat the barbecue. Trim the leeks to about 15 cm/6 inches long. Slice in half lengthways, and then crossways into 2.5-cm/1-inch pieces. Thread the leeks, tomatoes and mushrooms alternately onto 12 presoaked wooden skewers or metal skewers. Brush with melted butter and season to taste with salt and pepper.

2. Oil the barbecue rack. Cook the kebabs over medium–hot coals, turning frequently, for 6–10 minutes, or until thoroughly cooked. Transfer to serving plates, sprinkle with the cheese and serve.

JERK CHICKEN

SERVES: 4   **PREP TIME: 30 MINS PLUS 8 HRS MARINATING TIME**   **COOK TIME: 35 MINS**

INGREDIENTS

2 fresh red chillies, deseeded and chopped

2 tbsp corn oil, plus extra for brushing

2 garlic cloves, finely chopped

1 tbsp finely chopped onion

1 tbsp finely chopped spring onion

1 tbsp white wine vinegar

1 tbsp lime juice

2 tsp demerara sugar

1 tsp dried thyme

1 tsp ground cinnamon

1 tsp ground mixed spice

½ tsp freshly grated nutmeg

4 chicken quarters

salt and pepper

fresh coriander sprigs, to garnish

lime wedges, to serve

1. Place the chillies in a small bowl with the oil, garlic, onion, spring onion, vinegar, lime juice, sugar, thyme, cinnamon, mixed spice and nutmeg. Season to taste with salt and pepper and mash thoroughly with a fork.

2. Using a sharp knife, make a series of diagonal slashes in the chicken quarters and place them in a large non-metallic dish. Spoon the jerk seasoning over the chicken, rubbing it well into the slashes. Cover and leave to marinate in the refrigerator for up to 8 hours.

3. Preheat the grill. Remove the chicken from the marinade, discarding the marinade. Brush with oil and cook under the preheated grill, turning frequently, for 30–35 minutes, until the chicken is tender and the juices run clear when a skewer is inserted into the thickest part of the meat. Transfer to plates, garnish with coriander sprigs and serve with lime wedges.

RASPBERRY & WHITE CHOCOLATE S'MORES

SERVES: 4   PREP TIME: 5 MINS   COOK TIME: 5 MINS

INGREDIENTS

12 marshmallows, halved

8 graham crackers or digestive biscuits

4 tbsp white chocolate chips

12 raspberries

1. Preheat the barbecue. Place the three marshmallow halves on each cracker.

2. Toast the s'mores on the preheated barbecue until the marshmallows start to melt.

3. Top four of the crackers with white chocolate chips and raspberries, then invert the remaining biscuits on top, pressing lightly. Serve.

ROCKET & PARMESAN SALAD

SERVES: 4–6   PREP TIME: 10 MINS   COOK TIME: 5 MINS

INGREDIENTS

2 handfuls rocket leaves

1 small fennel bulb

5 tbsp olive oil

2 tbsp balsamic vinegar

50 g/1¾ oz pine kernels

100 g/3½ oz Parmesan cheese shavings

salt and pepper

1. Divide the rocket among serving plates.

2. Halve the fennel bulb and slice it finely. Arrange the sliced fennel over the rocket.

3. Whisk together the oil and vinegar with salt and pepper to taste. Drizzle a little of the dressing over each serving.

4. Toast the pine kernels in a dry frying pan until golden brown.

5. Top the salad with the Parmesan shavings and toasted pine kernels. Serve.

TURKEY WITH MOLE SAUCE

SERVES: 4–6   PREP TIME: 25 MINS   COOK TIME: 1½ HRS

INGREDIENTS

4 turkey portions, each cut into 4 pieces

about 500 ml/18 fl oz chicken stock, plus extra for thinning

about 250 ml/9 fl oz water

1 onion, chopped

1 whole garlic bulb, divided into cloves and peeled

1 celery stalk, chopped

1 bay leaf

1 bunch fresh coriander, finely chopped

500 ml/18 fl oz mole poblano or use ready-made mole paste, thinned as instructed on the packaging

4–5 tbsp sesame seeds, to garnish

1. Preheat the oven to 190°C/375°F/Gas Mark 5. Arrange the turkey in a large flameproof casserole. Pour the stock and water around the turkey, then add the onion, garlic, celery, bay leaf and half the coriander.

2. Bake in the preheated oven for 1–1½ hours, or until the turkey is very tender. Add extra liquid if needed.

3. Warm the mole sauce in a saucepan with enough stock to make it the consistency of thin cream.

4. To toast the sesame seeds for the garnish, place the seeds in an unoiled frying pan and dry-fry, shaking the pan, until lightly golden.

5. Arrange the turkey pieces on a serving plate and spoon the warmed mole sauce over the top. Sprinkle with the toasted sesame seeds and the remaining chopped coriander and serve.

ROCKET &
PARMESAN SALAD

SEPTEMBER

BEETROOT & EGG SOUP

SERVES: 6   PREP TIME: 25 MINS PLUS 3 HRS CHILLING TIME   COOK TIME: 20 MINS

INGREDIENTS

650 g/1 lb 7 oz cooked beetroots, peeled and chopped

2 lemons, peeled, deseeded and chopped

1.3 litres/2¼ pints vegetable stock

3 large eggs

1½ tbsp clear honey, plus extra for drizzling

salt and pepper

TO GARNISH

soured cream, chilled

snipped fresh chives

1. Put the beetroots and lemons into a large saucepan, pour in the stock and bring to the boil. Reduce the heat and simmer for 20 minutes.

2. Remove the pan from the heat and leave to cool slightly. Ladle the soup into a food processor, in batches if necessary, and process to a purée. Pass the soup through a sieve into a bowl to remove any membrane or fibres. Leave to cool completely.

3. Meanwhile, put the eggs, honey and a pinch of salt into a food processor and process until thoroughly combined. Gradually add the mixture to the soup, stirring constantly.

4. Cover with clingfilm and chill in the refrigerator for at least 3 hours. To serve, stir the soup and taste and adjust the seasoning, if necessary. Ladle into bowls, drizzle with honey, garnish with the soured cream and snipped chives and serve.

SCALLOPED POTATOES

SERVES: 8   PREP TIME: 20 MINS PLUS 15 MINS RESTING TIME   COOK TIME: 1 HR 10 MINS

INGREDIENTS

15 g/½ oz butter, plus extra for greasing

1 tbsp plain flour

225 ml/8 fl oz double cream

450 ml/16 fl oz milk

1 tsp salt

pinch of freshly grated nutmeg

pinch of freshly ground white pepper

4 fresh thyme sprigs

2 garlic cloves, finely chopped

2 kg/4 lb 8 oz baking potatoes, thinly sliced

115 g/4 oz Gruyère cheese or Cheddar cheese, grated

salt and pepper

1. Preheat the oven to 190°C/375°F/Gas Mark 5. Grease a 38 x 25-cm/15 x 10-inch ovenproof dish.

2. Melt the butter in a saucepan over a medium heat. Stir in the flour and cook, stirring constantly, for 2 minutes. Gradually whisk in the cream and milk and bring to simmering point. Add the salt, the nutmeg, white pepper, thyme and garlic, reduce the heat to low and simmer for 5 minutes. Remove the thyme sprigs.

3. Make a layer of half the potatoes in the prepared dish and season generously with salt and pepper. Top with half the sauce and cover with half the cheese. Repeat the layers with the remaining potatoes, sauce and cheese.

4. Bake in the preheated oven for about 1 hour, or until the top is browned and the potatoes are tender. Remove from the oven and leave to rest for 15 minutes before serving.

BEETROOT
& EGG SOUP

ROCKY ROAD
CHOCOLATE MUFFINS

MAKES: 12　　　PREP TIME: 15 MINS　　　COOK TIME: 20 MINS

INGREDIENTS

oil or melted butter, for greasing (if using)

225 g/8 oz plain flour

55 g/2 oz cocoa powder

1 tbsp baking powder

pinch of salt

115 g/4 oz caster sugar

100 g/3½ oz white chocolate chips

50 g/1¾ oz white mini marshmallows, cut in half

2 eggs

250 ml/9 fl oz milk

85 g/3 oz butter, melted and cooled

1. Preheat the oven to 200°C/400°F/Gas Mark 6. Grease a 12-cup muffin tin or line with 12 paper cases. Sift together the flour, cocoa powder, baking powder and salt into a large bowl. Stir in the sugar, chocolate chips and marshmallows.

2. Lightly beat the eggs in a large bowl then beat in the milk and butter. Make a well in the centre of the dry ingredients and pour in the beaten liquid ingredients. Gently stir until just combined; do not over-mix.

3. Spoon the mixture into the prepared muffin tin. Bake in the preheated oven for about 20 minutes until risen and firm to the touch.

4. Leave the muffins in the tin for 5 minutes then serve warm or transfer to a wire rack and leave to cool.

DRIED FRUIT & SUNFLOWER SEED COOKIES

MAKES: 18   PREP TIME: 15 MINS   COOK TIME: 15 MINS

INGREDIENTS

85 g/3 oz unsalted butter, softened, plus extra for greasing

85 g/3 oz light muscovado sugar

1 egg, beaten

225 g/8 oz plain flour

½ tsp freshly grated nutmeg

55 g/2 oz sultanas

30 g/1 oz sunflower seeds

demerara sugar, for sprinkling

1. Preheat the oven to 200°C/400°F/Gas Mark 6. Lightly grease a large baking sheet.

2. Put the butter and muscovado sugar into a mixing bowl or food processor and beat together until soft and fluffy. Add the egg and beat thoroughly, then stir in the flour, nutmeg, sultanas and sunflower seeds, mixing evenly to a fairly soft dough.

3. Break off small pieces of the dough and use your hands to roll them into walnut-sized balls. Arrange the balls on the prepared baking sheet and press to flatten slightly.

4. Sprinkle the cookies with a little demerara sugar and bake in the preheated oven for 12–15 minutes, or until golden brown. Transfer to a wire rack to cool.

APPLE & BLACKBERRY WAFFLES

SERVES: **4**   PREP TIME: **10 MINS**   COOK TIME: **ABOUT 10 MINS**

INGREDIENTS

150 g/5½ oz plain white flour

1½ tsp baking powder

pinch of salt

250 ml/9 fl oz milk

1 large egg

2 tbsp sunflower oil, plus extra for brushing

2 crisp eating apples, grated

200 g/7 oz blackberries

maple syrup, for drizzling

1. Preheat a waffle maker to high. Sift together the flour, baking powder and salt into a mixing bowl and make a well in the centre.

2. Add the milk and egg, then whisk to a smooth, bubbly batter. Add the oil and apple and beat well to mix.

3. Brush the waffle maker with a little oil, add a ladleful of batter and cook until puffed and golden. You will need to do this in batches, keeping the cooked waffles warm while you cook the remaining batter.

4. Serve the waffles hot in stacks of two, topped with blackberries and a drizzle of maple syrup.

FRIED CHICKEN WINGS

SERVES: 4   PREP TIME: 20 MINS   COOK TIME: 25 MINS

INGREDIENTS

12 chicken wings

1 egg

60 ml/4 tbsp milk

4 heaped tbsp plain flour

1 tsp paprika

225 g/8 oz breadcrumbs

55 g/2 oz butter

salt and pepper

1. Preheat the oven to 220°C/425°F/Gas Mark 7. Separate the chicken wings into three pieces each. Discard the bony tip. Beat the egg with the milk in a shallow dish. Combine the flour, paprika, and salt and pepper to taste in a separate shallow dish. Place the breadcrumbs in another shallow dish.

2. Dip the chicken pieces into the egg to coat well, then drain and roll in the seasoned flour. Remove, shaking off any excess, then roll the chicken in the breadcrumbs, gently pressing them onto the surface and shaking off any excess.

3. Put the butter in a shallow roasting tin large enough to hold all the chicken pieces in a single layer. Place the tin in the preheated oven and melt the butter. Remove from the oven and arrange the chicken, skin-side down, in the tin. Return to the oven and bake for 10 minutes. Turn and bake for a further 10 minutes, or until the chicken is tender and the juices run clear when a skewer is inserted into the thickest part of the meat.

4. Remove the chicken from the tin. Serve hot or at room temperature.

HUSH PUPPIES

MAKES: 30–35   PREP TIME: 20 MINS   COOK TIME: ABOUT 15 MINS

INGREDIENTS

280 g/10 oz polenta

70 g/2½ oz plain flour, sifted

1 small onion, finely chopped

1 tbsp caster sugar

2 tsp baking powder

½ tsp salt

175 ml/6 fl oz milk

1 egg, beaten

corn oil, for deep-frying

1. Stir together the polenta, flour, onion, sugar, baking powder and salt in a bowl and make a well in the centre.

2. Beat together the milk and egg in a jug, then pour into the dry ingredients and stir until a thick batter forms.

3. Heat enough oil for deep-frying in a large saucepan or deep-fryer to 180°C/350°F, checking the temperature with a thermometer.

4. Drop in as many teaspoonfuls of the batter as will fit without overcrowding the frying pan and cook, stirring constantly, until the hush puppies puff up and turn golden.

5. Remove from the oil with a slotted spoon and drain on kitchen paper. Reheat the oil, if necessary, and cook the remaining batter. Serve hot.

BANGERS & MASH

SERVES: 4   PREP TIME: 20 MINS   COOK TIME: 1 HR 20 MINS

INGREDIENTS

1 tbsp olive oil

8 good-quality sausages

ONION GRAVY

3 onions, halved and thinly sliced

70 g/2½ oz butter

125 ml/4 fl oz Marsala or port

125 ml/4 fl oz vegetable stock

salt and pepper

MASH

900 g/2 lb floury potatoes, such as King Edward, Maris Piper or Desirée, peeled and cut into chunks

55 g/2 oz butter

3 tbsp hot milk

2 tbsp chopped fresh parsley

1. Place a frying pan over a low heat with the oil and add the sausages. (Alternatively, you may wish to grill the sausages.) Cover the pan and cook for 25–30 minutes, turning the sausages from time to time, until browned all over.

2. Meanwhile, prepare the onion gravy by placing the onions in a frying pan with the butter and frying over a low heat until soft, stirring constantly. Continue to cook for around 30 minutes, or until the onions are brown and have started to caramelize.

3. Pour in the Marsala and stock and continue to bubble away until the onion gravy is really thick. Season to taste with salt and pepper.

4. To make the mash, bring a large saucepan of lightly salted water to the boil. Add the potatoes, bring back to the boil and cook for 15–20 minutes. Drain well and mash with a potato masher until smooth. Season to taste with salt and pepper. Add the butter, milk and parsley and stir well.

5. Serve the sausages with the mash, and the onion gravy spooned over the top.

09 SEPTEMBER

POTATO GNOCCHI

SERVES: 4   PREP TIME: 35 MINS   COOK TIME: 40 MINS

INGREDIENTS

450 g/1 lb floury potatoes

55 g/2 oz freshly grated Parmesan cheese

1 egg, beaten

200 g/7 oz plain flour, plus extra for dusting

WALNUT PESTO

40 g/1½ oz fresh flat-leaf parsley

2 tbsp capers, rinsed

2 garlic cloves

175 ml/6 fl oz extra virgin olive oil

70 g/2½ oz walnut halves

40 g/1½ oz freshly grated Parmesan cheese

salt and pepper

1. Boil the potatoes in their skins in a large saucepan of lightly salted water for 30–35 minutes, until tender. Drain well and leave to cool slightly.

2. Meanwhile, to make the walnut pesto, chop the parsley, capers and garlic, then put in a mortar with the oil, walnuts and salt and pepper to taste. Pound with a pestle to a coarse paste. Add the Parmesan cheese.

3. Peel the skins off the potatoes and pass the flesh through a sieve into a bowl. While still hot, season well with salt and pepper and add the Parmesan cheese. Beat in the egg and sift in the flour. Lightly mix together, then turn out onto a lightly floured work surface. Knead lightly until the mixture becomes a smooth dough.

4. Roll the dough out with your hands into a long log. Cut into 2.5-cm/ 1-inch pieces and gently press with a fork to give the traditional ridged effect. Transfer to a floured baking sheet and cover with a clean tea towel.

5. Bring a large saucepan of lightly salted water to the boil. Carefully add the gnocchi, in small batches, return to the boil and cook for 2–3 minutes, or until they rise to the surface. Remove with a slotted spoon and transfer to a warmed serving dish while you cook the remaining gnocchi.

6. Serve the gnocchi in serving bowls with a good spoonful of the walnut pesto on top.

10 SEPTEMBER

CHEESE & COURGETTE CASSEROLE

SERVES: 4   PREP TIME: 20 MINS   COOK TIME: ABOUT 10 MINS

INGREDIENTS

16 courgettes (about 500 g/1 lb 2 oz total weight)

55 g/2 oz butter, plus extra for greasing

40 g/1½ oz plain white flour

600 ml/1 pint milk

1 tsp Dijon mustard

115 g/4 oz mature Cheddar cheese, grated

8 fairly thin slices lean smoked or unsmoked cooked ham

40 g/1½ oz fresh white or wholemeal breadcrumbs

salt and pepper

snipped fresh chives or parsley, to garnish

1. Lightly grease a shallow ovenproof dish and set aside. Cook the courgettes in a saucepan of boiling water for 4–5 minutes or until tender. Drain well, set aside and keep warm.

2. Meanwhile, melt 40 g/1½ oz of the butter in a separate saucepan, then stir in the flour and cook gently for 1 minute, stirring. Remove the pan from the heat and gradually whisk in the milk. Return to the heat and bring gently to the boil, stirring continuously, until the sauce thickens. Simmer for 2–3 minutes, stirring. Remove the pan from the heat and stir in the mustard and 85 g/3 oz of the cheese. Season to taste with salt and pepper.

3. Preheat the grill to medium–high. Cut each slice of ham in half crossways, then wrap a half slice of ham around each courgette. Place the ham-wrapped courgettes in a single layer in the prepared dish and pour the cheese sauce evenly over the top to cover.

4. Mix together the remaining cheese and the breadcrumbs and sprinkle evenly over the cheese sauce. Dot with the remaining butter, then place under the grill for a few minutes until lightly browned and bubbling. Garnish with snipped fresh chives and serve.

POTATO
GNOCCHI

11 SEPTEMBER

CHICKEN FAJITAS

SERVES: 4   PREP TIME: 20 MINS PLUS 2–3 HRS CHILLING TIME   COOK TIME: ABOUT 10 MINS

INGREDIENTS

3 tbsp olive oil, plus extra for drizzling

3 tbsp maple syrup or honey

1 tbsp red wine vinegar

2 garlic cloves, crushed

2 tsp dried oregano

1–2 tsp dried red pepper flakes

4 skinless, boneless chicken breasts

2 red peppers, deseeded and cut into 2.5-cm/1-inch strips

8 tortillas, warmed

salt and pepper

1. Place the oil, maple syrup, vinegar, garlic, oregano, pepper flakes and salt and pepper to taste in a large, shallow dish or bowl and mix together.

2. Slice the chicken across the grain into 2.5-cm/1-inch thick slices. Toss in the marinade until well coated. Cover and chill in the refrigerator for 2–3 hours, turning occasionally.

3. Heat a griddle pan until hot. Lift the chicken slices from the marinade with a slotted spoon, lay on the griddle pan and cook over a medium–high heat for 3–4 minutes on each side, or until cooked through. Remove the chicken to a warmed serving plate and keep warm. Add the peppers, skin-side down, to the griddle pan and cook for 2 minutes on each side. Transfer to the serving plate. Serve with the warmed tortillas to be used as wraps.

12 SEPTEMBER

PAD THAI

SERVES: 4–6   PREP TIME: 15 MINS   COOK TIME: 10 MINS

INGREDIENTS

225 g/8 oz thick rice noodles

2 tbsp vegetable or groundnut oil

2 garlic cloves, chopped

2 fresh red chillies, deseeded and chopped

175 g/6 oz pork fillet, thinly sliced

115 g/4 oz raw prawns, peeled, deveined and chopped

8 fresh Chinese chives, snipped

2 tbsp Thai fish sauce

juice of 1 lime

2 tsp palm sugar or light brown sugar

2 eggs, beaten

115 g/4 oz fresh beansprouts

4 tbsp chopped fresh coriander

115 g/4 oz unsalted peanuts, chopped

1. Soak the noodles in enough lukewarm water to cover for 15 minutes, or cook according to the instructions on the packet, until soft. Drain well and set aside.

2. Heat a wok over a medium–high heat, then add the oil. Stir-fry the garlic, chillies and pork for 2–3 minutes. Add the prawns and stir-fry for a further 2–3 minutes.

3. Add the chives and noodles, then cover and cook for 1–2 minutes. Add the fish sauce, lime juice, sugar and eggs. Cook, stirring and tossing constantly to mix in the eggs.

4. Stir in the beansprouts, coriander and peanuts and mix well, then transfer to serving dishes. Serve.

CHICKEN
FAJITAS

SPICY FRIED EGGS

SERVES: 2　　**PREP TIME: 10 MINS**　　**COOK TIME: 20 MINS**

INGREDIENTS

2 tbsp olive oil

1 large onion, finely chopped

2 green or red peppers, deseeded and roughly chopped

1 garlic clove, finely chopped

½ tsp dried chilli flakes

4 plum tomatoes, peeled and roughly chopped

2 eggs

salt and pepper

1. Heat the oil in a large non-stick frying pan. Add the onion and cook until golden. Add the peppers, garlic and chilli flakes and cook until the peppers are soft.

2. Stir in the tomatoes and season to taste with salt and pepper. Place over a low heat and simmer for 10 minutes.

3. Using the back of a spoon, make two depressions in the mixture in the frying pan. Break the eggs into the depressions, season if liked and cover and cook for 3–4 minutes until the eggs are set. Serve.

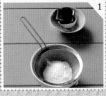

PEANUT BUTTER & JAM WAFFLE SANDWICH

SERVES: 4   **PREP TIME: 10 MINS**   **COOK TIME: 10 MINS**

INGREDIENTS

150 g/5½ oz plain flour

1½ tsp baking powder

1 tbsp caster sugar

pinch of salt

250 ml/9 fl oz milk

1 large egg

2 tbsp melted butter

icing sugar, for dusting

FILLING

4 tbsp crunchy peanut butter

4 tbsp strawberry jam or raspberry jam

1. Sift the flour, baking powder, sugar and salt into a bowl. Add the milk, egg and butter and whisk to a smooth batter. Leave to stand for 5 minutes.

2. Preheat a waffle maker to high. Pour the batter into the waffle maker and cook until golden brown. Repeat this process using the remaining batter, while keeping the cooked waffles warm.

3. Spread half the waffles with peanut butter and the remainder with jam. Sandwich the two together with the peanut butter and jam inside.

4. Dust with icing sugar and serve.

15 SEPTEMBER

FIGS WITH HONEY & ALMONDS

SERVES: 4   PREP TIME: 5 MINS   COOK TIME: NO COOKING

INGREDIENTS

8 large ripe figs

4 tbsp Greek-style yogurt or crème fraîche

4 tbsp clear honey

40 g/1½ oz toasted flaked almonds

ground cinnamon, for sprinkling

1. Cut the figs crossways almost to the base, then push the sides to open out. Divide between four serving plates.

2. Spoon the yogurt into the figs and drizzle the honey over.

3. Scatter the almonds on top and sprinkle lightly with cinnamon to serve.

16 SEPTEMBER

HAZELNUT SHORTBREAD FINGERS

MAKES: 12   PREP TIME: 15 MINS   COOK TIME: 15 MINS

INGREDIENTS

125 g/4½ oz unsalted butter, softened, plus extra for greasing

100 g/3½ oz caster sugar, plus extra for sprinkling

1 egg, beaten

200 g/7 oz plain flour

55 g/2 oz toasted hazelnuts, finely chopped

1. Preheat the oven to 180°C/350°F/Gas Mark 4. Lightly grease a 22-cm/8½-inch shallow square cake tin.

2. Put the butter and sugar into a mixing bowl and cream together with a hand mixer until smooth. Gradually add the egg, beating to mix evenly. Add the flour and hazelnuts and mix well, kneading lightly with your hands to a soft dough.

3. Press the dough into the prepared tin, pressing with your knuckles to spread evenly.

4. Bake in the preheated oven for about 15 minutes, or until firm and pale golden brown.

5. Cut the shortbread into 12 fingers with a sharp knife and sprinkle with sugar. Leave to cool in the tin until firm before removing.

SALAMI PASTA SALAD

SERVES: 4–6   PREP TIME: 25 MINS   COOK TIME: 10 MINS

INGREDIENTS

350 g/12 oz dried penne

2 tbsp pesto sauce

3 tbsp olive oil

1 orange pepper, deseeded and diced

1 yellow pepper, deseeded and diced

1 red onion, finely diced

85 g/3 oz stoned black olives

115 g/4 oz cherry tomatoes, halved

175 g/6 oz piece Milano salami, cut into small chunks

125 g/4½ oz mozzarella cheese, torn into small pieces

salt and pepper

fresh basil sprigs, to garnish

1. Bring a large, heavy-based saucepan of lightly salted water to the boil. Add the penne, bring back to the boil and cook for 8–10 minutes, or until just tender but still firm to the bite.

2. Drain the pasta well and transfer to a bowl. Mix together the pesto sauce and olive oil and stir into the hot pasta. Leave to cool, stirring occasionally.

3. Add the peppers, onion, olives, tomatoes, salami and mozzarella cheese to the pasta and toss well to mix. Season to taste with salt and pepper. Garnish with basil sprigs and serve.

SAUSAGE CIDER CASSEROLE

SERVES: 4   PREP TIME: 10 MINS   COOK TIME: 40–45 MINS

INGREDIENTS

1 tbsp sunflower oil

8 pork sausages

1 onion, sliced

1 large green pepper, deseeded and sliced

150 ml/5 fl oz dry cider

400 g/14 oz canned plum tomatoes

250 g/9 oz fresh or frozen sweetcorn kernels

2 tbsp Worcestershire sauce

1 tsp dried thyme

salt and pepper

crusty bread, to serve

1. Heat the oil in a large saucepan or flameproof casserole, add the sausages and fry, turning occasionally, for 6–8 minutes until golden. Remove from the pan and keep warm.

2. Add the onion and green pepper to the pan and stir-fry over a medium heat for 3–4 minutes until soft.

3. Return the sausages to the pan and stir in the cider. Bring to the boil, then add the tomatoes, sweetcorn, Worcestershire sauce and thyme. Season well with salt and pepper.

4. Bring to the boil, then reduce the heat, cover and simmer gently for 30–35 minutes. Serve hot with crusty bread.

EASY APPLE CAKE

SERVES: 8   PREP TIME: 15 MINS   COOK TIME: 50 MINS

INGREDIENTS

400 g/14 oz eating apples, peeled, cored and diced

2 tbsp apple juice

140 g/5 oz light muscovado sugar

125 g/4½ oz unsalted butter, at room temperature, plus extra for greasing

2 large eggs, beaten

225 g/8 oz self-raising flour

1½ tsp mixed spice

40 g/1½ oz hazelnuts, peeled and finely chopped

1. Preheat the oven to 190°C/375°F/Gas Mark 5. Grease a 20-cm/8-inch deep, round loose-based cake tin and base-line with greaseproof paper. Sprinkle the apples with the apple juice.

2. Reserve 1 tablespoon of the sugar, then put the sugar and butter into a mixing bowl and beat until pale and fluffy. Gradually add the eggs, beating thoroughly after each addition. Sift together the flour and spice into the mixture and evenly fold in with a metal spoon.

3. Stir the apples and juice into the mixture, then spoon into the prepared tin and level the surface with a palette knife.

4. Mix the hazelnuts with the reserved sugar and sprinkle over the surface of the cake.

5. Bake in the preheated oven for 45–50 minutes until firm and golden brown. Leave to cool for 10 minutes in the tin, then turn out onto a wire rack to cool completely.

PEAR & PECAN SPONGE CAKE

SERVES: 8 | PREP TIME: **20 MINS** | COOK TIME: **45 MINS**

INGREDIENTS

SPONGE

1 large egg

100 g/3½ oz light muscovado sugar

3 tbsp golden syrup

3 tbsp milk

3 tbsp sunflower oil

125 g/4½ oz self-raising flour

1 tsp ground ginger

1 tsp ground cinnamon

Greek-style yogurt or custard, to serve

TOPPING

15 g/½ oz butter

1 tbsp golden syrup

4 ripe pears

4 pecan nuts, halved

1. Preheat the oven to 180°C/350°F/Gas Mark 4. To make the topping, put the butter and golden syrup into a saucepan and heat gently, stirring, until melted. Pour into a 22-cm/8½-inch deep round cake tin, spreading to cover the base.

2. Thinly peel the pears, cut in half lengthways and use a teaspoon to scoop out the cores.

3. Place a pecan half in the cavity of each pear half and arrange cut side down in the tin.

4. To make the sponge, put the egg, sugar, golden syrup, milk and oil into a mixing bowl and beat together. Sift together the flour, ginger and cinnamon and stir into the egg mixture. Beat well to make a smooth batter.

5. Pour the batter over the pears. Bake in the preheated oven for 35–40 minutes, or until risen and springy to the touch.

6. Leave to cool in the tin for 5 minutes, then invert onto a serving plate and serve with yogurt.

21 SEPTEMBER

APPLE PANCAKES WITH MAPLE SYRUP

MAKES: 18   PREP TIME: 15 MINS   COOK TIME: 10 MINS

INGREDIENTS

200 g/7 oz self-raising flour

100 g/3½ oz caster sugar

1 tsp ground cinnamon

1 egg

200 ml/7 fl oz milk

2 apples, peeled and grated

1 tsp butter

3 tbsp maple syrup

1. Mix together the flour, sugar and cinnamon in a bowl and make a well in the centre. Beat together the egg and the milk and pour into the well. Using a wooden spoon, gently incorporate the dry ingredients into the liquid until well combined, then stir in the grated apple.

2. Gently heat the butter in a large non-stick frying pan. Add tablespoons of the pancake mixture to form small circles. Cook each pancake for about 1 minute, until it starts to bubble lightly on the top and looks set, then flip it over and cook the other side for 30 seconds, or until cooked through. The pancakes should be golden brown. Remove from the pan and repeat the process until all of the pancake batter has been used up. Serve with the maple syrup drizzled over the pancakes.

22 SEPTEMBER

BRAZIL NUT BRITTLE

MAKES: 20 PIECES   PREP TIME: 10 MINS PLUS COOLING TIME   COOK TIME: 10 MINS

INGREDIENTS

sunflower oil, for brushing

350 g/12 oz plain chocolate, broken into pieces

100 g/3½ oz shelled Brazil nuts, chopped

175 g/6 oz white chocolate, roughly chopped

175 g/6 oz fudge, roughly chopped

1. Brush the bottom and sides of a baking tin with oil.

2. Melt half the plain chocolate in a medium-sized saucepan over a low heat and spread in the prepared tin.

3. Sprinkle with the chopped Brazil nuts, white chocolate and fudge. Melt the remaining plain chocolate pieces and pour over the top.

4. Leave in a cool place to set, then break up into jagged pieces using the tip of a strong knife.

MINI MACAROONS

MAKES: 30 **PREP TIME: 25 MINS PLUS 30 MINS STANDING TIME** **COOK TIME: 15 MINS**

INGREDIENTS

75 g/2¾ oz ground almonds

115 g/4 oz icing sugar

2 large egg whites

50 g/1¾ oz caster sugar

½ tsp vanilla extract

selection of sugar sprinkles,
to decorate

BUTTERCREAM

85 g/3 oz unsalted butter, softened

1 tsp vanilla extract

175 g/6 oz icing sugar, sifted

edible pink, yellow and green food
colouring pastes or liquids

1. Place the ground almonds and icing sugar in a food processor and process for 15 seconds. Sift the mixture into a bowl. Line two baking sheets with greaseproof paper.

2. Place the egg whites in a large bowl and whisk until soft peaks form. Gradually whisk in the caster sugar to make a firm, glossy meringue. Whisk in the vanilla extract.

3. Using a spatula, fold the almond mixture into the meringue one third at a time. When all the dry ingredients are thoroughly incorporated, continue to cut and fold the mixture until it forms a shiny batter with a thick, ribbon-like consistency.

4. Pour the mixture into a piping bag fitted with a 1-cm/½-inch plain nozzle. Pipe 60 tiny rounds onto the prepared baking sheets. Tap the baking sheets firmly onto a work surface to remove air bubbles. Top with the sprinkles. Leave at room temperature for 30 minutes. Meanwhile, preheat the oven to 160°C/325°F/Gas Mark 3.

5. Bake in the preheated oven for 10–15 minutes. Cool for 10 minutes, then carefully peel the macaroons off the greaseproof paper. Leave to cool completely.

6. To make the buttercream, beat the butter and vanilla extract in a bowl until pale and fluffy. Gradually beat in the icing sugar until smooth and creamy. Divide the buttercream into three bowls and colour each with pink, yellow or green food colouring. Use to sandwich pairs of macaroons together.

BAKED BEANS WITH CORN

SERVES: 4–6   PREP TIME: 20 MINS   COOK TIME: 1 HR 35 MINS

INGREDIENTS

6 tbsp olive oil or butter

750 g/1 lb 10 oz onions, finely sliced

3–4 garlic cloves, finely chopped

1 tsp cumin seeds

1 tsp fresh or dried oregano leaves

500 g/1 lb 2 oz canned chopped tomatoes

500 g/1 lb 2 oz pumpkin, peeled, deseeded and cut into small dice

750 g/1 lb 10 oz cooked pinto beans

2 tbsp green olives, stoned and chopped

2 tbsp raisins

1 tbsp icing sugar

1 tsp dried chilli flakes

TOPPING

1.5 litres/2¾ pints fresh sweetcorn

375 ml/13 fl oz full-fat milk

1 egg, beaten

1. Heat 4 tablespoons of the oil in a heavy-based saucepan, add the onions and garlic and cook over a very low heat, stirring occasionally, for 20–30 minutes, or until the onions are soft and golden but not browned.

2. Add the cumin seeds, oregano and tomatoes and heat until bubbling, mashing the tomatoes down with a potato masher, for 10 minutes, or until you have a thick, sticky sauce.

3. Add the pumpkin and heat until bubbling. Reduce the heat to low, cover and cook for a further 10–15 minutes, or until the pumpkin is softened but not collapsed. Stir in the beans, olives and raisins. Reheat gently and simmer for 5 minutes to marry the flavours.

4. Preheat the oven to 180°C/350°F/Gas Mark 4. To make the topping, put the sweetcorn in a food processor with the milk and blend to a purée. Transfer to a saucepan and cook, stirring constantly, for 5 minutes, or until the mixture has thickened slightly. Remove from the heat and leave to cool to room temperature. Stir in the egg.

5. Spread the bean mixture in a baking dish and top with a thick layer of the sweetcorn mixture – the bean base and the topping should be of roughly equal thickness. Drizzle with the remaining oil or dot small pieces of butter over the surface and sprinkle with the sugar and chilli flakes.

6. Bake in the preheated oven for 30 minutes, or until browned and bubbling. Serve hot.

LASAGNE

SERVES: 4   PREP TIME: 30 MINS   COOK TIME: 1 HR 15 MINS

INGREDIENTS

2 tbsp olive oil

55 g/2 oz pancetta, chopped

1 onion, chopped

1 garlic clove, finely chopped

225 g/8 oz fresh beef mince

2 celery sticks, chopped

2 carrots, chopped

pinch of sugar

½ tsp dried oregano

400 g/14 oz canned chopped tomatoes

2 tsp Dijon mustard

140 g/5 oz Cheddar cheese, grated

300 ml/10 fl oz white sauce

225 g/8 oz no pre-cook lasagne sheets

115 g/4 oz Parmesan cheese, plus extra for sprinkling

1. Preheat the oven to 190°C/375°F/Gas Mark 5. Heat the oil in a large heavy-based saucepan. Add the pancetta and cook over a medium heat, stirring occasionally, for 3 minutes, or until the fat begins to run. Add the onion and garlic and cook, stirring occasionally, for 5 minutes, or until softened.

2. Add the beef and cook, breaking it up with a wooden spoon, until browned all over. Stir in the celery and carrots and cook for 5 minutes. Add the sugar, oregano and tomatoes and their can juices. Bring to the boil, reduce the heat and simmer for 30 minutes.

3. Meanwhile, to make the cheese sauce, stir the mustard and Cheddar cheese into the white sauce.

4. In a large, rectangular ovenproof dish, make alternate layers of meat sauce, lasagne sheets and Parmesan cheese. Pour the cheese sauce over the layers, covering them completely, and sprinkle with Parmesan cheese. Bake in the preheated oven for 30 minutes, or until golden brown and bubbling. Serve immediately.

BAKED BEANS
WITH CORN

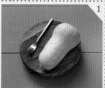

ROAST BUTTERNUT SQUASH

SERVES: 4   **PREP TIME: 40 MINS**   **COOK TIME: 1 HR 10 MINS**

INGREDIENTS

1 butternut squash, about 450 g/1 lb

1 onion, chopped

2–3 garlic cloves, crushed

4 small tomatoes, chopped

85 g/3 oz chestnut mushrooms, chopped

85 g/3 oz canned butter beans, drained, rinsed and roughly chopped

1 courgette, about 115 g/ 4 oz, trimmed and grated

1 tbsp chopped fresh oregano, plus extra to garnish

2 tbsp tomato purée

300 ml/10 fl oz water

4 spring onions, trimmed and chopped

1 tbsp Worcestershire sauce, or to taste

pepper

1. Preheat the oven to 190°C/375°F/Gas Mark 5. Prick the squash all over with a metal skewer then roast for 40 minutes, or until tender. Remove from the oven and leave to rest until cool enough to handle.

2. Cut the squash in half, scoop out and discard the seeds, then scoop out some of the flesh, making hollows in both halves. Chop the scooped-out flesh and put in a bowl. Place the two squash halves side by side in a large roasting tin.

3. Add the onion, garlic, tomatoes and mushrooms to the squash flesh in the bowl. Add the butter beans, courgette, oregano and pepper to taste and mix well. Spoon the filling into the two halves of the squash, packing it down as firmly as possible.

4. Mix the tomato purée with the water, spring onions and Worcestershire sauce in a small bowl and pour around the squash.

5. Cover loosely with a large sheet of foil and bake for 30 minutes, or until piping hot. Serve in bowls, garnished with some chopped oregano.

CHICKEN & WILD MUSHROOM CANNELLONI

SERVES: 4   **PREP TIME: 20 MINS**   **COOK TIME: 1 HR 50 MINS**

INGREDIENTS

butter, for greasing

2 tbsp olive oil

2 garlic cloves, crushed

1 large onion, finely chopped

225 g/8 oz wild mushrooms, sliced

350 g/12 oz fresh chicken mince

115 g/4 oz prosciutto, diced

150 ml/5 fl oz Marsala wine

200 g/7 oz canned chopped tomatoes

1 tbsp shredded fresh basil leaves

2 tbsp tomato purée

10–12 dried cannelloni tubes

1 x quantity Béchamel sauce

85 g/3 oz freshly grated Parmesan cheese

salt and pepper

1. Preheat the oven to 190°C/375°F/Gas Mark 5. Lightly grease a large ovenproof dish. Heat the olive oil in a heavy-based frying pan. Add the garlic, onion and mushrooms and cook over a low heat, stirring frequently, for 8–10 minutes. Add the chicken mince and prosciutto and cook, stirring frequently, for 12 minutes, or until browned all over. Stir in the Marsala, tomatoes and their can juices, basil and tomato purée and cook for 4 minutes. Season to taste with salt and pepper, then cover and simmer for 30 minutes. Uncover, stir and simmer for 15 minutes.

2. Bring a large, heavy-based saucepan of lightly salted water to the boil. Add the cannelloni, bring back to the boil and cook for 8–10 minutes, or until just tender but still firm to the bite. Using a slotted spoon, transfer to a plate and pat dry.

3. Using a teaspoon, fill the cannelloni tubes with the chicken and mushroom mixture. Transfer them to the dish. Pour the Béchamel sauce over them to cover completely and sprinkle with the grated Parmesan cheese.

4. Bake in the preheated oven for 30 minutes, or until golden brown and bubbling. Serve immediately.

MEATBALL SANDWICH

SERVES: 4 | PREP TIME: 20 MINS | COOK TIME: 15–20 MINS

INGREDIENTS

450 g/1 lb lean minced beef

1 small onion, grated

2 garlic cloves, crushed

25 g/1 oz fine white breadcrumbs

1 tsp hot chilli sauce

wholemeal flour, for dusting

groundnut oil, for shallow frying

salt and pepper

4 sub rolls or small baguettes, to serve

FILLING

1 tbsp olive oil

1 small onion, sliced

4 tbsp mayonnaise

55 g/2 oz sliced jalapeños (from a jar)

2 tbsp squeezy mustard

1. Place the minced beef, onion, garlic, breadcrumbs and chilli sauce into a bowl. Season to taste with salt and pepper and mix thoroughly. Shape the mixture into 20 small equal-sized balls using floured hands. Cover and chill for 10 minutes or until required.

2. Heat a shallow depth of oil in a wok or heavy frying pan until very hot, then fry the meatballs in batches for 6–8 minutes, turning often, until golden brown and firm. Drain on kitchen paper and keep hot.

3. To make the filling, heat the olive oil in a clean pan and fry the onion over a moderate heat, stirring occasionally, until soft and golden brown.

4. Split the rolls lengthwise and spread with mayonnaise. Arrange the onion, meatballs and jalapeños over the bottom half, squeeze the mustard over and top with the other half. Serve.

THE REUBEN SANDWICH

SERVES: 2 | PREP TIME: 25 MINS | COOK TIME: 5 MINS

INGREDIENTS

2 tbsp margarine, softened

4 slices rye bread

115–175 g/4–6 oz cooked salt beef

200 g/7 oz bottled sauerkraut, drained

115 g/4 oz Gruyère cheese, grated

vegetable oil, for frying

2 tbsp pickled gherkins, chopped, to serve

DRESSING

2 tbsp mayonnaise

2 tbsp ketchup or chilli sauce

150 g/5½ oz green pepper, deseeded and finely chopped

2 tbsp pimiento, finely chopped

1. To make the dressing, mix together all the dressing ingredients in a bowl until well blended.

2. Spread the margarine on one side of each slice of bread and lay margarine-side down. Spread the other sides with 1 tablespoon of the dressing.

3. Divide the salt beef between two slices, tucking in the sides to fit. Divide the sauerkraut and make an even layer on top of the salt beef, before covering with grated cheese. Top with the remaining slices of bread, margarine-side facing up, and press firmly to compress the layers.

4. Heat the oil in a non-stick griddle pan over a medium–high heat and carefully slide the sandwiches into the pan. Using a fish slice, press down on the tops of the sandwiches. Cook for 3 minutes, or until the undersides are crisp and golden. Carefully turn the sandwiches, press down again, and cook for a further 2 minutes, or until golden, the cheese is melted and the salt beef is hot.

5. Remove from the heat and transfer the sandwiches to a cutting board. Cut in half and serve with pickled gherkins.

STEAK & CHIPS

SERVES: 4   **PREP TIME: 20 MINS**   **COOK TIME: 1 HR**

INGREDIENTS

4 sirloin steaks, about 225 g/8 oz each

4 tsp Tabasco sauce

salt and pepper

CHIPS

450 g/1 lb potatoes, peeled

2 tbsp sunflower oil

WATERCRESS BUTTER

1 bunch watercress

85 g/3 oz unsalted butter, softened

1. To make the chips, preheat the oven to 200°C/400°F/Gas Mark 6. Cut the potatoes into thick, even-sized chips. Rinse them under cold running water and then dry well on a clean tea towel. Place in a bowl, add the oil and toss together until coated.

2. Spread the chips on a baking sheet and cook in the preheated oven for 40–45 minutes, turning once, until golden.

3. To make the watercress butter, finely chop enough watercress to fill 4 tablespoons. Place the butter in a small bowl and beat in the chopped watercress with a fork until fully incorporated. Cover with clingfilm and leave to chill in the refrigerator until required.

4. Preheat a griddle pan to high. Sprinkle each steak with 1 teaspoon of the Tabasco sauce, rubbing it in well. Season to taste with salt and pepper.

5. Cook the steaks in the preheated pan for 2½ minutes each side for rare, 4 minutes each side for medium and 6 minutes each side for well done. Transfer to serving plates and serve topped with the watercress butter and accompanied by the chips.

OCTOBER

SOUFFLÉ JACKET POTATOES

SERVES: 4 | PREP TIME: 10 MINS | COOK TIME: 1 HR 35 MINS

INGREDIENTS

4 large baking potatoes, about 400 g/14 oz each

oil, for brushing

2 tbsp milk or single cream

2 eggs, separated

100 g/3½ oz Cheddar cheese, grated

15 g/½ oz butter

4 spring onions, finely chopped

salt and pepper

1. Preheat the oven to 200°C/400°F/Gas Mark 6. Place the potatoes on a baking sheet, brush with oil and rub with salt. Bake in the preheated oven for 1–1¼ hours until tender. (Do not turn off the oven.)

2. Cut a slice from the top of the potatoes and scoop out the flesh, leaving about a 5-mm/¼-inch thick shell. Put the flesh into a bowl. Add the milk, egg yolks and half the cheese and mash together.

3. Melt the butter in a small saucepan, add the spring onions and stir-fry for 1–2 minutes until soft. Stir into the potato mixture and season to taste with salt and pepper.

4. Whisk the egg whites in a grease-free bowl until they hold soft peaks. Fold them lightly into the potato mixture, then spoon the mixture back into the shells.

5. Place the filled potatoes on the baking sheet and sprinkle the remaining cheese on top. Bake for 15–20 minutes until golden. Serve.

PORK CHOPS WITH APPLE SAUCE

SERVES: 4   PREP TIME: 20 MINS   COOK TIME: 40 MINS

INGREDIENTS

4 pork rib chops on the bone, each about 3 cm/1¼ inches thick, at room temperature

1½ tbsp sunflower oil or rapeseed oil

salt and pepper

APPLE SAUCE

450 g/1 lb cooking apples, such as Bramley, peeled, cored and diced

4 tbsp caster sugar, plus extra, if needed

finely grated zest of ½ lemon

½ tbsp lemon juice, plus extra, if needed

4 tbsp water

¼ tsp ground cinnamon

knob of butter

1. Preheat the oven to 200°C/400°F/Gas Mark 6.

2. To make the apple sauce, put the apples, sugar, lemon zest, lemon juice and water into a heavy-based saucepan over a high heat and bring to the boil, stirring to dissolve the sugar. Reduce the heat to low, cover and simmer for 15–20 minutes, until the apples are tender and fall apart when you mash them against the side of the pan. Stir in the cinnamon and butter and beat the apples until they are as smooth or chunky as you like. Stir in extra sugar or lemon juice, to taste. Remove the pan from the heat, cover and keep the apple sauce warm.

3. Meanwhile, pat the chops dry and season to taste with salt and pepper. Heat the oil in a large ovenproof frying pan over a medium–high heat. Add the chops and fry for 3 minutes on each side to brown.

4. Transfer the pan to the oven and roast the chops for 7–9 minutes until cooked through and the juices run clear when you cut the chops. Remove the pan from the oven, cover with foil and leave to stand for 3 minutes. Gently reheat the apple sauce, if necessary.

5. Transfer the chops to warmed plates and spoon over the pan juices. Serve accompanied by the apple sauce.

MINI SALMON & BROCCOLI PIES

MAKES: 8   PREP TIME: 35 MINS PLUS 30 MINS CHILLING TIME   COOK TIME: 45–50 MINS

INGREDIENTS

FILLING

125 g/4½ oz broccoli florets

125 g/4½ oz salmon fillet

25 g/1 oz butter

25 g/1 oz plain flour

275 ml/9½ fl oz warm milk

salt and pepper

salad, to serve

PASTRY

225 g/8 oz plain flour, plus extra for dusting

pinch of salt

115 g/4 oz butter

about 3 tbsp iced water

1 egg, lightly beaten with 1 tbsp water

1. Cook the broccoli in lightly salted boiling water for 5–10 minutes, until tender. Drain and leave to cool. Meanwhile, bring a saucepan of lightly salted water to the boil, then reduce the heat to very low. Add the fish and poach, turning once, for 5 minutes, until the flesh flakes easily. Remove from the pan and leave to cool.

2. Melt the butter in a saucepan, add the flour and cook over a low heat, stirring constantly, for 2 minutes. Gradually stir in the warm milk. Bring to the boil, stirring constantly, then simmer, stirring, until thickened and smooth. Season to taste, remove from the heat and leave to cool, stirring occasionally.

3. Meanwhile, make the pastry. Sift the flour and salt into a bowl. Add the butter and cut into the flour. Rub in with your fingertips until the mixture resembles breadcrumbs. Stir in the water and mix to a smooth dough, adding more water if necessary. Shape into a ball, cover and chill for 30 minutes.

4. Remove the skin and flake the flesh of the fish into a bowl. Break up the broccoli florets and add to the bowl. Stir in the white sauce and season to taste. Mix well.

5. Preheat the oven to 200°C/400°F/Gas Mark 6. Roll out the pastry on a lightly floured surface and stamp out 16 rounds with a 10-cm/4-inch cutter. Put 8 rounds into a muffin tin. Add spoonfuls of the salmon mixture without filling the pastry cases completely. Brush the edges of the remaining rounds with water and use to cover the pies, pressing with the tines of a fork to seal.

6. Brush the tops with the beaten egg mixture and bake for 20–25 minutes, until golden brown. Serve with salad.

BAKED SEA BASS

SERVES: 4   **PREP TIME: 20 MINS**   **COOK TIME: 50 MINS**

INGREDIENTS

1.3 kg/3 lb fresh sea bass or
2 x 750 g/1 lb 10 oz sea bass, gutted

2–4 sprigs fresh rosemary

½ lemon, thinly sliced

2 tbsp olive oil, plus extra for brushing

fresh bay leaves, to garnish

lemon wedges, to serve

GARLIC SAUCE

2 tsp coarse sea salt

2 tsp capers

2 garlic cloves, crushed

4 tbsp water

2 fresh bay leaves

1 tsp lemon juice or wine vinegar

2 tbsp olive oil

pepper

1. Preheat the oven to 190°C/375°F/Gas Mark 5. Scrape off the scales from the fish and cut off the sharp fins. Make diagonal cuts along both sides. Wash and dry thoroughly. Place a sprig of rosemary in the cavity of each of the smaller fish with half the lemon slices, or put two sprigs and all the lemon slices in the large fish.

2. Brush a roasting tin with oil then brush the fish with the rest of the oil. Cook in the preheated oven for 30 minutes for the small fish or 45–50 minutes for the large fish, until the thickest part of the fish is opaque.

3. To make the garlic sauce, crush the salt and capers with the garlic in a mortar with a pestle and then work in the water. Alternatively, work in a food processor until smooth.

4. Bruise the bay leaves and remaining sprigs of rosemary and put into a bowl. Add the garlic mixture, lemon juice and oil and pound together until the flavours are released. Season to taste with pepper.

5. Place the fish on a serving dish and, if liked, remove the skin. Spoon some of the sauce over the fish and serve the rest separately. Remove the bruised bay leaves, garnish with fresh bay leaves and serve with lemon wedges. Do not eat the bay leaves.

SOUTHERN-STYLE CHICKEN DRUMSTICKS

SERVES: 4 **PREP TIME: 15 MINS PLUS 1 HR CHILLING TIME** **COOK TIME: 30 MINS**

INGREDIENTS

8 chicken drumsticks

500 ml/18 fl oz milk

200 g/7 oz plain flour

1 tsp garlic salt

¼ tsp cayenne pepper

1 tbsp dried parsley

1 tsp dried thyme

1 large egg, beaten

sunflower oil, for deep-frying

1. Place the drumsticks in a large bowl and pour over the milk. Cover and chill in the refrigerator for 1 hour.

2. Put the chicken and milk into a large saucepan and heat over a medium heat until boiling. Reduce the heat, cover and simmer gently for 20 minutes until the chicken is cooked. Drain well and leave to cool slightly.

3. Mix together the flour, garlic salt, cayenne pepper, parsley and thyme in a shallow bowl. Put the egg into a separate shallow bowl. Dip the chicken drumsticks in the seasoned flour to coat evenly. Dip into the beaten egg, then dip again into the seasoned flour.

4. Heat enough oil for deep-frying in a large saucepan or deep-fryer to 170°C/340°F, checking the temperature with a thermometer. Lower the chicken drumsticks into the oil and fry in batches for 6–8 minutes. Check the chicken is tender and the juices run clear when a skewer is inserted into the thickest part of the meat. Keep the cooked chicken warm while you cook the remaining drumsticks.

5. Remove the chicken with a slotted spoon, drain on absorbent kitchen paper and serve.

LAMB CHOPS IN TOMATO SAUCE

SERVES: 4   PREP TIME: 25 MINS   COOK TIME: 30 MINS

INGREDIENTS

8 lamb chops

25 g/1 oz butter

2 tbsp olive oil

1 onion, finely chopped

2 garlic cloves, finely chopped

1 celery stick, finely chopped

40 g/1½ oz pancetta or bacon, diced

400 g/14 oz canned chopped tomatoes

2 tbsp tomato purée

brown sugar, to taste

2 tbsp chopped fresh basil

1 tbsp red wine vinegar

350 g/12 oz shelled fresh or frozen broad beans, grey skins removed

salt and pepper

1. Season the chops with salt and pepper to taste. Melt the butter with the oil in a large frying pan. Add the chops and cook over a medium heat for 1–1½ minutes on each side, until evenly browned. Remove the chops from the pan and set aside.

2. Add the onion, garlic, celery and pancetta to the pan and cook over a low heat, stirring occasionally, for 5 minutes, until the onion has softened. Stir in the tomatoes, tomato purée, sugar to taste, basil, vinegar and 100 ml/3½ fl oz of water and season to taste with salt and pepper. Increase the heat to medium and bring to the boil, then reduce the heat and simmer, stirring occasionally, for 10 minutes.

3. Return the chops to the pan and add the broad beans. Partially cover and simmer for 10 minutes, until the lamb is tender and cooked through. Transfer to a serving dish and serve.

ROAST VEGETABLES

SERVES: 4–6   PREP TIME: 25 MINS   COOK TIME: 1 HR

INGREDIENTS

3 parsnips, cut into 5-cm/2-inch chunks

4 baby turnips, cut into quarters

3 carrots, cut into 5-cm/2-inch chunks

450 g/1 lb butternut squash, peeled and cut into 5-cm/2-inch chunks

450 g/1 lb sweet potatoes, peeled and cut into 5-cm/2-inch chunks

2 garlic cloves, finely chopped

2 tbsp chopped fresh rosemary

2 tbsp chopped fresh thyme

2 tsp chopped fresh sage

3 tbsp olive oil

salt and pepper

chopped fresh mixed herbs, such as parsley, thyme and mint, to garnish

1. Preheat the oven to 220°C/425°F/Gas Mark 7.

2. Arrange all the vegetables in a single layer in a large roasting tin. Scatter over the garlic and the herbs. Pour over the oil and season well with salt and pepper.

3. Toss all the ingredients together until they are well mixed and coated with the oil (you can leave them to marinate at this stage to allow the flavours to be absorbed).

4. Roast the vegetables at the top of the preheated oven for 50–60 minutes until they are cooked and nicely browned. Turn the vegetables over halfway through the cooking time.

5. Serve with a good handful of fresh herbs scattered on top and a final sprinkling of salt and pepper to taste.

LAMB CHOPS IN
TOMATO SAUCE

08 OCTOBER

MUSHROOM & WALNUT OPEN TART

SERVES: 4　　PREP TIME: 20 MINS　　COOK TIME: 30–40 MINS

INGREDIENTS

1 tbsp olive oil

15 g/½ oz butter

1 red onion, sliced

1 garlic clove, crushed

500 g/1 lb 2 oz closed-cup chestnut mushrooms, sliced

85 g/3 oz walnuts, chopped

2 tbsp chopped fresh flat-leaf parsley, plus extra to garnish

500 g/1 lb 2 oz ready-made shortcrust pastry

plain flour, for dusting

beaten egg, for glazing

salt and pepper

1. Preheat the oven to 200°C/400°F/Gas Mark 6. Heat the oil and butter in a large frying pan, add the onion and stir-fry for 2–3 minutes until soft, but not brown.

2. Add the garlic and mushrooms and cook, stirring, for 3–4 minutes until soft. Cook until any liquid has evaporated, then remove from the heat and stir in the walnuts, parsley, and salt and pepper to taste.

3. Roll out the pastry on a lightly floured work surface to a 35-cm/14-inch round and place on a large baking sheet. Pile the mushroom mixture onto the pastry, leaving a 9-cm/3½-inch border around the edge.

4. Lift the edges of the pastry and tuck up around the filling, leaving an open centre. Brush the pastry with beaten egg to glaze.

5. Bake in the preheated oven for 25–30 minutes until the pastry is golden brown. Serve warm, sprinkled with parsley.

09 OCTOBER

BLUE CHEESE, FIG & WALNUT BREAD

MAKES: 1 LOAF　　PREP TIME: 30 MINS PLUS 30 MINS SOAKING TIME　　COOK TIME: 55 MINS

INGREDIENTS

butter, for greasing

85 g/3 oz dried figs, roughly chopped

4 tbsp Marsala

200 g/7 oz plain flour

1 tbsp baking powder

3 eggs

200 g/7 oz full-fat crème fraîche

175 g/6 oz blue cheese, such as Roquefort or Gorgonzola

75 g/2¾ oz walnuts, roughly chopped

salt and pepper

1. Lightly grease and line the base and sides of a 450-g/1-lb loaf tin with greaseproof paper. Put the figs in a small bowl, pour over the Marsala and leave to soak for 30 minutes or so.

2. Preheat the oven to 180°C/350°F/Gas Mark 4.

3. Sift the flour and baking powder into a large bowl. In a separate bowl, beat together the eggs and crème fraîche until smooth. Stir the egg mixture into the flour until everything is well combined. Season to taste with salt and a good grinding of pepper.

4. Crumble the blue cheese and add 150 g/5½ oz to the batter. Add the figs and the Marsala, then stir in half the walnuts. Turn the mixture into the prepared tin, scatter over the remaining cheese and walnuts and bake in the preheated oven for 40 minutes, or until the loaf is golden brown.

5. Cover the tin loosely with foil and return to the oven for a further 15 minutes, or until a skewer inserted into the centre of the loaf comes out clean.

6. Leave the loaf to cool slightly in the tin, then turn out onto a wire rack to cool completely.

MUSHROOM &
WALNUT OPEN TART

MASHED POTATOES

SERVES: 4 | PREP TIME: 10 MINS | COOK TIME: 25 MINS

INGREDIENTS

900 g/2 lb floury potatoes, such as King Edward, Maris Piper or Desirée

55 g/2 oz butter

3 tbsp hot milk

salt and pepper

1. Peel the potatoes, placing them in cold water as you prepare the others, to prevent them from going brown.

2. Cut the potatoes into even-sized chunks. Cook in a large saucepan of lightly salted boiling water over a medium heat, covered, for 20–25 minutes until they are tender. Test with the point of a knife, but do make sure you test right to the middle to avoid lumps.

3. Remove the pan from the heat and drain the potatoes. Return the potatoes to the hot pan and mash with a potato masher until smooth.

4. Add the butter and continue to mash until it is all mixed in, then add the milk (it is better hot because the potatoes absorb it more quickly to produce a creamier mash).

5. Taste the mash and season with salt and pepper as necessary. Serve.

CHORIZO & CHEESE QUESADILLAS

SERVES: 4 | PREP TIME: 20 MINS | COOK TIME: 20 MINS

INGREDIENTS

115 g/4 oz mozzarella cheese, grated

115 g/4 oz Cheddar cheese, grated

225 g/8 oz cooked chorizo sausage, outer casing removed, or ham, diced

4 spring onions, finely chopped

2 fresh green chillies, such as poblano, deseeded and finely chopped

8 tortillas

vegetable oil, for brushing

salt and pepper

1. Place the cheeses, chorizo, spring onions, chillies and salt and pepper to taste in a bowl and mix together. Divide the mixture between four tortillas, then top with the remaining tortillas.

2. Brush a large, non-stick or heavy-based frying pan with oil and heat over a medium heat. Add one quesadilla and cook, pressing it down with a spatula, for 4–5 minutes, or until the underside is crisp and lightly browned. Turn over and cook the other side until the cheese is melting. Remove from the pan and keep warm. Cook the remaining quesadillas individually.

3. Cut each quesadilla into quarters, arrange on serving plates and serve.

CHICKEN & VEGETABLE BAKE

SERVES: 4   PREP TIME: 20 MINS   COOK TIME: 45 MINS

INGREDIENTS

3 tbsp olive oil

2 leeks, sliced

2 garlic cloves, sliced

2 large skinless, boneless chicken breasts, about 175 g/ 6 oz each, cut into bite-sized pieces

2 sweet potatoes, peeled and cut into chunks

2 parsnips, scrubbed and sliced

1 red pepper, deseeded and cut into strips

1 yellow pepper, deseeded and cut into strips

250 g/9 oz mixed wild mushrooms, cleaned

400 g/14 oz tomatoes, roughly chopped

300 g/10½ oz cooked white long-grain rice

1 small bunch fresh parsley, chopped

125 g/4½ oz mature Cheddar cheese, grated

salt and pepper

1. Preheat the oven to 180°C/350°F/Gas Mark 4.

2. Heat the oil in a large frying pan over a medium heat, add the leeks and garlic and cook, stirring frequently, for 3–4 minutes until softened. Add the chicken and cook, stirring frequently, for 5 minutes. Add the sweet potatoes and parsnips and cook, stirring frequently, for 5 minutes, or until golden and beginning to soften. Add the peppers and mushrooms and cook, stirring frequently, for 5 minutes. Stir in the tomatoes, rice and parsley and season to taste with salt and pepper.

3. Spoon the mixture into an ovenproof dish, scatter over the Cheddar cheese and bake in the preheated oven for 20–25 minutes. Check the chicken is tender and cooked through. Serve.

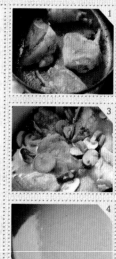

CHICKEN IN RIESLING

SERVES: 4–6   PREP TIME: 35 MINS   COOK TIME: 40 MINS

INGREDIENTS

1 chicken, about 1.6 kg/3 lb 8 oz, cut into 8 pieces

2 tbsp plain flour, seasoned with salt and pepper

55 g/2 oz butter, plus extra for the pasta

1 tbsp sunflower oil, plus extra if needed

4 shallots, finely chopped

400 g/14 oz chestnut mushrooms, sliced

2 tbsp brandy

300 ml/10 fl oz Riesling wine

2 carrots, thinly sliced

200 g/7 oz dried ribbon pasta, such as pappardelle or tagliatelle

100 ml/3½ fl oz crème fraîche or double cream

salt and pepper

1. Coat the chicken pieces with the seasoned flour, shaking off any excess, and set aside. Melt 30 g/1 oz of the butter with the oil in a flameproof casserole over a medium heat. Add the chicken pieces to the casserole and fry for 3–5 minutes until golden brown, removing each piece when it is browned and adding extra oil, if necessary. Wipe out the casserole.

2. Melt the remaining butter in the casserole. Add the shallots and fry, stirring, for 2–3 minutes, or until soft. Add the mushrooms and a pinch of salt and continue frying until they absorb the liquid they give off. Return the chicken to the casserole. Light the brandy in a ladle and pour over the chicken.

3. When the flames have died down, add the wine and carrots and enough water to cover all the ingredients. Bring to the boil, then reduce the heat to low and simmer for 20–25 minutes, or until the chicken is cooked through and the juices run clear when a skewer is inserted into the thickest part of the meat. Meanwhile, preheat the oven to 110°C/225°F/Gas Mark ¼.

4. Bring a large, heavy-based saucepan of lightly salted water to the boil. Add the pappardelle, bring back to the boil and cook for 8–10 minutes, or until just tender but still firm to the bite. Drain well, toss with butter and keep warm in the preheated oven. Using tongs and a slotted spoon transfer the chicken and the vegetables to a serving platter and keep warm in the oven. Skim any fat off the cooking juices, stir in the crème fraîche and bring to the boil, stirring, for 2–3 minutes to reduce. Taste and adjust the seasoning, if necessary, then pour the sauce over the chicken. Serve with the pasta.

BLACKBERRY CRUMBLE CUPCAKES

MAKES: 6 · PREP TIME: 20 MINS · COOK TIME: 30 MINS

INGREDIENTS

115 g/4 oz self-raising flour

½ tsp baking powder

115 g/4 oz butter, softened, plus extra for greasing

115 g/4 oz caster sugar

2 eggs

175 g/6 oz blackberries

whipped cream or custard, to serve

CRUMBLE TOPPING

85 g/3 oz self-raising flour

55 g/2 oz demerara sugar

55 g/2 oz butter, chilled and diced

1. Preheat the oven to 190°C/375°F/Gas Mark 5. Grease six 200-ml/7-fl oz ovenproof teacups or dishes (such as ramekins) with butter.

2. To make the crumble topping, mix the flour and sugar in a bowl. Add the butter and rub in until the mixture resembles coarse breadcrumbs.

3. To make the sponge, sift the flour and baking powder into a bowl. Add the butter, caster sugar and eggs and, using an electric hand-held whisk, beat together until smooth. Spoon the mixture into the cups or dishes and level the surface. Top with the blackberries. Spoon the crumble topping over the blackberries.

4. Put the cups or dishes on a baking sheet and bake in the preheated oven for 25–30 minutes until the crumble topping is golden brown. Serve warm with whipped cream.

15 OCTOBER

NUTTY FLAPJACKS

MAKES: 16 | PREP TIME: 10 MINS | COOK TIME: 25 MINS

INGREDIENTS

200 g/7 oz rolled oats

115 g/4 oz chopped hazelnuts

55 g/2 oz plain flour

115 g/4 oz butter, plus extra for greasing

2 tbsp golden syrup

85 g/3 oz light muscovado sugar

1. Preheat the oven to 180°C/350°F/Gas Mark 4. Grease a 23-cm/9-inch square cake tin.

2. Place the rolled oats, hazelnuts and flour in a large mixing bowl and stir together.

3. Place the butter, golden syrup and sugar in a saucepan over a low heat and stir until melted. Pour onto the dry ingredients and mix well. Spoon the mixture into the prepared cake tin and smooth the surface with the back of a spoon.

4. Bake in the preheated oven for 20–25 minutes, or until golden and firm to the touch. Mark into 16 pieces and leave to cool in the tin. When completely cold, cut with a sharp knife and remove from the tin.

16 OCTOBER

CHOCOLATE PEANUT BUTTER SQUARES

MAKES: 20 | PREP TIME: 20 MINS | COOK TIME: 35 MINS

INGREDIENTS

300 g/10½ oz milk chocolate

350 g/12 oz plain flour

1 tsp baking powder

225 g/8 oz butter

350 g/12 oz soft light brown sugar

175 g/6 oz rolled oats

70 g/2½ oz chopped mixed nuts

1 egg, beaten

400 g/14 oz canned condensed milk

70 g/2½ oz crunchy peanut butter

1. Preheat the oven to 180°C/350°F/Gas Mark 4.

2. Finely chop the chocolate. Sift the flour and baking powder into a large bowl. Add the butter to the flour mixture and rub in using your fingertips until the mixture resembles breadcrumbs. Stir in the sugar, rolled oats and nuts.

3. Put a quarter of the mixture into a bowl and stir in the chopped chocolate. Set aside.

4. Stir the egg into the remaining mixture, then press into the base of a 30 x 20-cm/12 x 8-inch baking tin. Bake in the preheated oven for 15 minutes.

5. Meanwhile, mix together the condensed milk and peanut butter. Pour the mixture over the base and spread evenly, then sprinkle the reserved chocolate mixture on top and press down lightly.

6. Return to the oven and bake for a further 20 minutes, until golden brown. Leave to cool in the tin, then cut into squares.

FRESH TOMATO
SOUP WITH PASTA

SERVES: 4   **PREP TIME: 15 MINS**   **COOK TIME: 55 MINS**

INGREDIENTS

1 tbsp olive oil

4 large plum tomatoes

1 onion, cut into quarters

1 garlic clove, thinly sliced

1 celery stick, roughly chopped

500 ml/18 fl oz chicken stock

55 g/2 oz dried soup pasta

salt and pepper

chopped fresh flat-leaf parsley,
to garnish

1. Pour the oil into a large heavy-based saucepan and add the tomatoes, onion, garlic and celery. Cover and cook over a low heat, occasionally shaking gently, for 45 minutes, until pulpy.

2. Transfer the mixture to a food processor and process to a smooth purée.

3. Push the purée through a sieve into a clean saucepan.

4. Add the stock and bring to the boil. Add the soup pasta, return to the boil and cook for 8–10 minutes, or until just tender but still firm to the bite. Season to taste with salt and pepper. Garnish with parsley and serve.

18 OCTOBER

MEATLOAF

SERVES: 4–6   PREP TIME: 20 MINS   COOK TIME: 45 MINS

INGREDIENTS

1 thick slice white bread, crusts removed

700 g/1 lb 9 oz fresh beef, pork or lamb mince

1 small egg

1 tbsp finely chopped onion

1 beef stock cube, crumbled

1 tsp dried mixed herbs

salt and pepper

TO SERVE

gravy

mashed potatoes

cooked runner beans

1. Preheat the oven to 180°C/350°F/Gas Mark 4. Put the bread into a small bowl and add enough water to soak. Leave to stand for 5 minutes, then drain and squeeze well to remove the water. Crumble the bread into small pieces.

2. Combine the bread with the beef, egg, onion, stock cube and herbs in a bowl and season to taste with salt and pepper. Shape into a loaf, then place on a baking sheet or in an ovenproof dish.

3. Bake the meatloaf in the preheated oven for 30–45 minutes, until the juices run clear when it is pierced with a skewer. Cut into slices and serve with gravy, mashed potatoes and runner beans.

19 OCTOBER

POT ROAST WITH POTATOES & DILL

SERVES: 6   PREP TIME: 30 MINS   COOK TIME: ABOUT 3 HRS

INGREDIENTS

2½ tbsp plain flour, seasoned with salt and pepper

1 rolled brisket joint, weighing 1.6 kg/3 lb 8 oz

2 tbsp vegetable oil

2 tbsp butter

1 onion, finely chopped

2 celery sticks, diced

2 carrots, peeled and diced

1 tsp dill seed

1 tsp dried thyme or oregano

350 ml/12 fl oz red wine

150–225 ml/5–8 fl oz beef stock

5 boiled potatoes, cut into chunks

1. Preheat the oven to 140°C/275°F/Gas Mark 1. Put 2 tablespoons of the flour in a shallow dish. Dip the meat to coat. Heat the oil in a flameproof casserole and brown the meat all over. Transfer to a plate. Add half the butter to the casserole and cook the onion, celery, carrots, dill seed and thyme for 5 minutes. Return the meat and juices to the casserole.

2. Pour in the wine and enough stock to reach one third of the way up the meat. Bring to the boil, cover and cook in the oven for 3 hours, turning the meat every 30 minutes. After it has been cooking for 2 hours, add the potatoes and more stock if necessary.

3. When ready, transfer the meat and vegetables to a warmed serving dish. Strain the cooking liquid to remove any solids, then return the liquid to the casserole.

4. Mix the remaining butter and flour to a paste. Bring the cooking liquid to the boil. Whisk in small pieces of the flour and butter paste, whisking constantly until the sauce is smooth. Pour the sauce over the meat and vegetables. Serve.

MEATLOAF

FISH &
POTATO STEW

SERVES: 4 PREP TIME: 25 MINS COOK TIME: 50 MINS

INGREDIENTS

1½ tbsp olive oil, plus extra for brushing

1 onion, finely chopped

3 large garlic cloves, 2 chopped and 1 halved

1 tbsp fennel seeds

½ tsp dried chilli flakes, or to taste

pinch of saffron threads

400 g/14 oz canned chopped tomatoes

125 ml/4 fl oz fish stock or water

2 bay leaves

500 g/1 lb 2 oz floury potatoes, thinly sliced

900 g/2 lb mixed fish, such as hake, monkfish and red snapper, boned, skinned and trimmed as necessary

2 red peppers, deseeded and sliced

2 tbsp chopped fresh parsley

salt and pepper

1. Preheat the oven to 180°C/350°F/Gas Mark 4.

2. Heat the oil in a saucepan over a medium heat. Add the onion and fry, stirring, for 2 minutes. Add the chopped garlic, fennel seeds, chilli flakes and saffron and continue frying for a further 1 minute, or until the onion is soft. Add the tomatoes, stock and bay leaves and season to taste with salt and pepper. Cover and bring to the boil, then reduce the heat to very low and simmer for 10 minutes. Taste and adjust the seasoning with salt and pepper, if necessary. Remove and discard the bay leaves.

3. Meanwhile, rub the garlic halves all over a 1.5-litre/2¾-pint ovenproof baking dish, pressing down firmly, then set aside the dish, discarding the garlic. Bring a large saucepan of lightly salted water to the boil, add the potatoes, bring back to the boil and cook for 8–10 minutes, or until they are starting to soften but still hold their shape. Drain well, pat dry and set aside.

4. Place the prepared dish on a baking sheet and arrange half the potatoes in a layer at the bottom of the dish. Place the fish and red peppers on top. Spoon over the tomato sauce, sprinkle with the parsley and shake the dish slightly. Arrange the remaining potatoes on top to cover all the other ingredients and lightly brush with oil. Bake in the preheated oven for 20–25 minutes, or until the fish and potatoes are tender when pierced with a skewer. Serve.

FETA &
SPINACH PARCELS

MAKES: 6   PREP TIME: 25 MINS   COOK TIME: 20 MINS

INGREDIENTS

2 tbsp olive oil, plus extra for greasing

1 bunch spring onions, chopped

500 g/1 lb 2 oz spinach leaves, roughly chopped

1 egg, beaten

125 g/4½ oz feta cheese, crumbled

½ tsp freshly grated nutmeg

6 sheets filo pastry

55 g/2 oz butter, melted

1 tbsp sesame seeds

salt and pepper

1. Preheat the oven to 200°C/400°F/Gas Mark 6. Grease a baking sheet with oil.

2. Heat the oil in a wok or large frying pan, add the onions and stir-fry for 1–2 minutes. Add the spinach and stir until the leaves are wilted. Cook, stirring occasionally, for 2–3 minutes. Drain off any free liquid and leave to cool slightly.

3. Stir the egg, cheese and nutmeg into the spinach and season well with salt and pepper.

4. Brush three sheets of pastry with butter. Place another three sheets on top and brush with butter. Cut each sheet down the middle to make six long strips in total. Place a spoonful of the spinach filling on the end of each strip.

5. Lift one corner of pastry over the filling to the opposite side, then turn over the opposite way to enclose. Continue to fold over down the strip to make a triangular parcel, finishing with the seam underneath.

6. Place the parcels on the baking sheet, brush with butter and sprinkle with the sesame seeds. Bake in the preheated oven for 12–15 minutes, or until golden brown and crisp. Serve.

22 OCTOBER

PAPRIKA PORK

SERVES: 4　**PREP TIME: 15 MINS**　**COOK TIME: 35 MINS**

INGREDIENTS

675 g/1 lb 8 oz pork fillet

2 tbsp sunflower oil

25 g/1 oz butter

1 onion, chopped

1 tbsp paprika

25 g/1 oz plain flour

300 ml/10 fl oz chicken stock

4 tbsp dry sherry

115 g/4 oz mushrooms, sliced

150 ml/5 fl oz soured cream

salt and pepper

1. Cut the pork into 4-cm/1½-inch cubes. Heat the oil and butter in a large saucepan. Add the pork and cook over a medium heat, stirring, for 5 minutes, or until browned. Transfer to a plate with a slotted spoon.

2. Add the chopped onion to the saucepan and cook, stirring occasionally, for 5 minutes, or until softened. Stir in the paprika and flour and cook, stirring constantly, for 2 minutes. Gradually stir in the stock and bring to the boil, stirring constantly.

3. Return the pork to the saucepan, add the sherry and sliced mushrooms and season to taste with salt and pepper. Cover and simmer gently for 20 minutes, or until the pork is tender. Stir in the soured cream and serve.

23 OCTOBER

THAI CHICKEN

SERVES: 4　**PREP TIME: 20 MINS PLUS 2 HRS MARINATING TIME**　**COOK TIME: 25 MINS**

INGREDIENTS

6 garlic cloves, coarsely chopped

1 tsp pepper

8 chicken legs

1 tbsp Thai fish sauce

4 tbsp dark soy sauce

fresh ginger, cut into matchsticks, to garnish

1. Put the garlic in a mortar, add the pepper and pound to a paste with a pestle. Using a sharp knife, make three to four diagonal slashes on both sides of the chicken legs. Spread the garlic paste over the chicken legs and place them in a dish. Add the fish sauce and soy sauce and turn the chicken to coat well. Cover with clingfilm and leave to marinate in the refrigerator for 2 hours.

2. Preheat the grill to medium–high. Drain the chicken legs, reserving the marinade. Put them on a grill rack and cook under the grill, turning and basting frequently with the reserved marinade, for 20–25 minutes, or until cooked through and tender. The juices should run clear when a skewer is inserted into the thickest part of the meat. Garnish with ginger and serve.

CRÈME BRÛLÉE

SERVES: 4–6   PREP TIME: 15 MINS PLUS 2 HRS CHILLING TIME   COOK TIME: 5 MINS

INGREDIENTS

225–300 g/8–10½ oz mixed soft fruits, such as blueberries and stoned fresh cherries

1½ –2 tbsp orange liqueur or orange flower water

250 g/9 oz mascarpone cheese

200 ml/7 fl oz crème fraîche

2–3 tbsp dark muscovado sugar

1. Prepare the fruit, if necessary, and lightly rinse, then place in the bases of 4–6 x 150-ml/5-fl oz ramekin dishes. Sprinkle the fruit with the liqueur.

2. Cream the mascarpone cheese in a bowl until soft, then gradually beat in the crème fraîche.

3. Spoon the cheese mixture over the fruit, smoothing the surface and ensuring that the tops are level. Chill in the refrigerator for at least 2 hours.

4. Sprinkle the tops with the sugar. Using a chef's blow torch, grill the tops until caramelized (about 2–3 minutes). Alternatively, cook under a preheated grill, turning the dishes, for 3–4 minutes, or until the tops are lightly caramelized all over.

5. Serve warm or chill in the refrigerator for 15–20 minutes before serving.

COCONUT FUDGE BALLS

MAKES: 16   PREP TIME: 15 MINS PLUS CHILLING TIME   COOK TIME: 5 MINS

INGREDIENTS

400 ml/14 fl oz canned condensed milk

140 g/5 oz desiccated coconut

½ tsp ground cinnamon

few drops edible yellow food colouring (optional)

1. Place the condensed milk in a saucepan and heat gently, stirring, for 1 minute.

2. Stir in 100 g/3½ oz of the coconut with the cinnamon and food colouring, if using. Cook over a moderate heat, stirring, for 3–4 minutes until the mixture thickens and begins to clump together in one piece.

3. Remove from the heat and leave to stand until the mixture is cool enough to handle. Break off bite-sized balls of the mixture and roll into small balls with your hands.

4. Put the remaining coconut into a bowl and roll the balls in it to coat evenly, then place on a chilled plate and leave to set.

26 OCTOBER

SLICED BEEF IN BLACK BEAN SAUCE

SERVES: 4–6   PREP TIME: 15 MINS   COOK TIME: 5 MINS

INGREDIENTS

3 tbsp groundnut oil

450 g/1 lb beef sirloin, thinly sliced

1 red pepper, deseeded and thinly sliced

1 green pepper, deseeded and thinly sliced

1 bunch spring onions, sliced

2 garlic cloves, crushed

1 tbsp grated fresh ginger

2 tbsp black bean sauce

1 tbsp sherry

1 tbsp soy sauce

1. Heat 2 tablespoons of the oil in a wok and stir-fry the beef on a high heat for 1–2 minutes. Remove and keep to one side.

2. Add the remaining oil and peppers and stir-fry for 2 minutes.

3. Add the spring onions, garlic and ginger and stir-fry for 30 seconds.

4. Add the black bean sauce, sherry and soy sauce, then stir in the beef and heat until bubbling. Serve.

27 OCTOBER

FRENCH ONION SOUP

SERVES: 6   PREP TIME: 15 MINS   COOK TIME: 1½ HRS

INGREDIENTS

3 tbsp olive oil

675 g/1 lb 8 oz onions, thinly sliced

4 garlic cloves, 3 chopped and 1 halved

1 tsp sugar

2 tsp chopped fresh thyme, plus extra sprigs to garnish

2 tbsp plain flour

125 ml/4 fl oz dry white wine

2 litres/3½ pints vegetable stock

6 slices French bread

300 g/10½ oz Gruyère cheese, grated

1. Heat the oil in a large, heavy-based saucepan over a medium–low heat, add the onions and cook, stirring occasionally, for 10 minutes, or until they are just beginning to brown. Stir in the chopped garlic, sugar and chopped thyme, then reduce the heat and cook, stirring occasionally, for 30 minutes, or until the onions are golden brown.

2. Sprinkle in the flour and cook, stirring constantly, for 1–2 minutes. Stir in the wine. Gradually stir in the stock and bring to the boil, skimming off any scum that rises to the surface, then reduce the heat and simmer for 45 minutes. Meanwhile, preheat the grill to medium.

3. Toast the bread on both sides under the grill, then rub the toast with the cut edges of the halved garlic clove.

4. Ladle the soup into six flameproof bowls set on a baking sheet. Float a piece of toast in each bowl and divide the grated cheese between them. Place under the grill for 2–3 minutes, or until the cheese has just melted. Garnish with thyme sprigs and serve.

BEAN CASSEROLE WITH POTATOES, CORN & PUMPKIN

SERVES: 4–6   **PREP TIME: 35 MINS PLUS SOAKING TIME**   **COOK TIME: 2 HRS 45 MINS**

INGREDIENTS

250 g/9 oz dried butter beans

500 g/1 lb 2 oz yellow-fleshed potatoes, peeled and cubed

500 g/1 lb 2 oz pumpkin or butternut squash, deseeded and cubed

500 ml/18 fl oz fresh or frozen sweetcorn kernels

salt and pepper

chopped fresh basil leaves and crumbled feta cheese, to serve

FLAVOURING SALSA

2–3 yellow or red chillies, deseeded and chopped

1 small onion, finely chopped

6 spring onions, green parts included, finely chopped

2–3 garlic cloves, finely chopped

2 tbsp olive oil

1. Soak the beans in cold water overnight. Drain, rinse and transfer to a large saucepan with enough water to cover by two fingers' width. Do not add salt. Bring to the boil, then reduce the heat and simmer very gently for 1½–2 hours, or until the beans are tender.

2. Meanwhile, put all the flavouring salsa ingredients in a small saucepan and cook over a medium heat, stirring frequently, for 5 minutes to marry the flavours. Set aside.

3. When the beans are tender, add the potatoes and pumpkin and top up with enough boiling water to submerge all the ingredients. Return to the boil, then reduce the heat, cover and cook gently for 20–30 minutes, or until the vegetables are tender. Season to taste with salt and pepper.

4. Stir in the sweetcorn kernels and reheat until bubbling. Stir in the flavouring salsa and cook for a further 10 minutes to marry the flavours and reduce the cooking juices. The dish should be juicy but not soupy. Sprinkle with the chopped basil and crumbled cheese and serve.

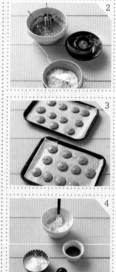

PUMPKIN WHOOPIE PIES

MAKES: 12   PREP TIME: 30 MINS   COOK TIME: 10 MINS

INGREDIENTS

275 g/9¾ oz plain flour

½ tsp baking powder

½ tsp bicarbonate of soda

1½ tsp ground cinnamon

¼ tsp salt

200 g/7 oz soft light brown sugar

125 ml/4 fl oz sunflower oil

1 large egg, beaten

1 tsp vanilla extract

115 g/4 oz canned pumpkin purée

CINNAMON & MAPLE FILLING

200 g/7 oz full fat soft cheese

85 g/3 oz unsalted butter, softened

2 tbsp maple syrup

1 tsp ground cinnamon

85 g/3 oz icing sugar, sifted

1. Preheat the oven to 180°C/350°F/Gas Mark 4. Line two to three large baking sheets with greaseproof paper. Sift together the plain flour, baking powder, bicarbonate of soda, cinnamon and salt.

2. Place the sugar and oil in a large bowl and beat with an electric whisk for 1 minute. Whisk in the egg and vanilla extract then the pumpkin purée. Stir in the sifted flour mixture and beat until thoroughly incorporated.

3. Pipe or spoon 24 mounds of the mixture onto the prepared baking sheets, spaced well apart to allow for spreading. Bake, one sheet at a time, in the preheated oven for 8–10 minutes until risen and just firm to the touch. Cool for 5 minutes then using a palette knife transfer to a cooling rack and leave to cool completely.

4. For the cinnamon and maple filling, place the soft cheese and butter in a bowl and beat together until well blended. Beat in the maple syrup, cinnamon and icing sugar until smooth.

5. To assemble, spread or pipe the filling over the flat side of half the cakes. Top with the rest of the cakes.

PUMPKIN & GRUYÈRE STEW

SERVES: 4–6   **PREP TIME: 25 MINS**   **COOK TIME: 1 HR 15 MINS**

INGREDIENTS

1 large pumpkin

300 ml/10 fl oz double cream

3 garlic cloves, thinly sliced

1 tbsp fresh thyme leaves

125 g/4½ oz Gruyère cheese, grated

salt and pepper

crusty bread, to serve

1. Preheat the oven to 180°C/350°F/Gas Mark 4.

2. Cut horizontally straight through the top quarter of the pumpkin to form a lid. Scoop out the seeds. Put the pumpkin in a large, deep ovenproof dish. Heat together the cream and garlic in a saucepan until just below boiling point. Remove from the heat, season to taste with salt and pepper and stir in the thyme. Pour into the pumpkin and pop the lid on top.

3. Bake in the preheated oven for 1 hour, or until the flesh is tender – the exact cooking time will depend on the size of the pumpkin. Take care not to overcook the pumpkin, or it may collapse. Remove from the oven, lift off the lid and scatter over the Gruyère cheese. Return to the oven and bake for a further 10 minutes.

4. Serve the soft pumpkin flesh with a generous portion of the cheesy cream and crusty bread.

HALLOWEEN MUD PIE

SERVES: 6–8   PREP TIME: 30 MINS   COOK TIME: 35–40 MINS

INGREDIENTS

85 g/3 oz plain chocolate

85 g/3 oz unsalted butter

85 g/3 oz light muscovado sugar

2 eggs, beaten

100 ml/3½ fl oz single cream

1 tsp vanilla extract

PASTRY

175 g/6 oz plain flour, plus extra for dusting

25 g/1 oz cocoa powder

40 g/1½ oz light muscovado sugar

85 g/3 oz unsalted butter

2–3 tbsp cold water

TOPPING

250 ml/9 fl oz whipping cream

85 g/3 oz plain chocolate

1. Preheat the oven to 200°C/400°F/Gas Mark 6. To make the pastry, sift the flour and cocoa powder into a bowl and stir in the sugar. Rub in the butter with your fingertips until the mixture resembles fine breadcrumbs. Add just enough water to bind to a dough.

2. Roll out the dough on a lightly floured work surface to a round large enough to line a 20-cm/8-inch, 3-cm/1¼-inch deep flan tin. Use the pastry to line the tin. Prick the base with a fork, cover with a piece of greaseproof paper and fill with baking beans, then blind-bake the base in the preheated oven for 10 minutes. Remove from the oven and take out the greaseproof paper and beans. Reduce the oven temperature to 180°C/350°F/Gas Mark 4.

3. Put the chocolate and butter into a saucepan and heat over a low heat, stirring, until melted. Put the sugar and eggs into a bowl and whisk together until smooth, then stir in the chocolate mixture, cream and vanilla extract.

4. Pour the chocolate mixture into the pastry case and bake in the oven for 20–25 minutes, or until just set. Leave to cool.

5. To make the topping, whip the cream until it just holds its shape, then spread over the pie. Melt the chocolate in a bowl set over a saucepan of simmering water, making sure the bowl doesn't come in contact with the water, then spoon into a piping bag and pipe decorations over the cream. Serve cold.

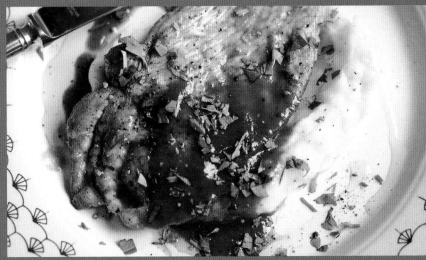

01 NOVEMBER

BEEF WITH HERB DUMPLINGS

SERVES: 6 | PREP TIME: 35 MINS | COOK TIME: 2 HRS 20 MINS

INGREDIENTS

2 tbsp sunflower oil

2 large onions, thinly sliced

8 carrots, sliced

4 tbsp plain flour

1.25 kg/2 lb 12 oz stewing steak, cut into cubes

425 ml/15 fl oz stout

2 tsp muscovado sugar

2 bay leaves

1 tbsp chopped fresh thyme

HERB DUMPLINGS

115 g/4 oz self-raising flour

55 g/2 oz shredded suet

2 tbsp chopped fresh parsley

about 4 tbsp water

1. Preheat the oven to 160°C/325°F/Gas Mark 3. Heat the oil in a flameproof casserole. Add the onions and carrots and cook over a low heat, stirring occasionally, for 5 minutes, or until the onions are softened. Meanwhile, place the flour in a polythene bag. Add the stewing steak to the bag, tie the top and shake well to coat. Do this in batches, if necessary.

2. Remove the vegetables from the casserole with a slotted spoon and reserve. Add the stewing steak to the casserole, in batches, and cook, stirring frequently, until browned all over. Return all the meat and the onions and carrots to the casserole and sprinkle in any remaining flour. Pour in the stout and add the sugar, bay leaves and thyme. Bring to the boil, cover and transfer to the preheated oven to bake for 1¾ hours.

3. To make the herb dumplings, sift the flour into a bowl. Stir in the suet and parsley and add enough of the water to make a soft dough. Shape into small balls between the palms of your hands. Add to the casserole and return to the oven for 30 minutes. Remove and discard the bay leaves. Serve.

02 NOVEMBER

CHICKEN-FRIED STEAK

SERVES: 4 | PREP TIME: 20 MINS | COOK TIME: 45 MINS

INGREDIENTS

4 x 175 g/6 oz minute steaks

2 eggs, beaten

4 tbsp milk

140 g/5 oz plain flour

1 tbsp paprika

½ tsp white pepper

vegetable oil, for frying

salt and pepper

GRAVY

115 g/4 oz pork sausage meat

3 spring onions, chopped

3 tbsp butter

35 g/1¼ oz plain flour

600 ml/1 pint milk

1. Generously season both sides of the steaks with salt and pepper. Put the eggs and milk into a pie dish, whisk together and set aside. Put the flour, paprika and white pepper into a second pie dish and mix well to combine. One at a time, dip the steaks into the egg mixture, turning to coat completely, and then dredge in the flour, coating on both sides. Place the egged and floured steaks on a plate and leave to stand for 10 minutes.

2. Add about 5 mm/¼ inch of the oil to a large frying pan and place over a medium–high heat. When the oil begins to shimmer, add the steaks and cook for about 3–4 minutes on each side, until golden brown and cooked through. Remove from the pan and drain for about 2 minutes on a wire rack set over some kitchen paper. If working in batches, keep the cooked steaks warm in a low oven until the remainder have been cooked.

3. To make the gravy, cook the sausages until browned, breaking up the meat into small pieces. Add the white parts of the spring onion and the butter and sauté for a few minutes, until the onions are translucent.

4. Stir in the flour and cook for 3 minutes. Gradually whisk in the milk until combined. When it reaches simmering point, reduce the heat to low and cook, stirring occasionally, for 15 minutes. If the gravy thickens too much, add some more milk. Serve the gravy over the steaks.

BEEF WITH HERB
DUMPLINGS

MINI YORKSHIRE PUDDINGS

MAKES: 6   **PREP TIME: 15 MINS**   **COOK TIME: 35 MINS**

INGREDIENTS

30 g/1 oz beef dripping or 2 tbsp sunflower oil

140 g/5 oz plain flour

½ tsp salt

2 eggs

225 ml/8 fl oz milk

1. Grease six metal pudding moulds with the dripping, then divide the remaining dripping between the moulds. Preheat the oven to 220°C/425°F/Gas Mark 7, placing the moulds in the oven so the dripping can melt while the oven heats.

2. Sift together the flour and salt into a large mixing bowl and make a well in the centre. Break the eggs into the well, add the milk and beat, gradually drawing in the flour from the side to make a smooth batter. Remove the moulds from the oven and spoon in the batter until they are about half full.

3. Bake in the preheated oven for 30–35 minutes, without opening the door, until the puddings are well risen, puffed and golden brown. Serve.

TURKEY STEAKS WITH CHILLI MAPLE GLAZE

SERVES: 4   PREP TIME: 10 MINS   COOK TIME: 15 MINS

INGREDIENTS

4 turkey breast steaks, about 125 g/4½ oz each

2 tbsp olive oil

1 garlic clove, crushed

4 tbsp maple syrup

2 tbsp tomato purée

2 tbsp Worcestershire sauce

3 tbsp lime juice

1½ tsp hot chilli sauce

salt and pepper

chopped fresh flat-leaf parsley, to garnish

1. Place the turkey breasts between two pieces of clingfilm and beat with a rolling pin until very thin. Season to taste with salt and pepper.

2. Heat the oil in a large frying pan, add the turkey and fry over a fairly high heat, turning once, for 3–4 minutes until golden brown.

3. Mix together the garlic, maple syrup, tomato purée, Worcestershire sauce, lime juice and chilli sauce, then spoon over the turkey.

4. Turn the turkey in the glaze to coat, then reduce the heat to low, cover the pan and cook very gently for 8–10 minutes until the turkey is tender and thoroughly cooked.

5. Adjust the seasoning to taste, sprinkle with parsley and serve.

CHICKEN MOLE POBLANO

| SERVES: 4 | PREP TIME: 30 MINS | COOK TIME: 1 HR 20 MINS |

INGREDIENTS

3 tbsp olive oil

4 chicken pieces, about 175 g/6 oz each, halved

1 onion, chopped

2 garlic cloves, finely chopped

1 hot dried red chilli, reconstituted and finely chopped

1 tbsp sesame seeds, toasted, plus extra to garnish

1 tbsp chopped almonds

½ tsp each of ground cinnamon, cumin and cloves

3 tomatoes, peeled and chopped

2 tbsp raisins

350 ml/12 fl oz chicken stock

1 tbsp peanut butter

25 g/1 oz plain chocolate, grated, plus extra to garnish

salt and pepper

1. Heat the oil in a large frying pan. Add the chicken and cook until browned on all sides. Remove the chicken pieces with a slotted spoon and set aside.

2. Add the onion, garlic and chilli and cook for 5 minutes, or until softened. Add the sesame seeds, almonds and spices and cook, stirring, for 2 minutes. Add the tomatoes, raisins, stock, peanut butter and chocolate and stir well.

3. Season to taste with salt and pepper and simmer for 5 minutes. Transfer the mixture to a food processor and process until smooth (you may need to do this in batches). Return the mixture to the frying pan, add the chicken and bring to the boil. Reduce the heat, cover and simmer for 1 hour, or until the chicken is very tender, adding more liquid if necessary. Check the juices run clear when a skewer is inserted into the thickest part of the meat.

4. Serve garnished with sesame seeds and a little grated chocolate.

CHICKEN & CORN SOUP

| SERVES: 6 | PREP TIME: 35 MINS | COOK TIME: 50 MINS |

INGREDIENTS

1 roasted chicken, about 1.3 kg/3 lb

½ tsp saffron threads

3 tbsp corn oil

2 onions, thinly sliced

3 celery sticks, sliced

1.7 litres/3 pints vegetable stock

8 black peppercorns

1 mace blade

115 g/4 oz egg noodles

400 g/14 oz frozen sweetcorn

pinch of dried sage

2 tbsp chopped fresh parsley

salt and pepper

1. Remove the skin from the chicken, cut the meat off the bones and cut into small pieces. Put the saffron into a bowl, pour in hot water to cover and leave to soak.

2. Heat the oil in a saucepan. Add the onions and celery and cook over a low heat, stirring occasionally, for 5 minutes, until softened. Increase the heat to medium, pour in the stock, add the peppercorns and mace and bring to the boil. Reduce the heat and simmer for 25 minutes.

3. Increase the heat to medium, add the chicken, noodles, sweetcorn, sage, parsley and saffron with its soaking water, season to taste with salt and pepper and bring back to the boil. Reduce the heat and simmer for a further 20 minutes.

4. Remove the pan from the heat, taste and adjust the seasoning, if necessary, and ladle into serving bowls.

CHICKEN MOLE
POBLANO

SQUASH, SWEET POTATO & GARLIC SOUP

SERVES: 4–6   PREP TIME: 35 MINS   COOK TIME: 1 HR 20 MINS

INGREDIENTS

1 acorn or butternut squash

1 sweet potato, about 350 g/12 oz

4 shallots

2 tbsp olive oil

5–6 garlic cloves, unpeeled

850 ml/1½ pints chicken stock

100 ml/3½ fl oz crème fraîche

pepper

snipped fresh chives, to garnish

1. Preheat the oven to 190°C/375°F/Gas Mark 5. Cut the squash, sweet potato and shallots in half lengthways, through to the stem end. Scoop the seeds out of the squash. Brush the cut sides with the oil.

2. Place the vegetables, cut-side down, in a shallow roasting tin and add the garlic. Roast in the preheated oven for about 40 minutes until tender and light brown. Cool.

3. When cool, scoop the flesh from the sweet potato and squash halves and place in a saucepan with the shallots. Peel the garlic and add the soft insides to the other vegetables.

4. Add the stock. Bring just to the boil, reduce the heat and simmer, partially covered, for about 30 minutes, stirring occasionally, until the vegetables are very tender.

5. Leave the soup to cool slightly, then transfer to a food processor and process until smooth, working in batches, if necessary. (If using a food processor, strain off the cooking liquid and set aside. Process the soup solids with enough cooking liquid to moisten them, then combine with the remaining liquid.)

6. Return the soup to the rinsed-out saucepan. Season with pepper to taste, then simmer for 5–10 minutes, until completely heated through. Ladle into serving bowls and swirl over the crème fraîche. Garnish with extra pepper and snipped chives and serve.

BUTTERNUT SQUASH & MUSHROOM RISOTTO

SERVES: 4   PREP TIME: 35 MINS   COOK TIME: 1 HR

INGREDIENTS

2 tbsp olive oil

1 large onion,
finely chopped

6 sage leaves,
finely chopped

2 tsp chopped fresh
thyme leaves

700 g/1 lb 9 oz butternut squash,
peeled, deseeded and cut into
2 cm/¾ inch chunks

225 g/8 oz chestnut mushrooms,
sliced

300 ml/10 fl oz vegetable stock

200 ml/7 fl oz dry white wine

350 g/12 oz risotto rice

55 g/2 oz freshly grated
Parmesan cheese

salt and pepper

crispy fried sage leaves,
to garnish

1. Preheat the oven to 200°C/400°F/Gas Mark 6. Heat the oil in a large saucepan. Add the onion, sage and thyme. Cover and cook over a low heat for 5 minutes until the onion turns translucent.

2. Stir in the butternut squash, mushrooms, stock and wine. Bring to the boil, then remove from the heat and ladle everything in the pan into a large ovenproof casserole. Stir in the rice.

3. Cover the casserole with a tight fitting lid and bake for 40–45 minutes until the rice and vegetables are tender. Stir in half the cheese, then season to taste with salt and pepper. Serve sprinkled with the remaining cheese and fried sage leaves to garnish.

HAM & MUSHROOM QUICHE

SERVES: 4–6   PREP TIME: 30 MINS PLUS 30 MINS CHILLING TIME   COOK TIME: 45–50 MINS

INGREDIENTS

15 g/½ oz butter

1 small onion, finely chopped

115 g/4 oz closed-cup mushrooms, sliced

140 g/5 oz cooked ham, diced

2 eggs, beaten

200 ml/7 fl oz single cream

55 g/2 oz Gruyère cheese, grated

salt and pepper

PASTRY

200 g/7 oz plain flour, plus extra for dusting

100 g/3½ oz butter

2–3 tbsp cold water

1. To make the pastry, sift the flour into a bowl and rub in the butter with your fingertips until the mixture resembles fine breadcrumbs. Stir in just enough water to bind to a soft dough.

2. Roll out the dough on a lightly floured work surface and use to line a 23-cm/9-inch flan tin. Press into the edges, trim the excess and prick the base with a fork. Chill in the refrigerator for 15 minutes.

3. Preheat the oven to 200°C/400°F/Gas Mark 6. Prick the base with a fork, cover with a piece of greaseproof paper and fill with baking beans, then blind-bake the base in the preheated oven for 10 minutes until lightly browned. Remove from the oven and take out the greaseproof paper and beans, then bake for a further 10 minutes.

4. Melt the butter in a frying pan, add the onion and fry for 2 minutes, then add the mushrooms and fry, stirring, for a further 2–3 minutes. Add the ham, then spread the mixture evenly in the pastry case.

5. Put the eggs into a bowl with the cream and beat together, then season to taste with salt and pepper. Pour into the pastry case and sprinkle with the cheese. Bake for 20–25 minutes until golden brown and just set.

10 NOVEMBER
CHUNKY POTATO & SPINACH CURRY

SERVES: 4   PREP TIME: 30 MINS   COOK TIME: 25 MINS

INGREDIENTS

4 tomatoes

2 tbsp groundnut or vegetable oil

2 onions, cut into thick wedges

2.5-cm/1-inch piece fresh ginger, peeled and finely chopped

1 garlic clove, chopped

2 tbsp ground coriander

450 g/1 lb peeled potatoes, cut into chunks

600 ml/1 pint vegetable stock

1 tbsp red curry paste

225 g/8 oz spinach leaves

cooked rice or noodles, to serve

1. Put the tomatoes in a heatproof bowl and cover with boiling water. Leave for 2–3 minutes, then plunge into cold water and peel off the skins. Cut each tomato into quarters and remove and discard the seeds and central core. Set aside.

2. Heat the oil in a preheated wok, add the onions, ginger and garlic and stir-fry over a medium–high heat for 2–3 minutes until starting to soften. Add the coriander and potatoes and stir-fry for 2–3 minutes. Add the stock and curry paste and bring to the boil, stirring occasionally. Reduce the heat and simmer gently for 10–15 minutes until the potatoes are tender.

3. Add the spinach and the tomato quarters and cook, stirring, for 1 minute, or until the spinach has wilted. Serve with rice.

11 NOVEMBER
PAN-FRIED HOT & SPICY SALMON

SERVES: 4   PREP TIME: 5 MINS   COOK TIME: 5 MINS

INGREDIENTS

½ tsp dried crushed chillies

2-cm/¾-inch piece fresh ginger, grated

1 tbsp sesame oil

finely grated rind and juice of 1 lemon

4 salmon fillet pieces

1 tbsp sunflower oil

salt and pepper

sautéed potatoes and seasonal vegetables, to serve

1. Put the chillies, ginger, sesame oil, lemon rind and half the lemon juice into a non-metallic bowl and mix together.

2. Add the salmon to the mixture and turn to coat evenly. Cover and leave to stand for 5 minutes. Season to taste with salt and pepper.

3. Preheat a heavy-based frying pan or griddle pan. Add the sunflower oil, then place the salmon in the pan skin-side down. Cook for about 2 minutes until the skin is golden and crisp, then turn and cook the other side for about 2 minutes until golden and just firm.

4. Squeeze the remaining lemon juice over the salmon and serve with sautéed potatoes and vegetables.

VEGETABLE CHILLI

SERVES: 4 • PREP TIME: 35 MINS • COOK TIME: 1 HR 10 MINS

INGREDIENTS

1 aubergine, cut into 2.5-cm/1-inch slices

1 tbsp olive oil, plus extra for brushing

1 large red onion, finely chopped

2 red or yellow peppers, deseeded and finely chopped

3–4 garlic cloves, finely chopped or crushed

800 g/1 lb 12 oz canned chopped tomatoes

1 tbsp mild chilli powder

½ tsp ground cumin

½ tsp dried oregano

2 small courgettes, quartered lengthways and sliced

400 g/14 oz canned kidney beans, drained and rinsed

450 ml/16 fl oz water

1 tbsp tomato purée

6 spring onions, finely chopped

115 g/4 oz Cheddar cheese, grated

salt and pepper

1. Brush the aubergine slices on one side with olive oil. Heat half the oil in a large, heavy-based frying pan over a medium–high heat. Add the aubergine slices, oiled-side up, and cook for 5–6 minutes, or until browned on one side. Turn the slices over, cook on the other side until browned and transfer to a plate. Cut into bite-sized pieces.

2. Heat the remaining oil in a large saucepan over a medium heat. Add the onion and peppers and cook, stirring occasionally, for 3–4 minutes, or until the onion is just softened, but not browned.

3. Add the garlic and cook for a further 2–3 minutes, or until the onion is beginning to colour.

4. Add the tomatoes, chilli powder, cumin and oregano. Season to taste with salt and pepper. Bring just to the boil, reduce the heat, cover and simmer gently for 15 minutes.

5. Add the courgettes, aubergine pieces and kidney beans. Stir in the water and the tomato purée. Return to the boil, then cover and continue simmering for 45 minutes, or until the vegetables are tender. Taste and adjust the seasoning if necessary. Ladle into serving bowls and top with spring onions and cheese.

CINNAMON SWIRLS

MAKES: 12   PREP TIME: 30 MINS PLUS 1 HR 10 MINS STANDING TIME   COOK TIME: 30 MINS

INGREDIENTS

225 g/8 oz strong white flour

½ tsp salt

10 g/¼ oz easy-blend dried yeast

2 tbsp butter, cut into small pieces, plus extra for greasing

1 egg, lightly beaten

125 ml/4 fl oz lukewarm milk

2 tbsp maple syrup, for glazing

FILLING

4 tbsp butter, softened

2 tsp ground cinnamon

50 g/1¾ oz soft light brown sugar

50 g/1¾ oz currants

1. Grease a baking sheet with a little butter.

2. Sift the flour and salt into a mixing bowl. Stir in the yeast. Rub in the butter with your fingertips until the mixture resembles breadcrumbs. Add the egg and milk and mix to form a dough.

3. Form the dough into a ball, place in a greased bowl, cover and leave to stand in a warm place for about 40 minutes, or until doubled in size.

4. Lightly knock back the dough for 1 minute, then roll out to a rectangle measuring 30 x 23 cm/12 x 9 inches.

5. To make the filling, cream together the butter, cinnamon and sugar until light and fluffy. Spread the filling evenly over the dough rectangle, leaving a 2.5-cm/1-inch border all around. Sprinkle the currants evenly over the top.

6. Roll up the dough from one of the long edges, and press down to seal. Cut the roll into 12 slices. Place them, cut-side down, on the baking sheet, cover and leave to stand for 30 minutes. Meanwhile, preheat the oven to 190°C/375°F/Gas Mark 5.

7. Bake the buns in the preheated oven for 20–30 minutes, or until well risen. Brush with the maple syrup and leave to cool slightly before serving.

CHOCOLATE FUDGE BROWNIES

MAKES: 16   PREP TIME: 25 MINS   COOK TIME: 45 MINS

INGREDIENTS

200 g/7 oz low-fat soft cheese

½ tsp vanilla extract

225 g/8 oz caster sugar

2 eggs

85 g/3 oz butter, plus extra for greasing

3 tbsp cocoa powder

100 g/3½ oz self-raising flour

50 g/1¾ oz pecan nuts, chopped

FUDGE ICING

55 g/2 oz butter

1 tbsp milk

75 g/2¾ oz icing sugar

2 tbsp cocoa powder

1. Preheat the oven to 180°C/350°F/Gas Mark 4. Lightly grease and line a shallow 20-cm/8-inch square cake tin.

2. Place the cheese, vanilla extract and 5 teaspoons of the sugar in a large bowl and beat together until smooth.

3. Place the eggs and remaining sugar in a separate bowl and beat together until light and fluffy. Place the butter and cocoa powder in a small saucepan and heat gently, stirring until the butter melts and the mixture combines, then stir it into the egg mixture.

4. Fold in the flour and nuts, pour half of the batter into the tin and smooth the top. Carefully spread the cheese mixture over, then cover it with the remaining batter. Bake in the preheated oven for 40–45 minutes. Leave to cool in the tin.

5. To make the fudge icing, melt the butter with the milk in a pan. Stir in the icing sugar and cocoa powder. Spread the icing over the brownies, leave to set, then cut into squares or rectangles.

CINNAMON
SWIRLS

RATATOUILLE

| SERVES: 4 | PREP TIME: 30 MINS | COOK TIME: ABOUT 1 HR |

INGREDIENTS

150 ml/5 fl oz olive oil

2 onions, sliced

2 garlic cloves

2 aubergines, roughly chopped

4 courgettes, roughly chopped

2 yellow peppers, deseeded and chopped

2 red peppers, deseeded and chopped

1 bouquet garni

1. Heat the oil in a large saucepan. Add the onions and cook over a low heat, stirring occasionally, for 5 minutes, or until softened. Add the garlic and cook, stirring frequently for a further 2 minutes.

2. Add the aubergines, courgettes and peppers. Increase the heat to medium and cook, stirring occasionally, until the peppers begin to colour. Add the bouquet garni, reduce the heat, cover and simmer gently for 40 minutes.

3. Stir in the chopped tomatoes and season to taste with salt and pepper. Re-cover the saucepan and simmer gently for a further 10 minutes. Remove and discard the bouquet garni. Serve warm or cold.

PRAWNS FU YUNG

| SERVES: 4–6 | PREP TIME: 10 MINS | COOK TIME: 10 MINS |

INGREDIENTS

1 tbsp vegetable or groundnut oil

115 g/4 oz large prawns, peeled and deveined

4 eggs, lightly beaten

1 tsp salt

pinch of white pepper

2 tbsp finely chopped Chinese chives

1. Heat a wok over a high heat and add the oil. Add the prawns and stir-fry for about 4 minutes, or until just pink.

2. Season the eggs with the salt and pepper and pour over the prawns. Stir-fry for 1 minute, then add the chives.

3. Cook for a further 4 minutes, stirring all the time, until the eggs are cooked through but still soft in texture. Serve.

CHICKEN GUMBO

SERVES: 4–6   PREP TIME: 30 MINS   COOK TIME: 2½ HRS

INGREDIENTS

1 chicken, weighing 1.5 kg/3 lb 5 oz, cut into 6 pieces

2 celery sticks, 1 broken in half and 1 finely chopped

1 carrot, chopped

2 onions, 1 sliced and 1 chopped

2 bay leaves

¼ tsp salt

4 tbsp corn or groundnut oil

50 g/1¾ oz plain flour

2 large garlic cloves, crushed

1 green pepper, cored, deseeded and diced

450 g/1 lb fresh okra, trimmed, then cut crossways into 1-cm/½-inch slices

225 g/8 oz andouille sausage or Polish kielbasa, sliced

2 tbsp tomato purée

1 tsp dried thyme

½ tsp salt

½ tsp cayenne pepper

¼ tsp pepper

400 g/14 oz canned plum tomatoes

cooked long-grain rice and hot pepper sauce, to serve

1. Put the chicken into a large saucepan with water to cover over a medium–high heat and bring to the boil, skimming the surface to remove the foam. When the foam stops rising, reduce the heat to medium, add the celery stick halves, carrot, sliced onion, 1 bay leaf and salt and simmer for 20 minutes, or until the chicken is tender and the juices run clear when a skewer is inserted into the thickest part of the meat. Strain the chicken, reserving 1 litre/1¾ pints of the liquid. When the chicken is cool enough to handle, remove and discard the skin, bones and flavourings. Cut the flesh into bite-sized pieces and reserve.

2. Heat the oil in a large saucepan over a medium–high heat for 2 minutes. Reduce the heat to low, sprinkle in the flour and stir to make the roux. Stir constantly for 30 minutes, or until the roux turns hazelnut-brown. If black specks appear, it is burnt and you will have to start again.

3. Add the chopped celery, chopped onion, garlic, green pepper and okra to the saucepan. Increase the heat to medium–high and cook, stirring frequently, for 5 minutes. Add the sausage and cook, stirring frequently, for 2 minutes.

4. Stir in the remaining ingredients, including the second bay leaf and the reserved cooking liquid. Bring to the boil, crushing the tomatoes with a wooden spoon. Reduce the heat to medium–low and simmer, uncovered, for 30 minutes, stirring occasionally.

5. Add the chicken to the pan and simmer for a further 30 minutes. Taste and adjust the seasoning, if necessary. Remove the bay leaves and spoon the gumbo over the rice. Serve with a bottle of hot pepper sauce on the side.

BRAISED BEEF WITH RED WINE & CRANBERRIES

SERVES: 4 | PREP TIME: 15 MINS | COOK TIME: 1 HR 40 MINS

INGREDIENTS

2 tbsp olive oil

6 shallots, quartered

600 g/1 lb 5 oz braising beef, cubed

1 tbsp plain flour

300 ml/10 fl oz red wine

2 tbsp tomato purée

1 tbsp Worcestershire sauce

2 bay leaves

100 g/3½ oz fresh or frozen cranberries

salt and pepper

mashed potatoes and seasonal vegetables, to serve

1. Heat the oil in a large, flameproof casserole, add the shallots and fry, stirring, for 2–3 minutes until beginning to brown. Remove from the pan and keep warm.

2. Add the beef and cook, stirring, for 3–4 minutes, or until evenly coloured. Stir in the flour and cook for 1 minute.

3. Add the wine and bring to the boil, then boil for 1 minute. Return the shallots to the pan with the tomato purée, Worcestershire sauce, bay leaves and salt and pepper to taste. Stir in the cranberries.

4. Reduce the heat to low, cover tightly with a lid and leave to simmer very gently for 1–1½ hours until the beef is tender.

5. Remove the bay leaves, adjust the seasoning to taste and serve with mashed potatoes and vegetables.

19 NOVEMBER

BAKED SWEET POTATO WITH GARLIC SALSA

SERVES: 4–6   PREP TIME: 20 MINS   COOK TIME: 1 HR 5 MINS

INGREDIENTS

1 kg/2 lb 4 oz sweet potatoes

chopped fresh coriander,
to garnish

GARLIC SALSA

2 tbsp olive oil

4 garlic cloves, crushed

juice of 3–4 oranges
(about 150 ml/5 fl oz)

juice and grated rind of 1 lemon

½ tsp sea salt

1. Preheat the oven to 180°C/350°F/Gas Mark 4.

2. Wash the sweet potatoes and pat dry. Bake in the preheated oven for 40 minutes, then test for softness with a knife – they may take up to a further 20 minutes to cook, depending on their variety and shape.

3. Meanwhile, make the garlic salsa. Heat the oil and garlic in a small saucepan, add the citrus juices, lemon rind and salt and leave to bubble for 3–4 minutes, or until blended.

4. When the sweet potatoes are perfectly tender, remove from the oven. When cool enough to handle, remove the skins and dice the flesh into bite-sized pieces.

5. Fold the diced sweet potato into the dressing. Serve at room temperature with the chopped coriander sprinkled over.

20 NOVEMBER

FARFALLE WITH GORGONZOLA & HAM

SERVES: 4   PREP TIME: 15 MINS   COOK TIME: 20 MINS

INGREDIENTS

225 ml/8 fl oz crème fraîche

225 g/8 oz chestnut mushrooms,
quartered

400 g/14 oz dried farfalle

85 g/3 oz Gorgonzola cheese,
crumbled

1 tbsp chopped fresh flat-leaf parsley,
plus extra sprigs to garnish

175 g/6 oz cooked ham, diced

salt and pepper

1. Pour the crème fraîche into a saucepan, add the mushrooms and season to taste with salt and pepper. Bring to just below the boil, then lower the heat and simmer very gently, stirring occasionally, for 8–10 minutes, until the cream has thickened.

2. Meanwhile, bring a large, heavy-based saucepan of lightly salted water to the boil. Add the farfalle, bring back to the boil and cook for 8–10 minutes, or until just tender but still firm to the bite.

3. Remove the pan of mushrooms from the heat and stir in the Gorgonzola cheese until it has melted. Return the pan to a very low heat and stir in the chopped parsley and ham.

4. Drain the pasta and add it to the sauce. Toss lightly, then divide among serving plates, garnish with the sprigs of parsley and serve.

VEGETABLE & BLACK BEAN SPRING ROLLS

SERVES: 4   PREP TIME: **30 MINS**   COOK TIME: **15 MINS**

INGREDIENTS

2 tbsp groundnut or vegetable oil, plus extra for deep-frying

4 spring onions, cut into 5-cm/2-inch lengths and shredded lengthways

2.5-cm/1-inch piece fresh ginger, peeled and finely chopped

1 large carrot, peeled and cut into matchsticks

1 red pepper, deseeded and cut into matchsticks

6 tbsp black bean sauce

55 g/2 oz fresh beansprouts

200 g/7 oz canned water chestnuts, drained and roughly chopped

5-cm/2-inch piece cucumber, cut into matchsticks

8 x 20-cm/8-inch square spring roll wrappers

sweet chilli dipping sauce, to serve (optional)

1. Heat the oil in a preheated wok, add the spring onions, ginger, carrot and red pepper and stir-fry over a medium–high heat for 2–3 minutes. Add the black bean sauce, beansprouts, water chestnuts and cucumber and stir-fry for 1–2 minutes. Leave to cool.

2. Remove the spring roll wrappers from the packet, but keep them in a pile, covered with clingfilm, to prevent them drying out. Lay one wrapper on a work surface in front of you in a diamond shape and brush the edges with water. Put a spoonful of the filling near one corner and fold the corner over the filling. Roll over again and then fold the side corners over the filling. Roll up to seal the filling completely. Repeat with the remaining wrappers and filling.

3. Heat the oil for deep-frying in the wok to 180°C/350°F, or until a cube of bread browns in 30 seconds. Add the rolls, in 2–3 batches, and cook for 2–3 minutes until crisp and golden all over. Remove with a slotted spoon, drain on kitchen paper and keep warm while you cook the remaining rolls. Serve with the sweet chilli dipping sauce, if using.

FRENCH BEAN CASSEROLE

SERVES: 4–6 | **PREP TIME: 10 MINS** | **COOK TIME: 40–45 MINS**

INGREDIENTS

500 g/1 lb 2 oz French beans, cut into 4-cm/1½-inch lengths

300 ml/10 fl oz canned condensed mushroom soup

225 ml/8 fl oz milk

1 tsp soy sauce

1 tbsp corn oil

15 g/½ oz butter

1 onion, sliced into rings

salt

1. Preheat the oven to 180°C/350°F/Gas Mark 4. Bring a saucepan of lightly salted water to the boil and add the beans. Bring back to the boil and cook for 5 minutes. Drain well.

2. Put the soup, milk and soy sauce into a bowl and mix together, then stir in the beans. Tip into a 1.4-litre/2½-pint casserole and distribute evenly. Bake in the preheated oven for 25–30 minutes, until bubbling and golden.

3. Meanwhile, heat the oil and butter in a frying pan, add the onion rings and fry over a fairly high heat, stirring frequently, until golden brown and crisp. Remove and drain on absorbent kitchen paper.

4. Arrange the onion rings on top of the casserole and bake for a further 5 minutes. Serve hot.

MASHED SWEET POTATOES WITH PARSLEY BUTTER

SERVES: 4   **PREP TIME: 10 MINS**   **COOK TIME: 25 MINS**

INGREDIENTS

70 g/2½ oz butter, softened

2 tbsp chopped fresh parsley

900 g/2 lb sweet potatoes, scrubbed

salt

1. Reserving 25 g/1 oz, put the butter into a bowl with the parsley and beat together. Turn out onto a square of foil or clingfilm, shape into a block and chill in the refrigerator until required.

2. Cut the sweet potatoes into even-sized chunks. Bring a large saucepan of lightly salted water to the boil, add the sweet potatoes, bring back to the boil and cook, covered, for 15–20 minutes until tender.

3. Drain the potatoes well, then cover the pan with a clean tea towel and leave to stand for 2 minutes. Remove the skins and mash with a potato masher until fluffy.

4. Add the reserved butter to the potatoes and stir in evenly. Spoon the mash into a serving dish and serve hot, topped with chunks of parsley butter.

24 NOVEMBER

THANKSGIVING ROAST TURKEY

SERVES: 8–10   PREP TIME: 20 MINS   COOK TIME: 2 HRS 45 MINS

INGREDIENTS

3 kg/6 lb 8 oz oven-ready turkey

1 onion, halved

fresh thyme sprigs

85 g/3 oz butter, softened

100 ml/3½ fl oz maple syrup

1 tbsp finely chopped fresh thyme

250 ml/9 fl oz chicken stock

1 tbsp lemon juice

salt and pepper

traditional trimmings, to serve

1. Preheat the oven to 180°C/350°F/Gas Mark 4. Put the turkey into a roasting tin and put the onion and thyme sprigs into the cavity.

2. Put the butter, maple syrup and chopped thyme into a bowl and mix together. Lift the turkey skin away from the breast and spread a little of the butter mixture on the meat. Replace the skin and brush more of the glaze over.

3. Sprinkle the turkey with salt and pepper and roast in the preheated oven for 2½ hours, basting occasionally with the glaze and juices. If the skin begins to over-brown, cover it loosely with foil.

4. Roast the turkey until there is no trace of pink in the juices when pierced through the thickest part of the leg. Remove from the oven, cover with foil and leave to rest for about 20 minutes before carving.

5. Skim any fat from the pan juices and stir in the stock and lemon juice. Bring to the boil and boil until slightly reduced, then adjust the seasoning to taste with salt and pepper.

6. Serve the turkey with the gravy and trimmings.

25 NOVEMBER

CREAMED SPINACH WITH NUTMEG

SERVES: 4   PREP TIME: 5 MINS   COOK TIME: 5 MINS

INGREDIENTS

15 g/½ oz butter

900 g/2 lb young spinach leaves

4 tbsp single cream

½ tsp freshly grated nutmeg

salt and pepper

1. Melt the butter in a large frying pan or wok, add the spinach and cook, stirring, until the leaves are wilted.

2. Continue to cook over a medium heat, stirring occasionally, until most of the free liquid has evaporated.

3. Stir in the cream and nutmeg, and season to taste with salt and pepper. Serve.

THANKSGIVING
ROAST TURKEY

APPLE PIE

SERVES: 6–8   PREP TIME: 40 MINS PLUS 30 MINS CHILLING TIME   COOK TIME: 50 MINS

INGREDIENTS

175 g/6 oz plain flour

pinch of salt

85 g/3 oz butter, cut into pieces

85 g/3 oz lard, cut into small pieces

about 1–2 tbsp water

beaten egg or milk, for glazing

FILLING

750 g–1 kg/1 lb 10 oz–2 lb 4 oz cooking apples, peeled, cored and sliced

125 g/4½ oz soft light brown sugar, plus extra for sprinkling

½ –1 tsp ground cinnamon

1. Sift the flour and salt into a mixing bowl. Add the butter and lard, and rub in with your fingertips until the mixture resembles fine breadcrumbs. Add enough cold water to mix to a firm dough. Wrap in clingfilm and chill for 30 minutes.

2. Preheat the oven to 220°C/425°F/Gas Mark 7. Thinly roll out almost two thirds of the pastry and use to line a deep 23-cm/9-inch pie dish.

3. For the filling, mix the apples with the sugar and cinnamon, and pack into the pastry case.

4. Roll out the remaining pastry to form a lid. Dampen the edges of the pie rim with water and position the lid, pressing the edges firmly together. Trim and crimp the edges. Use the pastry trimmings to cut out leaves or other shapes. Dampen and attach to the top of the pie. Glaze the pie with beaten egg, make one or two slits in the top and place the pie on a baking sheet.

5. Bake in the preheated oven for 20 minutes, then reduce the temperature to 180°C/350°F/Gas Mark 4 and bake for a further 30 minutes, or until the pastry is a light golden brown. Sprinkle with sugar and serve hot or cold.

PUMPKIN PIE

SERVES: 4–6   PREP TIME: 40 MINS   COOK TIME: 1 HR

INGREDIENTS

plain flour, for dusting

350 g/12 oz ready-made shortcrust pastry

400 g/14 oz pumpkin purée

2 eggs, lightly beaten

150 g/5½ oz sugar

1 tsp ground cinnamon

½ tsp ground ginger

¼ tsp ground cloves

½ tsp salt

350 ml/12 fl oz canned evaporated milk

EGGNOG WHIPPED CREAM

350 ml/12 fl oz double cream

55 g/2 oz icing sugar

1 tbsp brandy, or to taste

1 tbsp light or dark rum, or to taste

freshly grated nutmeg, to decorate

1. Preheat the oven to 200°C/400°F/Gas Mark 6. Very lightly dust a rolling pin with flour and use to roll out the pastry on a lightly floured work surface into a 30-cm/12-inch round. Line a 23-cm/9-inch deep pie dish with the pastry, trimming the excess. Prick the base with a fork, cover with a piece of greaseproof paper and fill with baking beans, then blind-bake the base in the preheated oven for 10 minutes until lightly browned. Remove from the oven and take out the greaseproof paper and beans. Reduce the oven temperature to 180°C/350°F/Gas Mark 4.

2. Meanwhile, put the pumpkin purée, eggs, sugar, cinnamon, ginger, cloves and salt into a bowl and beat together, then beat in the evaporated milk. Pour the mixture into the pastry case, return to the oven, and bake for 40–50 minutes until the filling is set and a knife inserted in the centre comes out clean. Transfer to a wire rack and set aside to cool completely.

3. While the pie is baking, make the eggnog whipped cream. Put the cream in a bowl and beat until it has thickened and increased in volume. Just as it starts to stiffen, sift over the icing sugar and continue beating until it holds stiff peaks. Add the brandy and rum and beat, taking care not to overbeat or the mixture will separate. Cover and chill until required. When ready to serve, grate some nutmeg over the whipped cream. Serve.

APPLE PIE

DINNER PARTY ROLLS

MAKES: 12   **PREP TIME: 40 MINS PLUS 1 HR 10 MINS RESTING TIME**   **COOK TIME: 15 MINS**

INGREDIENTS

125 ml/4 fl oz milk

4 tbsp water

5 tbsp butter, softened, plus extra for brushing

350 g/12 oz strong white flour, plus extra for dusting

1 sachet easy-blend dried yeast

1 tbsp sugar

½ tsp salt

1 large egg, beaten

sunflower oil, for greasing

1. Put the milk, water and 2 tablespoons of the butter into a small saucepan and heat to 43–45°C/110–113°F. Put the flour, yeast, sugar and salt into a large bowl, stir and make a well in the centre. Slowly pour in 6 tablespoons of the milk mixture, then add the egg and beat, drawing in the flour from the side. Add the remaining milk, tablespoon by tablespoon, until a soft dough forms.

2. Grease a bowl and set aside. Turn out the dough onto a lightly floured work surface and knead for 8–10 minutes, until smooth and elastic. Shape the dough into a ball, roll it around in the greased bowl, cover with clingfilm and set aside for 1 hour, or until doubled in size.

3. Turn out the dough onto a lightly floured work surface and knock back. Cover with the upturned bowl and leave to rest for 10 minutes. Meanwhile, preheat the oven to 200°C/400°F/Gas Mark 6 and dust a baking sheet with flour. Melt the remaining butter in a small saucepan over a medium heat.

4. Lightly flour a rolling pin and use to roll out the dough to a thickness of 5 mm/¼ inch. Using a floured 8-cm/3¼-inch round cutter, cut out 12 rounds, re-rolling the trimmings, if necessary. Brush the middle of a dough round with butter. Use a floured chopstick or pencil to make an indentation just off centre, then fold along the indentation and pinch the edges together to seal. Place on the prepared sheet, cover with a tea towel and leave to rise while you shape the remaining rolls.

5. Lightly brush the tops of the rolls with butter and bake in the preheated oven for 12–15 minutes, until the rolls are golden brown and the bases sound hollow when tapped. Transfer to a wire rack to cool. Serve warm or at room temperature.

SPICED APPLE MACAROONS

MAKES: 16   **PREP TIME: 40 MINS PLUS 30 MINS STANDING TIME**   **COOK TIME: 25 MINS**

INGREDIENTS

75 g/2¾ oz ground almonds

115 g/4 oz icing sugar

1 tsp ground cinnamon

2 large egg whites

50 g/1¾ oz caster sugar

½ tsp freshly grated nutmeg

FILLING

450 g/1 lb cooking apples, peeled, cored and chopped

3 tbsp caster sugar

1 tbsp water

1. Place the ground almonds, icing sugar and cinnamon in a food processor and process for 15 seconds. Sift the mixture into a bowl. Line two baking sheets with greaseproof paper.

2. Place the egg whites in a large bowl and whisk until holding soft peaks. Gradually whisk in the caster sugar to make a firm, glossy meringue.

3. Using a spatula, fold the almond mixture into the meringue one third at a time. When all the dry ingredients are thoroughly incorporated, continue to cut and fold the mixture until it forms a shiny batter with a thick, ribbon-like consistency.

4. Pour the mixture into a piping bag fitted with a 1-cm/½ -inch plain nozzle. Pipe 32 small rounds onto the prepared baking sheets. Tap the baking sheets firmly onto a work surface to remove air bubbles. Sprinkle over the grated nutmeg. Leave at room temperature for 30 minutes. Meanwhile, preheat the oven to 160°C/325°F/Gas Mark 3.

5. Bake in the preheated oven for 10–15 minutes. Cool for 10 minutes, then carefully peel the macaroons off the greaseproof paper. Leave to cool completely.

6. To make the filling, place the apples, sugar and water in a small pan. Cover and simmer for 10 minutes, until soft. Mash with a fork to make a purée, then leave to cool. Use to sandwich pairs of macaroons together.

WHISKY FLUMMERY

INGREDIENTS

3 tbsp fine oatmeal or porridge oats

225 ml/8 fl oz double cream

finely grated rind and juice of 1 small orange

3 tbsp clear honey

2 tbsp whisky

150 g/5½ oz raspberries

1. Sprinkle the oatmeal into a dry frying pan and stir over a medium heat for 1–2 minutes until lightly toasted. Remove and cool.

2. Put the cream into a bowl and whisk until thick, then gradually add the orange rind and juice, honey and whisky, whisking until it just holds its shape.

3. Reserving four raspberries for decoration, stir the remainder into the mixture with the oatmeal. Spoon into serving dishes and serve chilled, topped with the reserved raspberries.

DECEMBER

YULE LOG

SERVES: 8   **PREP TIME: 40 MINS PLUS COOLING TIME**   **COOK TIME: 15 MINS**

INGREDIENTS

butter, for greasing

150 g/5½ oz caster sugar, plus extra for sprinkling

4 eggs, separated

1 tsp almond extract

115 g/4 oz self-raising flour, plus extra for dusting

280 g/10 oz plain chocolate, broken into squares

225 ml/8 fl oz double cream

2 tbsp rum

holly and icing sugar, to decorate

1. Preheat the oven to 190°C/375°F/Gas Mark 5. Grease and line a 40 x 28-cm/16 x 11-inch Swiss roll tin, then dust with flour.

2. Reserve 2 tablespoons of the caster sugar and whisk the remainder with the egg yolks in a bowl until thick and pale. Stir in the almond extract. Whisk the egg whites in a separate grease-free bowl until soft peaks form. Gradually whisk in the reserved sugar until stiff and glossy. Sift half the flour over the egg yolk mixture and fold in, then fold in one quarter of the egg whites. Sift and fold in the remaining flour, followed by the remaining egg whites. Spoon the mixture into the tin, spreading it out evenly with a palette knife. Bake in the preheated oven for 15 minutes, until lightly golden.

3. Sprinkle caster sugar over a sheet of greaseproof paper and turn out the cake on to the paper. Roll up and leave to cool.

4. Place the chocolate in a heatproof bowl. Bring the cream to boiling point in a small saucepan, then pour it over the chocolate and stir until the chocolate has melted. Beat with an electric mixer until smooth and thick. Reserve about one third of the chocolate mixture and stir the rum into the remainder. Unroll the cake and spread the chocolate and rum mixture over. Re-roll and place on a plate or silver board. Spread the reserved chocolate mixture evenly over the top and sides. Mark with a fork so that the surface resembles tree bark. Just before serving, decorate with holly and a sprinkling of icing sugar to resemble snow.

PECAN PIE

SERVES: 8   **PREP TIME: 35 MINS PLUS 30 MINS CHILLING TIME**   **COOK TIME: ABOUT 1 HR**

INGREDIENTS

PASTRY

200 g/7 oz plain flour, plus extra for dusting

115 g/4 oz unsalted butter

2 tbsp caster sugar

FILLING

70 g/2½ oz unsalted butter

100 g/3½ oz light muscovado sugar

140 g/5 oz golden syrup

2 large eggs, beaten

1 tsp vanilla extract

115 g/4 oz pecan nuts

1. To make the pastry, place the flour in a bowl and rub in the butter with your fingertips until it resembles fine breadcrumbs. Stir in the sugar and add enough cold water to mix to a firm dough. Wrap in clingfilm and chill for 15 minutes, until firm enough to roll out.

2. Preheat the oven to 200°C/400°F/Gas Mark 6. Roll out the pastry on a lightly floured surface and use to line a 23-cm/9-inch loose-based round tart tin. Prick the base with a fork. Chill for 15 minutes.

3. Place the tart tin on a baking sheet, cover with a piece of greaseproof paper and fill with baking beans. Blind-bake the base in the preheated oven for 10 minutes until lightly browned. Remove from the oven and take out the greaseproof paper and beans. Put back in the oven and bake for a further 5 minutes. Reduce the oven temperature to 180°C/350°F/Gas Mark 4.

4. To make the filling, place the butter, sugar and golden syrup in a saucepan and heat gently until melted. Remove from the heat and quickly beat in the eggs and vanilla extract.

5. Roughly chop the nuts and stir into the mixture. Pour into the pastry case and bake for 35–40 minutes, until the filling is just set. Serve warm or cold.

YULE LOG

TURKEY SOUP WITH RICE, MUSHROOMS & SAGE

SERVES: 4–5   PREP TIME: 20 MINS   COOK TIME: ABOUT 1 HR

INGREDIENTS

3 tbsp butter

1 onion, finely chopped

1 celery stick, finely chopped

25 large fresh sage leaves, finely chopped

4 tbsp plain flour

1.2 litres/2 pints turkey or chicken stock

100 g/3½ oz brown rice

250 g/9 oz mushrooms, sliced

200 g/7 oz cooked turkey, diced

200 ml/7 fl oz double cream

salt and pepper

sprigs of fresh sage, to garnish

freshly grated Parmesan cheese, to serve

1. Melt half the butter in a large saucepan over a medium–low heat. Add the onion, celery and sage and cook for 3–4 minutes, until the onion is softened, stirring frequently. Stir in the flour and continue cooking for 2 minutes.

2. Slowly add about one quarter of the stock and stir well, scraping the bottom of the pan to mix in the flour. Pour in the remaining stock, stirring to combine completely, and bring just to the boil.

3. Stir in the rice and season to taste with salt and pepper. Reduce the heat and simmer gently, partially covered, for about 30 minutes until the rice is just tender, stirring occasionally.

4. Meanwhile, melt the remaining butter in a large frying pan over a medium heat. Add the mushrooms and season to taste with salt and pepper. Cook for about 8 minutes, until they are golden brown, stirring occasionally at first, then more often after they start to colour. Add the mushrooms to the soup.

5. Add the turkey to the soup and stir in the cream. Continue simmering for about 10 minutes, until heated through. Taste and adjust the seasoning, if necessary. Ladle into serving bowls, garnish with sage and serve with Parmesan cheese.

BACON-WRAPPED SAUSAGES

MAKES: 8   **PREP TIME: 15 MINS**   **COOK TIME: 20 MINS**

INGREDIENTS

8 pork sausages

2 tbsp mild mustard

24 ready-to-eat prunes

8 rashers smoked bacon

1. Preheat the grill. Using a sharp knife, cut a slit along the length of each sausage about three-quarters of the way through. Spread the mustard inside the slits and press 3 prunes into each sausage.

2. Stretch the bacon with the back of a knife until each rasher is quite thin. Wrap a rasher of bacon around each sausage.

3. Place the sausages on a grill rack and cook under the grill, turning occasionally, for 15–20 minutes until cooked through and browned all over.

LAYERED CASSEROLE

SERVES: 4–6 | **PREP TIME: 20 MINS** | **COOK TIME: ABOUT 1 HR**

INGREDIENTS

3 tbsp olive oil

600 g/1 lb 5 oz parsnips, peeled and thinly sliced

1 tsp fresh thyme leaves

1 tsp caster sugar

300 ml/10 fl oz double cream

600 g/1 lb 5 oz tomatoes, thinly sliced

1 tsp dried oregano

150 g/5½ oz Cheddar cheese, grated

salt and pepper

1. Preheat the oven to 180°C/350°F/Gas Mark 4.

2. Heat the oil in a frying pan over a medium heat, add the parsnips, thyme, sugar and salt and pepper to taste and cook, stirring frequently, for 6–8 minutes until golden and softened.

3. Spread half the parsnips over the base of a gratin dish. Pour over half the cream, then arrange half the tomatoes in an even layer across the parsnips. Season to taste with salt and pepper and scatter over half the oregano. Sprinkle over half the Cheddar cheese. Top with the remaining parsnips and tomatoes. Sprinkle with the remaining oregano, season to taste with salt and pepper and pour over the remaining cream. Scatter over the remaining cheese.

4. Cover with foil and bake in the preheated oven for 40 minutes, or until the parsnips are tender. Remove the foil and return to the oven for a further 5–10 minutes until the top is golden and bubbling. Serve.

LAYERED
CASSEROLE

BANANA WALNUT LOAF CAKE

| MAKES: 1 LOAF | PREP TIME: 10 MINS | COOK TIME: ABOUT 1 HR |

INGREDIENTS

250 g/9 oz plain flour

1½ tsp baking powder

200 g/7 oz light muscovado sugar

55 g/2 oz chopped walnuts

2 large eggs

100 ml/3½ fl oz sunflower oil, plus extra for greasing

2 ripe bananas, mashed

100 ml/3½ fl oz milk

1 tsp vanilla extract

8 walnut halves

1. Preheat the oven to 180°C/350°F/Gas Mark 4. Grease a 1-litre/1¾-pint loaf tin and line with greaseproof paper.

2. Sift together the flour and baking powder into a mixing bowl and stir in the sugar and chopped walnuts.

3. Put the eggs, oil, bananas, milk and vanilla extract into a bowl and beat together, then stir into the dry ingredients and mix together.

4. Spoon the mixture into the prepared tin, smoothing it level with a palette knife. Arrange the walnut halves over the surface.

5. Bake in the preheated oven for about 1 hour, or until risen, firm and golden brown. Leave to cool in the tin for 15 minutes, then turn out onto a wire rack to cool completely.

SMOKED SALMON RISOTTO

SERVES: 4   PREP TIME: 20 MINS   COOK TIME: 15–20 MINS

INGREDIENTS

50 g/1¾ oz unsalted butter

1 onion, finely chopped

½ small fennel bulb, very finely chopped

500 g/1 lb 2 oz arborio or carnaroli rice

300 ml/10 fl oz white wine or vermouth

1.2 litres/2 pints hot fish stock

150 g/5½ oz hot smoked salmon flakes

150 g/5½ oz smoked salmon slices

2 tbsp fresh chervil leaves or chopped flat-leaf parsley

salt and pepper

1. Melt half the butter in a large saucepan over a medium heat, add the onion and fennel and cook, stirring frequently, for 5–8 minutes until transparent and soft. Add the rice and stir well to coat the grains in the butter. Cook, stirring, for 3 minutes, then add the wine, stir and leave to simmer until most of the liquid has been absorbed.

2. With the stock simmering in a separate saucepan, add 1 ladleful to the rice and stir well. Cook, stirring constantly, until nearly all the liquid has been absorbed before adding another ladleful of stock. Continue to add the remaining stock in the same way until the rice is cooked but still firm to the bite and most or all of the stock has been added.

3. Remove from the heat and stir in the two types of salmon and the remaining butter. Season to taste with salt and pepper and serve scattered with the chervil.

08 DECEMBER
CRANBERRY & PINE KERNEL BISCOTTI

MAKES: 18–20   PREP TIME: 35 MINS PLUS 3–4 MINS COOLING TIME   COOK TIME: 35 MINS

INGREDIENTS

butter or oil, for greasing

85 g/3 oz light muscovado sugar

1 large egg

140 g/5 oz plain flour, plus extra for dusting

½ tsp baking powder

1 tsp ground mixed spice

55 g/2 oz dried cranberries

55 g/2 oz pine kernels, toasted

1. Preheat the oven to 180°C/350°F/Gas Mark 4. Grease a baking sheet.

2. Whisk together the sugar and egg until pale and thick enough to form a trail.

3. Sift the flour, baking powder and allspice and fold into the mixture. Stir in the cranberries and pine kernels and mix lightly to a smooth dough.

4. With lightly floured hands, shape the mixture into a long roll, about 28 cm/11 inches long. Press to flatten slightly.

5. Lift the dough onto the baking sheet and bake in the preheated oven for 20–25 minutes, until golden. Do not turn off the oven.

6. Cool for 3–4 minutes, then cut into 1.5-cm/⅝ -inch thick slices and arrange on the baking sheet.

7. Bake in the oven for 10 minutes, or until golden. Remove from the oven, transfer to a wire rack and leave to cool.

09 DECEMBER
CHRISTMAS TREE COOKIES

MAKES: 12   PREP TIME: 35 MINS PLUS 45 MINS CHILLING TIME   COOK TIME: ABOUT 10 MINS

INGREDIENTS

150 g/5½ oz plain flour, plus extra for dusting

1 tsp ground cinnamon

½ tsp ground nutmeg

½ tsp ground ginger

70 g/2½ oz unsalted butter, diced, plus extra for greasing

3 tbsp honey

white icing (optional) and narrow, gold or silver ribbon, to decorate

1. Sift the flour and spices into a bowl and rub in the butter until the mixture resembles breadcrumbs. Add the honey and mix together well to form a soft dough. Wrap the dough in clingfilm and chill in the refrigerator for 30 minutes.

2. Meanwhile, preheat the oven to 180°C/350°F/Gas Mark 4 and lightly grease two baking sheets with butter. Divide the dough in half. Roll out one piece of dough on a floured work surface to about 5 mm/¼ inch thick. Cut out tree shapes using a cutter or cardboard template. Repeat with the remaining piece of dough.

3. Put the biscuits on the prepared baking sheets and, using a cocktail stick, make a hole through the top of each biscuit large enough to thread the ribbon through. Chill in the refrigerator for 15 minutes.

4. Bake the biscuits in the preheated oven for 10–12 minutes until golden. Leave to cool on the baking sheets for 5 minutes, then transfer to a wire rack to cool completely. Decorate the trees with white icing, or simply leave them plain, then thread a length of ribbon through each hole and knot.

SNOWFLAKE CHRISTMAS WHOOPIE PIES

MAKES: 14   PREP TIME: 40 MINS   COOK TIME: ABOUT 10 MINS

INGREDIENTS

200 g/7 oz plain flour

2 tsp baking powder

large pinch of salt

55 g/2 oz ground almonds

115 g/4 oz butter, softened

150 g/5½ oz caster sugar, plus extra for sprinkling

1 large egg, beaten

1 tsp almond extract

100 ml/3½ fl oz milk

1 tbsp edible silver balls

BUTTERCREAM

150 g/5½ oz unsalted butter, softened

8 tbsp double cream

280 g/10 oz icing sugar, sifted

ICING

115 g/4 oz icing sugar

1–2 tbsp warm water

1. Preheat the oven to 180°C/350°F/Gas Mark 4. Line two to three large baking sheets with greaseproof paper. Sift together the plain flour, baking powder and salt. Stir in the ground almonds.

2. Place the butter and sugar in a large bowl and beat with an electric whisk until pale and fluffy. Beat in the egg and almond extract followed by half the flour mixture then the milk. Stir in the rest of the flour mixture and beat until thoroughly incorporated.

3. Pipe or spoon 28 mounds of the mixture onto the prepared baking sheets, spaced well apart to allow for spreading. Bake in the preheated oven, one sheet at a time, for 10–12 minutes until risen and just firm to the touch. Cool for 5 minutes then using a palette knife transfer to a wire rack and leave to cool completely.

4. For the buttercream, place the butter in a bowl and beat with an electric whisk for 2–3 minutes until pale and creamy. Beat in the cream then gradually beat in the icing sugar and continue beating for 2–3 minutes until the buttercream is very light and fluffy.

5. For the icing, sift the icing sugar into a bowl and gradually stir in enough water to make a smooth, thick icing that is thick enough to coat the back of a wooden spoon.

6. To assemble, spread or pipe the buttercream on the flat side of half of the cakes. Top with the rest of the cakes. Spoon the icing into a small paper piping bag, snip the end and pipe snowflake patterns on the top of the whoopie pies. Decorate with silver balls and sprinkle with caster sugar. Leave to set.

11 DECEMBER

TUSCAN CHRISTMAS CAKE

SERVES: 14   **PREP TIME: 50 MINS**   **COOK TIME: 1½ HRS**

INGREDIENTS

115 g/4 oz hazelnuts

115 g/4 oz almonds

85 g/3 oz chopped mixed peel

55 g/2 oz ready-to-eat dried apricots, finely chopped

55 g/2 oz candied pineapple, finely chopped

grated rind of 1 orange

55 g/2 oz plain flour

2 tbsp cocoa powder

1 tsp ground cinnamon

¼ tsp ground coriander

¼ tsp freshly grated nutmeg

¼ tsp ground cloves

115 g/4 oz caster sugar

175 g/6 oz clear honey

1. Preheat the oven to 180°C/350°F/Gas Mark 4. Line a 20-cm/8-inch round loose-based cake tin with greaseproof paper.

2. Spread out the hazelnuts on a baking sheet and toast in the preheated oven for 10 minutes, until golden brown. Tip them onto a tea towel and rub off the skins.

3. Meanwhile, spread out the almonds on a baking sheet and toast in the oven for 10 minutes, until golden. Watch carefully as they can burn easily.

4. Reduce the oven temperature to 150°C/300°F/Gas Mark 2. Chop all the nuts and place in a large bowl. Add the candied peel, apricots, pineapple and orange rind to the nuts and mix well.

5. Sift the flour, cocoa, cinnamon, coriander, nutmeg and cloves into the bowl and mix well.

6. Put the caster sugar and honey into a saucepan and set over a low heat, stirring, until the sugar has dissolved. Bring to the boil and cook for 5 minutes, until thickened and beginning to darken.

7. Stir the nut mixture into the saucepan and remove from the heat.

8. Spoon the mixture into the prepared cake tin and smooth the surface. Bake in the oven for 1 hour, then transfer to a wire rack to cool. When cold, carefully remove from the tin and peel off the greaseproof paper.

12 DECEMBER

GOLDEN CHRISTMAS CAKE

SERVES: 16–18   **PREP TIME: 50 MINS**   **COOK TIME: 2 HRS**

INGREDIENTS

175 g/6 oz dried apricots, chopped

85 g/3 oz dried mango, chopped

85 g/3 oz dried pineapple, chopped

175 g/6 oz sultanas

55 g/2 oz chopped stem ginger

55 g/2 oz chopped mixed peel

finely grated rind and juice of 1 orange

4 tbsp brandy

175 g/6 oz unsalted butter

100 g/3½ oz light muscovado sugar

4 eggs, beaten

2 tbsp clear honey

175 g/6 oz self-raising flour

2 tsp ground allspice

85 g/3 oz pecan nuts

1. Place the chopped apricots, mango and pineapple in a bowl with the sultanas, stem ginger and mixed peel. Stir in the orange rind, orange juice and brandy. Cover the bowl and leave to soak overnight.

2. Preheat the oven to 160°C/325°F/Gas Mark 3. Grease a 23-cm/9-inch round springform cake tin and line with greaseproof paper.

3. Cream together the butter and sugar until the mixture is pale and fluffy. Add the eggs to the mixture, beating well between each addition. Stir in the honey.

4. Sift the flour with the allspice and fold into the mixture using a metal spoon. Add the soaked fruit and pecan nuts, stirring thoroughly to mix. Spoon the mixture into the prepared tin, spreading evenly, then make a slight dip in the centre.

5. Place the tin in the centre of the preheated oven and bake for 1½–2 hours, or until golden brown and firm to the touch and a skewer inserted into the centre comes out clean. Leave to cool in the tin.

6. Turn the cake out, remove the greaseproof paper and re-wrap in clean greaseproof paper and foil. Store in a cool place for at least 1 month before icing.

TUSCAN
CHRISTMAS CAKE

POTATO LATKES

SERVES: 8 **PREP TIME: 10 MINS** **COOK TIME: 10–15 MINS**

INGREDIENTS

1 kg/2 lb 4 oz floury potatoes

1 onion

25 g/1 oz plain flour

1 egg, beaten

sunflower oil, for shallow frying

salt and pepper

soured cream, to serve

1. Finely grate the potatoes and onion. Put them into a sieve and press out as much liquid as possible, then spread out on a clean tea towel. Roll and twist to remove any remaining moisture.

2. Place the grated vegetables in a bowl and stir in the flour. Stir in the egg and season well with salt and pepper.

3. Heat a shallow depth of oil in a frying pan until medium–hot. Drop heaped tablespoonfuls of the mixture into the pan, pressing with a spatula to flatten, and fry in batches, turning once, for 8–10 minutes until golden brown and cooked through.

4. Drain the latkes on kitchen paper and keep warm while you cook the remaining mixture. Serve hot with soured cream.

COMPOTE OF DRIED FRUITS

SERVES: 4–6 · **PREP TIME: 5 MINS** · **COOK TIME: 20 MINS**

INGREDIENTS

140 g/5 oz ready-to-eat dried apricots, halved

140 g/5 oz ready-to-eat prunes

140 g/5 oz ready-to-eat dried apple rings, halved

55 g/2 oz dried cranberries

500 ml/18 fl oz orange juice

2 pieces stem ginger in syrup, drained and chopped, 2 tbsp syrup reserved

whipped cream or yogurt, to serve

1. Put the apricots, prunes, apple rings and cranberries into a saucepan and pour over the orange juice.

2. Bring to the boil over a medium heat, then stir in the ginger and reserved syrup. Reduce the heat to low, cover and simmer gently for about 15 minutes until the fruit is soft.

3. Lift out the fruit with a slotted spoon and place in a serving dish. Simmer the juice, uncovered, for 3–4 minutes until reduced and slightly thickened.

4. Pour the syrup over the fruit and serve warm or cold with whipped cream.

CRANBERRY APPLE MERINGUES

SERVES: 4   PREP TIME: **10 MINS**   COOK TIME: **20 MINS**

INGREDIENTS

500 g/1 lb 2 oz cooking apples or firm eating apples

1 tbsp apple juice

175 g/6 oz caster sugar

100 g/3½ oz dried cranberries

2 egg whites

1. Preheat the oven to 200°C/400°F/Gas Mark 6. Peel, core and chop the apples, place in a saucepan and sprinkle with the apple juice.

2. Add 70 g/2½ oz of the sugar and the cranberries, stir and heat gently until boiling. Cover the pan, reduce the heat and simmer gently, stirring occasionally, for 8–10 minutes until the fruit is just tender.

3. Divide the fruit between four 350-ml/12-fl oz ovenproof dishes and place on a baking sheet.

4. Put the egg whites into a grease-free bowl and whisk until they hold soft peaks. Gradually whisk in the remaining sugar until the mixture holds stiff peaks.

5. Spoon the meringue on top of the fruit, swirling with a knife. Bake in the preheated oven for 10–12 minutes until the meringue is lightly browned. Serve warm.

16 DECEMBER

MIXED NUT ROAST

SERVES: 4 | **PREP TIME: 35 MINS** | **COOK TIME: 35 MINS**

INGREDIENTS

2 tbsp butter, plus extra for greasing

2 garlic cloves, chopped

1 large onion, chopped

50 g/1¾ oz pine kernels, toasted

75 g/2¾ oz hazelnuts, toasted

50 g/1¾ oz ground walnuts

50 g/1¾ oz ground cashew nuts

100 g/3½ oz fresh wholemeal breadcrumbs

1 egg, lightly beaten

2 tbsp chopped fresh thyme

250 ml/9 fl oz vegetable stock

salt and pepper

fresh thyme sprigs, to garnish

cranberry sauce, to serve

1. Preheat the oven to 180°C/350°F/Gas Mark 4. Grease a loaf tin with butter and line it with greaseproof paper. Melt the butter in a saucepan over a medium heat. Add the garlic and onion and cook, stirring, for 5 minutes, until softened. Remove from the heat. Grind the pine kernels and hazelnuts. Stir all the nuts into the saucepan, add the breadcrumbs, egg, thyme and stock and season to taste with salt and pepper.

2. Spoon the mixture into the loaf tin and level the surface. Cook in the preheated oven for 30 minutes, or until cooked through and golden. The loaf is cooked when a skewer inserted into the centre comes out clean.

3. Remove the nut roast from the oven and turn out onto a serving dish. Garnish with thyme sprigs and serve with cranberry sauce.

17 DECEMBER

POACHED SALMON

SERVES: 8–12 | **PREP TIME: 15 MINS** | **COOK TIME: 25 MINS**

INGREDIENTS

4 litres/7 pints water

6 tbsp white wine vinegar

1 large onion, sliced

2 carrots, sliced

1½ tbsp salt

1 tsp black peppercorns

one 2.7-kg/6-lb salmon, cleaned, with gills and eyes removed

TO SERVE

green salad leaves

1 cucumber, thinly sliced

lemon wedges

1. To make a court-bouillon (stock) in which to poach the fish, put the water, vinegar, onion, carrots, salt and peppercorns in a large fish kettle or covered roasting tin and bring to the boil. Reduce the heat and simmer for 20 minutes. Remove the trivet (if using a fish kettle) and lay the salmon on it. Lower it into the court-bouillon, cover, return to simmering point and cook for 5 minutes. Turn off the heat and leave the fish, covered, to cool in the liquid.

2. When the fish is cold, lift it out of the kettle on the trivet and drain well. Using two fish slices, carefully transfer to a board. Using a sharp knife, remove the head, then slit the skin along the backbone and peel off. Carefully turn the fish over and peel off the skin on the other side.

3. To serve, line a serving platter with green salad leaves and cucumber and carefully transfer the salmon to the platter. Serve with lemon wedges.

MIXED NUT
ROAST

CHOCOLATE BRANDY TRUFFLES

MAKES: ABOUT 26 · **PREP TIME: 20 MINS PLUS COOLING TIME** · **COOK TIME: 5 MINS**

INGREDIENTS

200 g/7 oz plain chocolate

150 ml/5 fl oz double cream

3 tbsp brandy

2 tbsp icing sugar

cocoa powder, for dusting

1. Break the chocolate into small pieces and place in a bowl.

2. Pour the cream into a small saucepan and heat over a low heat until almost boiling. Remove from the heat and add the chocolate, stirring until melted and smooth.

3. Stir in the brandy and sugar and beat well with a wooden spoon. Leave to cool until the mixture is firm enough to hold its shape.

4. Put the cocoa powder into a shallow bowl and use some to lightly dust your hands. Use a teaspoon to scoop small pieces of mixture and roll into balls with your hands.

5. Roll the balls in the cocoa powder until lightly coated, then chill until firm.

6. Serve the truffles piled on a dish, or in small paper cases.

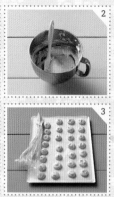

CHRISTMAS MACAROONS

MAKES: 16   PREP TIME: 40 MINS PLUS 30 MINS STANDING TIME   COOK TIME: 15 MINS

INGREDIENTS

75 g/2¾ oz ground almonds

115 g/4 oz icing sugar

1 tsp ground mixed spice

2 large egg whites

50 g/1¾ oz golden caster sugar

½ tsp freshly grated nutmeg

1 tsp gold dragées

FILLING

55 g/2 oz unsalted butter, softened

juice and finely grated rind of ½ orange

1 tsp ground mixed spice

115 g/4 oz icing sugar, sifted

25 g/1 oz glacé cherries, finely chopped

1. Place the ground almonds, icing sugar and mixed spice in a food processor and process for 15 seconds. Sift the mixture into a bowl. Line two baking sheets with greaseproof paper.

2. Place the egg whites in a large bowl and whisk until they hold soft peaks. Gradually whisk in the caster sugar to make a firm, glossy meringue. Using a spatula, fold the almond mixture into the meringue one third at a time. When all the dry ingredients are thoroughly incorporated, continue to cut and fold the mixture until it forms a shiny batter with a thick, ribbon-like consistency.

3. Pour the mixture into a piping bag fitted with a 1-cm/½ -inch plain nozzle. Pipe 32 small rounds onto the prepared baking sheets. Tap the baking sheets firmly onto a work surface to remove air bubbles. Sprinkle half the macaroons with the grated nutmeg and gold dragées. Leave at room temperature for 30 minutes. Meanwhile, preheat the oven to 160°C/325°F/Gas Mark 3.

4. Bake in the preheated oven for 10–15 minutes. Cool for 10 minutes, then carefully peel the macaroons off the greaseproof paper. Leave to cool completely.

5. To make the filling, beat the butter and orange juice and rind in a bowl until fluffy. Gradually beat in the mixed spice and icing sugar until smooth and creamy. Fold in the glacé cherries. Use to sandwich pairs of macaroons together.

20 DECEMBER

BRUSSELS SPROUTS WITH CHESTNUTS

SERVES: 4   PREP TIME: 10 MINS   COOK TIME: 10 MINS

INGREDIENTS

350 g/12 oz Brussels sprouts, trimmed

3 tbsp butter

100 g/3½ oz canned whole chestnuts

pinch of grated nutmeg

salt and pepper

flaked almonds, to garnish

1. Bring a large saucepan of lightly salted water to the boil. Add the Brussels sprouts and cook for 5 minutes. Drain thoroughly.

2. Melt the butter in a large saucepan over a medium heat. Add the Brussels sprouts and cook, stirring, for 3 minutes, then add the chestnuts and nutmeg. Season to taste with salt and pepper and stir well. Cook for a further 2 minutes, stirring, then remove from the heat. Transfer to a serving dish, scatter over the almonds and serve.

21 DECEMBER

PORK, CRANBERRY & HERB STUFFING

SERVES: 6   PREP TIME: 20 MINS   COOK TIME: 35 MINS

INGREDIENTS

1 tbsp vegetable oil, plus extra for oiling

1 onion, finely chopped

2 celery sticks, chopped

450 g/1 lb pork sausage meat

50 g/1¾ oz fresh white or wholemeal breadcrumbs

50 g/1¾ oz dried cranberries

70 g/2½ oz fresh cranberries

1 tbsp chopped fresh parsley

1 tbsp chopped fresh sage

1 tbsp chopped fresh thyme leaves

1 large egg, beaten

salt and pepper

1. Heat the oil in a heavy-based frying pan over a medium heat, add the onion and celery and cook, stirring frequently, for 10 minutes until the onion is transparent and soft.

2. Meanwhile, preheat the oven to 190°C/375°F/Gas Mark 5 and oil a baking sheet. Break up the sausage meat in a large bowl. Add the breadcrumbs, dried and fresh cranberries and the herbs and mix together well. Add the cooked onion and celery, then the egg. Season well with salt and pepper and mix together thoroughly.

3. Form the stuffing into balls, place on the prepared baking sheet and bake in the preheated oven for 25 minutes. Alternatively, spoon into two foil tins, level the surface and bake for 45 minutes.

MANGO & MACADAMIA STUFFING

SERVES: 4–6   PREP TIME: 10 MINS   COOK TIME: 30 MINS

INGREDIENTS

25 g/1 oz butter, plus extra for greasing

1 small onion, finely chopped

1 celery stick, diced

175 g/6 oz fresh white breadcrumbs

1 egg, beaten

1 tbsp Dijon mustard

1 small mango, peeled, stoned and diced

85 g/3 oz macadamia nuts, chopped

salt and pepper

1. Preheat the oven to 200°C/400°F/Gas Mark 6. Grease a 700-ml/1¼-pint ovenproof dish.

2. Melt the butter in a saucepan, add the onion and fry, stirring, for 3–4 minutes until soft. Add the celery and cook for a further 2 minutes.

3. Remove from the heat and stir in the breadcrumbs, egg and mustard. Add the mango and nuts, then season to taste with salt and pepper.

4. Spread the mixture into the prepared dish and bake in the preheated oven for 20–25 minutes until golden and bubbling.

CRANBERRY SAUCE

SERVES: 8   PREP TIME: 20 MINS   COOK TIME: 5 MINS

INGREDIENTS

thinly pared rind and juice of 1 lemon

thinly pared rind and juice of 1 orange

350 g/12 oz cranberries, thawed if frozen

140 g/5 oz caster sugar

2 tbsp arrowroot, mixed with 3 tbsp cold water

1. Place the lemon and orange rind in a heavy-based saucepan. If using fresh cranberries, rinse well and remove any stalks. Add the berries, lemon and orange juice and sugar to the saucepan and cook over a medium heat, stirring occasionally, for 5 minutes, or until the berries begin to burst.

2. Strain the juice into a clean saucepan and reserve the cranberries. Stir the arrowroot mixture into the juice, then bring to the boil, stirring constantly, until the sauce is smooth and thickened. Remove from the heat and stir in the reserved cranberries.

3. Transfer the cranberry sauce to a bowl and leave to cool, then cover with clingfilm and chill in the refrigerator until ready to use.

GLAZED GAMMON

SERVES: 8   PREP TIME: 20 MINS   COOK TIME: 4 HRS 20 MINS

INGREDIENTS

one 4-kg/8¾ -lb gammon joint

1 apple, cored and chopped

1 onion, chopped

300 ml/10 fl oz dry cider

6 black peppercorns

1 bouquet garni

1 bay leaf

about 50 cloves

4 tbsp Demerara sugar

1. Put the gammon in a large saucepan and add enough cold water to cover. Bring to the boil and skim off the scum that rises to the surface. Reduce the heat and simmer for 30 minutes. Drain the gammon and return to the saucepan. Add the apple, onion, cider, peppercorns, bouquet garni, bay leaf and a few of the cloves. Pour in enough fresh water to cover and return to the boil. Reduce the heat, cover and simmer for 3 hours 20 minutes.

2. Preheat the oven to 200°C/400°F/Gas Mark 6. Take the saucepan off the heat and set aside to cool slightly. Remove the gammon from the cooking liquid and, while it is still warm, loosen the rind with a sharp knife, then peel it off and discard. Score the fat into diamond shapes and stud with the remaining cloves. Place the gammon on a rack in a roasting tin and sprinkle with the sugar. Roast in the oven, basting occasionally with the cooking liquid, for 20 minutes. Serve hot, or cold later.

CRANBERRY
SAUCE

TRADITIONAL ROAST TURKEY

SERVES: 4   PREP TIME: 25 MINS PLUS 25 MINS STANDING TIME   COOK TIME: 3 HRS 15 MINS

INGREDIENTS

1 oven-ready turkey, weighing 5 kg/11 lb

1 garlic clove, finely chopped

100 ml/3½ fl oz red wine

75 g/2¾ oz butter

seasonal vegetables, to serve

STUFFING

100 g/3½ oz button mushrooms

1 onion, chopped

1 garlic clove, chopped

85 g/3 oz butter

100 g/3½ oz fresh breadcrumbs

2 tbsp finely chopped fresh sage

1 tbsp lemon juice

salt and pepper

PORT & CRANBERRY SAUCE

100 g/3½ oz sugar

250 ml/9 fl oz port

175 g/6 oz fresh cranberries

1. Preheat the oven to 200°C/400°F/Gas Mark 6.

2. To make the stuffing, clean and chop the mushrooms, put them in a saucepan with the onion, garlic and butter and cook for 3 minutes. Remove from the heat and stir in the remaining stuffing ingredients. Rinse the turkey and pat dry with kitchen paper. Fill the neck end with stuffing and truss with string.

3. Put the turkey in a roasting tin. Rub the garlic over the bird and pour the wine over. Add the butter and roast in the oven for 30 minutes. Baste, then reduce the temperature to 180°C/350°F/Gas Mark 4 and roast for a further 40 minutes. Baste again and cover with foil. Roast for a further 2 hours, basting regularly. Check that the bird is cooked by inserting a knife between the legs and body. If the juices run clear, it is cooked. Remove from the oven, cover with foil and leave to stand for 25 minutes.

4. Meanwhile, put the sugar, port and cranberries in a saucepan. Heat over a medium heat until almost boiling. Serve the turkey with seasonal vegetables and the port and cranberry sauce.

TRADITIONAL
ROAST TURKEY

TURKEY CLUB SANDWICHES

MAKES: 6   PREP TIME: 30 MINS   COOK TIME: 10 MINS

INGREDIENTS

12 pancetta or streaky bacon rashers

18 slices white bread

12 slices cooked turkey breast meat

3 plum tomatoes, sliced

6 Little Gem lettuce leaves

6 stuffed olives

salt and pepper

MAYONNAISE

2 large egg yolks

1 tsp English mustard powder

1 tsp salt

300 ml/10 fl oz groundnut oil

1 tsp white wine vinegar

1. First make the mayonnaise. Put the egg yolks in a bowl, add the mustard powder, pepper to taste and salt and beat together well. Pour the oil into a jug. Using an electric or hand-held whisk, begin to whisk the egg yolks, adding just 1 drop of the oil. Make sure that this has been thoroughly absorbed before adding another drop and whisking well.

2. Continue adding the oil 1 drop at a time until the mixture thickens and stiffens – at this point, whisk in the vinegar and then continue to dribble in the remaining oil very slowly in a thin stream, whisking constantly, until you have used up all the oil and you have a thick mayonnaise. Cover and refrigerate while you prepare the other sandwich components.

3. Grill or fry the pancetta until crisp, drain on kitchen paper and keep warm. Toast the bread until golden, then cut off the crusts. You will need three slices of toast for each sandwich. For each sandwich, spread the first piece of toast with a generous amount of mayonnaise, top with two slices of turkey, keeping the edges neat, and then top with a couple of slices of tomato. Season to taste with salt and pepper. Add another slice of toast and top with two pancetta rashers and one lettuce leaf. Season to taste again, add a little more mayonnaise, then top with the final piece of toast. Push a cocktail stick or a decorative sparkler through a stuffed olive, and then push this through the sandwich to hold it together.

CRANBERRY & ORANGE PIES

MAKES: 12   PREP TIME: 25 MINS   COOK TIME: 30 MINS

INGREDIENTS

butter, for greasing

175 g/6 oz frozen cranberries

1 tbsp cornflour

3 tbsp freshly squeezed orange juice

2 star anise

55 g/2 oz caster sugar, plus extra for sprinkling

225 g/8 oz ready-made sweet shortcrust pastry, chilled

flour, for dusting

milk, for glazing

1. Preheat the oven to 180°C/350°F/Gas Mark 4. Lightly grease a 12-cup mini muffin tin.

2. Put the still-frozen cranberries in a medium saucepan with the cornflour and orange juice. Add the star anise and cook uncovered over a low heat, stirring from time to time, for 5 minutes, or until the cranberries have softened. Add the sugar and cook for 5 minutes more, then leave to cool.

3. Roll the pastry out thinly on a lightly floured surface. Using a fluted cookie cutter, stamp out 12 circles, each 6 cm/2½ inches in diameter. Press these gently into the prepared tin, re-rolling the trimmings as needed. Squeeze any remaining trimmings together and reserve. Brush the top edges of the pie cases with a little milk. Discard the star anise, then spoon in the filling.

4. Roll the remaining pastry out thinly on a lightly floured surface. Using a fluted pastry wheel, cut thin strips of pastry. Arrange these over each pie and brush with a little milk. Sprinkle with a little sugar. Bake in the preheated oven for 20 minutes, covering with foil after 10 minutes if the tops are browning too quickly. Leave to cool in the tin for 10 minutes, then loosen with a round-bladed knife and transfer to a wire rack to cool.

TURKEY CLUB
SANDWICHES

MULLED WINE

MAKES: 3.3 LITRES/5¾ PINTS   PREP TIME: 20 MINS   COOK TIME: 15 MINS

INGREDIENTS

5 oranges

50 cloves

thinly pared rind and juice
of 4 lemons

850 ml/1½ pints water

115 g/4 oz caster sugar

2 cinnamon sticks

2 litres/3½ pints red wine

150 ml/5 fl oz brandy

1. Prick the skins of three of the oranges all over with a fork and stud with the cloves, then set aside. Thinly pare the rind and squeeze the juice from the remaining oranges.

2. Put the orange rind and juice, lemon rind and juice, water, sugar and cinnamon in a heavy-based saucepan and bring to the boil over a medium heat, stirring occasionally, until the sugar has dissolved. Boil for 2 minutes without stirring, then remove from the heat, stir once and leave to stand for 10 minutes. Strain the liquid into a heatproof jug, pressing down on the contents of the sieve to extract all the juice.

3. Pour the wine into a separate saucepan and add the strained spiced juices, the brandy and the clove-studded oranges. Simmer gently without boiling, then remove the saucepan from the heat. Strain into heatproof glasses and serve.

EGGNOG

SERVES: 4–6   PREP TIME: 5 MINS   COOK TIME: NO COOKING

INGREDIENTS

1 egg

1 tbsp icing sugar

2 measures brandy

warm milk

freshly grated nutmeg, to decorate

1. Whisk the first three ingredients together, strain into tall glasses and top up with milk. Sprinkle with the nutmeg and serve.

RICH CHICKEN CASSEROLE

SERVES: 4   **PREP TIME: 15 MINS**   **COOK TIME: ABOUT 1 HR 10 MINS**

INGREDIENTS

2 tbsp olive oil

8 chicken thighs

1 medium red onion, sliced

2 garlic cloves, crushed

1 large red pepper, deseeded and thickly sliced

thinly pared rind and juice of 1 small orange

125 ml/4 fl oz chicken stock

400 g/14 oz canned chopped tomatoes

25 g/1 oz sun-dried tomatoes, thinly sliced

1 tbsp chopped fresh thyme

50 g/1¾ oz pitted black olives

salt and pepper

thyme sprigs and orange rind, to garnish

1. In a heavy or non-stick large frying pan, heat the oil and fry the chicken over a fairly high heat, turning occasionally until golden brown. Using a slotted spoon, drain off any excess fat from the chicken and transfer to a flameproof casserole.

2. Fry the onion, garlic and red pepper in the pan over a moderate heat for 3–4 minutes. Transfer the vegetables to the casserole.

3. Add the orange rind and juice, chicken stock, canned tomatoes and sun-dried tomatoes and stir to combine.

4. Bring to the boil then cover the casserole with a lid and simmer very gently over a low heat for about 1 hour, stirring occasionally. Add the thyme and olives, then adjust the seasoning with salt and pepper to taste.

5. Check the chicken is tender and the juices run clear when a skewer is inserted into the thickest part of the meat. Scatter over the thyme sprigs and orange rind to garnish and serve.

TROPICAL FRUIT DESSERT

SERVES: 6   **PREP TIME: 20 MINS**   **COOK TIME: NO COOKING**

INGREDIENTS

14 amaretti

3 tbsp white rum

100 ml/3½ fl oz orange juice

1 papaya, halved, deseeded, peeled and chopped

½ small pineapple, cored and chopped

2 kiwi fruit, peeled and chopped

300 ml/10 fl oz whipping cream

1 tsp vanilla extract

toasted flaked coconut, to decorate

1. Roughly crumble the amaretti into a glass serving bowl and sprinkle with the rum and orange juice.

2. Mix together the papaya, pineapple and kiwi fruit and spread over the amaretti.

3. Whisk the cream with the vanilla extract until it just holds its shape, then spoon over the fruit.

4. Scatter the toasted coconut over the cream and serve chilled.

apple
Apple & Blackberry Waffles 258
Apple & Spice Porridge 56
Apple Pancakes with Maple Syrup 274
Apple Pie 340
Cranberry Apple Meringues 362
Easy Apple Cake 271
Spiced Apple Macaroons 343
Apricot Almond Tart 145
asparagus
Asparagus & Tomato Tart 134
Asparagus with Lemon Butter Sauce 106
Avocado, Feta & Rocket Salad 204

bacon
Bacon-Wrapped Chicken Burgers 238
Bacon-Wrapped Sausages 351
Cheese & Bacon Burgers 194
Romaine, Bacon & Blue Cheese Salad 210
Slow-Cooked Potato Stew 28
Toasted Muffins with Blueberries & Bacon 152
Baked Beans with Corn 276
banana
Banana Walnut Loaf Cake 354
Chocolate Banana Splits 218
Hot Banana Butterscotch 16
Bass, Baked Sea 288
bean
Bean Casserole with Potatoes, Corn &
Pumpkin 309
French Bean Casserole 336
beef
Beef Enchiladas 83
Beef Medallions with Orange, Lime &
Honey 94
Beef, Spring Onion & Pak Choi Stir-Fry 155
Beef with Herb Dumplings 316
Beef Wraps with Lime & Honey 232
Braised Beef with Red Wine & Cranberries 332
Cheese & Bacon Burgers 194
Chicken-Fried Steak 316
Chilli Beef Stir-Fry Salad 122
Chilli Con Carne 72
Fiery Beef Tacos 72
Grilled Fillet Steak 196
Grilled Italian Sausages with Double Chilli
Salsa 212
Hearty Beef Stew 10
Hot Sesame Beef 13
Meatball Sandwich 280
Meatloaf 300
Minced Beef & Mashed Potatoes 26
Peppered Sirloin Steak with Brandy & Cream
Sauce 174
Pot Roast with Potatoes & Dill 300
Simple Savoury Beef 225
Sliced Beef in Black Bean Sauce 308
Sliced Sirloin with Parmesan 182
Spare Ribs in Barbecue Sauce 228
Steak & Chips 281
Tequila-Marinated Beef Steaks 170

The Reuben Sandwich 280
Whole Roast Rib of Beef 17
Winter Beef Stew with Herb Dumplings 21
Beetroot & Egg Soup 254
Blackberry Crumble Cupcakes 297
blueberry
Blueberry & Cranberry Squares 190
Blueberry Frozen Yogurt 202
Brazil Nut Brittle 274
Bread & Butter Pudding 42
Broccoli & Stilton Soup 53
Brussels Sprouts with Chestnuts 368

Caesar Salad 193
Cake Pops, Mini 70
Calamari with Prawns & Broad Beans 136
carrot
Carrot & Coriander Soup 74
Carrot Cake 242
Cauliflower Cheese 48
cheese
Baked Cheese & Aubergine Layers 75
Baked Chilli Cheese Sandwiches 154
Baked Tuna & Ricotta Rigatoni 14
Blue Cheese, Fig & Walnut Spread 292
Cauliflower Cheese 48
Cheese & Bacon Burgers 194
Cheese & Courgette Casserole 262
Cheesy Sweetcorn Fritters 176
Chicken with Goat's Cheese 184
Chorizo & Cheese Quesadillas 294
Corn on the Cob with Blue Cheese
Dressing 240
Farfalle with Gorgonzola & Ham 334
Feta & Spinach Parcels 303
Macaroni Cheese 63
Pasta with Rocket & Mozzarella 170
Penne in Tomato Sauce with Two Cheeses 15
Pizza Margherita 140
Pumpkin & Blue Gruyère Stew 311
Baked Tuna & Ricotta Rigatoni 14
Roasted Vegetable & Feta Cheese Wraps 245
Rocket & Parmesan Salad 250
Romaine, Bacon & Blue Cheese Salad 210
Tomato & Herb Ricotta Tart 235
Tomato & Mozarella Stacks 134
Tuna & Cheese Quiche 137
Vegetable Kebabs with Blue Cheese 246
cheesecake
Mini Peach Cheesecake Crumbles 130
New York Cheesecake 125
chicken
Bacon-Wrapped Chicken Burgers 238
Barbecued Chicken 228
Barbecued Chicken with Tarragon Butter 201
Cajun Chicken 169
Chicken & Broccoli Casserole 60
Chicken & Corn Soup 320
Chicken & Vegetable Bake 295
Chicken & Wild Mushroom Cannelloni 279
Chicken Breasts Braised with Baby

Vegetables 142
Chicken Casserole Provençal 44
Chicken Chow Mein 40
Chicken Fajitas 264
Chicken Fried Rice 84
Chicken Gumbo 331
Chicken in Riesling 296
Chicken Mole Poblano 320
Chicken Pasta Salad, Honey & Mustard 149
Chicken Pot Pie 23
Chicken Satay Skewers with Peanut Sauce 148
Chicken Soup with Leeks & Rice 18
Chicken with Creamy Penne 90
Chicken with Goat's Cheese 184
Chicken with Tomato & Cinnamon Sauce 22
Fried Chicken Wings 260
Fried Chicken with Tomato & Bacon Sauce 87
Golden Chicken Casserole 26
Jerk Chicken 247
Mini Chicken Pot Pies 121
Mustard & Honey Drumsticks 106
Piri Piri Chicken 140
Quick Chicken Stew 146
Rich Chicken Casserole 377
Roast Chicken 59
Southern-Style Chicken Drumsticks 289
Sticky Lime Chicken 244
Thai Chicken 304
chilli
Baked Chilli Cheese Sandwiches 154
Barbecued Tuna with Chilli & Ginger Sauce 172
Chilli Beef Stir-Fry Salad 122
Chilli, Ham & Spinach Pasta 44
Chilli-Prawn Tacos 198
Chorizo, Chilli & Chickpea Casserole 91
Fish Goujons with Chilli Mayonnaise 133
New Potatoes with Garlic & Chilli Butter 88
Turkey Steaks with Chilli Maple Glaze 319
Vegetable Chilli 327
Vegetarian Chilli Burgers 180
chocolate
Chocolate & Nut Oat Bars 71
Chocolate & Orange Slices 234
Chocolate Banana Splits 218
Chocolate Brandy Truffles 366
Chocolate Chip Cookies 157
Chocolate Fudge Brownies 328
Chocolate Fudge Cake 78
Chocolate Peanut Butter Squares 298
Chocolate Pretzels 116
Dark Chocolate Roulade 104
Halloween Mud Pie 312
Raspberry & White Chocolate S'Mores 248
Real Hot Chocolate 32
Rocky Road Chocolate Muffins 256
Yule Log 348
Christmas cake
Golden Christmas Cake 358
Tuscan Christmas Cake 358
Churros 30

Quick Reference Index

Turbot Goujons with Caper Mayonnaise 222
Turbot Steaks with Parsley, Lemon & Garlic 114
Wine-Steamed Mussels 194

Ham

Bacon-Wrapped Chicken Burgers 238
Bacon-Wrapped Sausages 351
Baked Ham with Hoisin & Honey Glaze 8
Cheese & Bacon Burgers 194
Chorizo & Cheese Quesadillas 294
Farfalle with Gorgonzola & Ham 334
Glazed Gammon 370
Ham & Mushroom Quiche 324
Meatloaf 300
Paprika Pork 304
Pork Chops Braised with Shallots 64
Pork Chops with Apple Sauce 286
Pork, Cranberry & Herb Stuffing 368
Quick Pan Braise of Ham Chunks 110
Romaine, Bacon & Blue Cheese Salad 210
Sausage Cider Casserole 270
Slow-Cooked Potato Stew 28
Toasted Muffins with Blueberries & Bacon 152

Lamb

Irish Stew 82
Lamb Chops in Tomato Sauce 290
Lamb Koftas with Yogurt, Thyme & Lemon
    Dip 207
Lamb Stew 47
Meatloaf 300
Moroccan Lamb Stew 112
Peppered Lamb Fillet 107

Pasta

Chicken & Wild Mushroom Cannelloni 279
Chilli, Ham & Spinach Pasta 44
Farfalle with Gorgonzola & Ham 334
Fresh Tomato Soup with Pasta 299
Fusilli with Courgettes & Lemon 132
Honey & Mustard Chicken Pasta Salad 149
Lasagne 276
Macaroni & Seafood Bake 92
Pasta with Pesto 74
Pasta with Rocket & Mozzarella 170
Penne in Tomato sauce with two Cheeses 15
Penne with Turkey Meatballs 84
Pepperoni Pasta 110
Salami Pasta Salad 269
Spaghetti Alla Carbonara 14
Spaghetti Bolognese 58
Spaghetti with Fresh Pea Pesto 146
Spaghetti with Meatballs 122
Spaghetti with Tomatoes & Black Olives 214

Potatoes

Bangers & Mash 261
Bean Casserole with Potatoes, Corn &
    Pumpkin 309
Champ 82
Chunky Potato & Spinach Curry 326
Fish & Potato Stew 302
Fresh Potato Salad 139
Mashed Potatoes 294
New Potatoes with Garlic & Chilli Butter 88
Pot Roast with Potatoes & Dill 300
Potato Gnocchi 262
Potato Kebabs with Feta 211
Potato Latkes 360
Potato Stew, Slow-Cooked 28
Roast Potatoes 48
Scalloped Potatoes 254
Soufflé Jacket Potatoes 284
Tartiflette 92

Soups

Barley, Lentil & Onion Soup 12
Beetroot & Egg Soup 254
Broccoli & Stilton Soup 53
Carrot & Coriander Soup 74
Chicken & Corn Soup 320
Chicken Soup with Leeks & Rice 18
Chilled Pea Soup 217
French Onion Soup 308
Fresh Tomato Soup with Pasta 299
Gazpacho 205
Prawn Noodle Soup 178
Squash, Sweet Potato & Garlic Soup 322
Turkey & Lentil Soup 10
Turkey Soup with Rice, Mushrooms & Sage 350

Turkey

Creamy Turkey & Broccoli Gnocchi 34
Lemon Turkey with Spinach 111
Mexican Turkey Burgers 182
Mexican Turkey Steak 208
Paprika Turkey Strips 61
Penne with Turkey Meatballs 84
Spicy Turkey & Sausage Kebabs 208
Tarragon Turkey 238
Thanksgiving Roast Turkey 338
Traditional Roast Turkey 372
Turkey & Lentil Soup 10
Turkey Casserole with Cabbage & Dill 76
Turkey Club Sandwiches 374
Turkey Salad Pitta 184
Turkey Soup with Rice, Mushrooms & Sage 350
Turkey Steaks with Butter Beans 118
Turkey Steaks with Chilli Maple Glaze 319
Turkey Steaks with Prosciutto & Sage 34

Turkey Steaks with Tarragon Sauce 76
Turkey Teriyaki 168
Turkey with Mole Sauce 250

Vegetarian Dishes (* see also Pasta, Potatoes, Soups)

Asparagus & Tomato Tart 134
Asparagus with Lemon Butter Sauce 106
Avocado, Feta & Rocket Salad 204
Baked Beans with Corn 276
Baked Sweet Potato with Garlic Salsa 334
Bean Casserole with Potatoes, Corn &
    Pumpkin 309
Brussels Sprouts with Chestnuts 368
Caesar Salad 193
Caramelized Onion Tart 52
Champ 82
Chunky Potato & Spinach Curry 326
Coleslaw 224
Corn on the Cob with Blue Cheese Dressing 240
Courgettes with Butter & Lemon 236
Creamed Spinach with Nutmeg 338
French Bean Casserole 336
Garlic & Herb Bread Spiral 152
Hush Puppies 260
Lamb's Lettuce & Cucumber Salad with Figs 160
Layered Casserole 352
Leek & Goat's Cheese Tartlets 68
Mashed Sweet Potatoes with Parsley Butter 337
Mini Yorkshire Puddings 318
Mixed Nut Roast 364
Mixed Vegetable Bruschetta 210
Mushroom & Walnut Open Tart 292
Nachos 138
Potato Gnocchi 262
Pumpkin & Gruyère Stew 311
Ratatouille 330
Red Salad with Beetroot & Radish 148
Roast Butternut Squash 278
Roast Summer Vegetables 196
Roast Vegetables 290
Roasted Pepper & Garlic Focaccia 143
Roasted Vegetable & Feta Cheese Wraps 245
Spring Onion & Ricotta Tarts 119
Summer Couscous Salad 237
Sweetcorn & Chive Fritters 112
Tofu Parcels 185
Vegetable & Black Bean Spring Rolls 335
Vegetable Couscous 118
Vegetable Kebabs with Blue Cheese 246
Vegetarian Chilli Burgers 180
Vegetarian Hot Dogs 181
Warm Bulgar Wheat Salad 62
Winter Salad Slaw 16